D1236757

Children at Risk

Children
at Risk

GARY A. CROW

SCHOCKEN BOOKS · NEW YORK

TO

Joe West

Robert ⁓ ⁓ ⁓ ⁓ ⁓ Library

SEP 22 1978

Tallahassee, Florida

First published by SCHOCKEN BOOKS 1978

Copyright © 1978 by Schocken Books Inc.

Library of Congress Cataloging in Publication Data

Crow, Gary A., 1942–
  Children at risk.

  Bibliography: p. 268
  Includes index.
  1. Learning, Psychology of.
  2. Classroom management.   3. Teaching.   I. Title.
LB1051.C729   372.1′1′02   77-87859

Manufactured in the United States of America

Contents

Acknowledgments

A project of this nature has necessarily involved a very large number of people. Special thanks are first given to Harold Silverman of the Wright State University College of Education. He has been involved with the project since its inception and has been generous with his advice and criticism through each of its stages.

James Steiner has contributed his medical experience and expertise to the book through carefully reviewing the material for medical accuracy and consistency. Although he cannot, in any way, be held responsible for the final material, his contribution has been invaluable.

Jean Wiseman contributed much thought and energy through helping organize the Early Identification Index and coordinate some of the activities of the graduate students involved in the initial phase of the project. Thanks is also given to Harry Bailey for his involvement in that part of the process. In addition, the efforts of the graduate students involved in the project are here gratefully acknowledged.

Through the initial phase of the project, the care with which Robin Willoby handled recording and transcribing much of the data and supporting documentation was impressive. Her efforts are very much appreciated.

Linda Anderson has again contributed more to the process of turning a project into a book than could reasonably have been requested or expected. She has typed, read, retyped, and reread the manuscript with patience and with a real interest in the final quality and success of this book. Her hard work and enthusiasm has probably made the difference between "a project we are working on" and "a completed book."

George Dallas and Adele McDowell both contributed their experience and expertise through carefully reviewing draft copies of the manuscript and providing important comments and suggestions. Their contribution is evident to me and is very much appreciated.

Barbara Abma, Devinder Yakhmi, and Mike Miller are here acknowledged for the many hours they spent talking with me about the special needs, problems, and difficulties experienced by young children and about ways in which caring people can respond.

Sue Pedretti has made a very special contribution to this book. Using the English language clearly and correctly is not always an easy matter, unless you happen to have a special sensitivity to and facility for the language. Ms. Pedretti's work with draft copies of the manuscript has, I think, made the book more readable, more grammatically correct, and freer from sex/role bias. Although she should not be held responsible for the form and flow of the book, her contribution is present throughout.

Finally, and with that special appreciation that cannot really be stated but is reserved only for a wife and children, let me say thanks to Letha, Carene, Lisha, and Bret for putting up with me and "hanging in there" through the process.

ONE

Introduction

This is a handbook to be used by people who work with young children. Focus is on kids from five to eight years old, and the perspective is that of early elementary teachers. Even with this emphasis, though, the information and illustrations included will be of specific usefulness to elementary teachers and principals, nurses, guidance counselors, psychologists, and other school personnel. Recreation leaders, youth workers, religious educators, and parents of young children will find that the development and presentation of the one hundred most significant signs and symptoms of early childhood difficulty are both interesting and informative. Nonetheless, the major attempt is to communicate relevant and useful ideas and information to teachers.

Do adults who work with children and accept responsibility for caring and concern always understand who children are and what they need? Do we always know when to help, how to help, and why help is needed? Are our efforts always effective and in a child's best interest? At the center of our efforts in using our knowledge, skill, experience, and caring must be the child's welfare and well-being. Even when a particular action in retrospect seems to have been ill-advised, our efforts should always be governed by a few principles that recur throughout this handbook.

First, we know both professionally and intuitively that children need our maximum effort and involvement. Whether we are working with three children or thirty, we do as much as we can do. When we see problems or difficulties involving one or several children, then our efforts will be governed by the principle that it is always better to become overinvolved or to overrespond than to be underinvolved or to underrespond. We may be accused of exaggerating a problem, but should never be guilty of not appreciating the real seriousness of a child's problems or difficulties. For example, if a child receives a hard bump on the head as a result of an accident at school, we will respond as if he or she had received a "concussion"—just to be on the safe side. We will get him or her to lie down; we will apply ice or a cold compress to the bump; we will notify the school nurse if our school has one; we will be sure that the child's parents are notified; and we will strongly encourage them to take the child to the doctor— just to be sure everything is okay. We will be sure that an adult stays with the child until his or her parent comes to get him or her; and if the child has to remain at school, we will be sure that he or she is awakened at least once in every hour. Of course, if the child's parent takes him or her home, we will encourage them to do the same thing until they get the child to the doctor. Is this an excessive response for a hard bump on the head? All of this may be more than was actually necessary; but we can be sure that we have done enough in the event that the bad bump really was a concussion.

Next, we always start out by taking a child's complaints and expressed difficulties seriously. Of course, we know that children can exaggerate their problems and difficulties, and we know that children occasionally imitate the problems and difficulties of other children, especially if another child has received special attention. Nonetheless, we begin by believing. Usually, we have time to use our experience and ingenuity to test whether or not the child actually has a serious problem or difficulty. We start by assuming that he or she really does have the problem and then we give it a little time to understand what is going on. Based on the results of this serious attention to the possible problem or difficulty, we respond. Alternatively, if the particular sign or symptom demands an immediate response, we respond. If the child was "putting us on," we have unnecessarily used some time and energy. However, if the problem was real, we have dealt with it in a responsible and effective manner.

Next, we know that a child's healthy physical growth and development is essential to healthy emotional, social, and academic functioning. We know that physical problems and difficulties frequently underlie apparent social, emotional, and academic problems. Our first hypothesis with any difficulty a child may have, then, is that he or she may be experiencing physical problems. We will, thus, be sure that this possibility is explored and thoroughly evaluated before coming to any conclusions suggesting emotional, social, or intellectual explanations for a child's difficulties. The point deserves emphasis. Almost any apparently emotional, social, or intellectual problem or difficulty a child may experience can have origins or components related to physical problems.

In addition to these principles, we know that children are growing and developing people who have a lot of problems related to growth and development, many of which are only apparent problems and are functions of natural variability and variation. Although we never assume that a child will simply grow out of his or her difficulties without first understanding the nature and extent of the problem for the specific child, we are very aware of fairly wide variations in behavior and adjustment, giving the child plenty of room to grow and develop in his or her unique and special way. We know that physical problems in young children usually do not vary significantly between the ages of five and eight. Academic and classroom performance and adjustment is a different proposition, though. For example, five-year-olds may frequently reverse or rotate numbers or letters, may have difficulty getting things in the right order, and may have difficulty attending to a task at the desk or table. These problems are much less frequently seen in eight-year-olds; and when they are seen they warrant additional concern and attention. A five-year-old may experience difficulty negotiating new relationships in the world of peers and playmates. Second and third graders, though, should be showing fairly good social skills and involvements. A five-year-old may become noticeably emotionally upset when mother leaves him or her at school. A seven-year-old, though, will usually involve himself or herself in school with some enthusiasm while mother remains at home, goes to work, or is involved in other activities. The principle is that some problems are only problems relative to the age of the child, while others are problems regardless of the age of the child. Generally, physical problems and family or environmental problems are not age related, while emotional, social, and academic/classroom problems or symptoms are.

Finally, we do all we can to make all needed resources available to every child. Throughout this handbook, discussion will be focused on using school psychologists, school nurses, speech and hearing therapists, counselors, and other school-based personnel, if they are available. If not, specific ideas and suggestions are presented for finding and utilizing such resources within your community. Occasionally, though, needed resources may not be available either in the school or in the community. What then? As you will see, there is still a lot you can do to help the child with special difficulties. At a minimum, your relationship with the child and your understanding of his or her problem will help. In addition, your understanding will lead to things you can do within the relationship to increase the child's chances of healthy growth and development while running no risk of harming the child or interfering with his or her continuing growth. Although it is extremely important to recognize and understand our limitations, it is equally important that we understand and feel comfortable with what we do know and can do to help.

Although these principles will not be repetitiously reiterated throughout the pages of this handbook, it is essential that you keep focus on them as we begin to think about our shared concern for young children. It is unusual to talk with a group of teachers or parents without someone asking, "How do you recognize serious problems or potentially serious problems in young children? How can we tell if our kids are having problems?" On the one hand, the questions seem relatively simple and straight-forward. On the other hand, responding to these questions raises several complex and difficult issues. First, children are multidimensional beings. They have a physical dimension, an emotional dimension, a moral/spiritual dimension, a social dimension, a sexual dimension, and an intellectual dimension. Each of these aspects and all of them collectively hold the potential for problem development. Recognition of difficulties in one dimension, then, is a somewhat different proposition than recognition of difficulties in other dimensions. Similarly, recognition of difficulty in some dimensional combinations is a somewhat different matter than recognition of difficulties in other combinations. Second, "problems" vary from extremely serious to relatively insignificant. When thinking about how to recognize problems, it is thus important to be able to separate the more significant from the less significant. Finally, some signs and symptoms only become "problematic" if they recur with sufficient frequency to cause concern, while others need only occur once to be alarming. For example, significant weakness in one side of the body relative to the other would be an alarming symptom were it noticed only once. Alternatively, a five-year-old would need to stutter and stammer fairly regularly before there would be any cause for concern.

Since the problem of recognition of childhood difficulties is a continuing and frequently expressed concern of everyone who deals with small children, a response is needed that goes beyond simply recognizing the difficulty and complexity of the questions. To deal with recognizing problems for all children in all situations would require hundreds of volumes and life times of research and study. I have therefore focused on the most significant one hundred signs and symptoms of early childhood difficulty observable by teachers at school. The one hundred signs and symptoms to be discussed are listed in Figure 1. Why these signs and symptoms but not others? First, a general research question was posed: "How can signs and symptoms of difficulty or of potential difficulty in young children be recognized?" This question, of course, assumes a preliminary question: "What kinds of things represent signs and symptoms of difficulty in young children?" It was clear that the universe of children would need to be narrowed and defined before a set of signs and symptoms could be developed. Somewhat arbitrarily and following my special interest in younger children, I decided that the focus would be on early elementary-age children, that is, on children in kindergarten through the third grade. This limited the research universe to boys and girls from five through eight years old. Limiting the population allowed the general questions to be further focused: "What are the possible signs and symptoms of difficulty in children five through eight years old?"

Signs and symptoms of difficulty in children five to eight years old still represented an unmanageable universe, although one substantially narrowed from the universe of all children. The author's work with teachers and with the Wright State University College of Education in Dayton, Ohio, naturally led to asking the research question from the point of view of teachers: "What signs and symptoms of difficulty in young children are important for teachers to be aware of and to recognize?" A thorough review of education literature conducted by the author yielded 450 signs and symptoms of difficulty in young children. It is important to note that the literature was not approached with the intent of reviewing the development and understanding of signs and symptoms but solely for the purpose of isolating and extracting specific signs and symptoms of difficulty in young children. Some signs and symptoms received detailed discussion in the literature, while others were only mentioned in passing. Nevertheless, all items were tabulated without regard to the significance attributed to the sign or symptom by any particular author. Undoubtedly, the 450 signs and symptoms of early childhood difficulty culled from the literature are not totally exhaustive. Also, as the reader will note when reviewing Appendix I, a few of the 450 items would be more appropriately seen as "factors" related to problems and difficulties and not as actual signs or symptoms of problems and difficulties. I sincerely

**Fig. 1. The 100 Most Significant Signs and Symptoms of Early Child-
hood Difficulty***

1. Sudden deterioration in the quality of work. (24)
2. Seems to feel incapable of doing his/her work. (30)
3. Seems to feel defeated before even beginning to do his/her work. (31)
4. Seems not to be working up to ability. (32)
5. Cannot keep up with his/her peer group academically. (35)
6. Reverses and rotates numbers and letters. (36)
7. Consistently has difficulty identifying body parts. (38)
8. Easily distracted by surroundings and minor noises. (39)
9. Consistently looks at books or pictures upside down. (41)
10. Has difficulty applying him/herself. (41)
11. Has difficlty repeating three to five numbers in sequence. (42)
12. Appears to have occasional memory lapses. (43)
13. Frequently rocks in his/her desk or chair. (44)
14. Works inconsistently; seems to know something one day but not the next. (45)
15. Shows apparently inability to follow simple directions. (46)
16. Grasps his/her pencil or crayon too tightly, occasionally tearing holes in the paper. (46)
17. Scribbles when asked to draw a picture of a person. (47)
18. Shows an inability to draw a circle, square, or cross. (47)
19. Answers oral questions by completely changing the subject. (46)
20. Pulls out hair. (54)
21. Repeatedly inflicts pain on self. (55)
22. Shows constant nail biting, nose picking, or scratching. (57)
23. Frequently annoys others to draw attention to self. (59)
24. Is repeatedly cruel to other children. (61)
25. Intentionally seriously injures another child. (61)
26. Shows repeated cruelty to animals. (62)
27. Has consistent difficulty on school bus or on the way to and from school. (73)
28. Has frequent temper tantrums. (63)
29. Runs away from home or school repeatedly. (65)
30. Seems not to learn from previous experiences. (68)
31. Consistently fails to follow school rules. (68)

*Bracketed numbers refer to page in text where symptom is discussed.

32. Frequently defies authority. (71)
33. Steals repeatedly. (72)
34. Is excessively or indiscriminately affectionate toward adults. (75)
35. Seems unlovable. (77)
36. Vomiting. (84)
37. Difficulty swallowing. (85)
38. Frequent or severe stomachaches. (86)
39. Rash on face or other parts of the body. (88)
40. Frequent wheezing. (90)
41. Frequent wet, productive cough. (91)
42. Diarrhea. (92)
43. Shows evidence of having been sexually molested. (100)
44. Shows evidence that parents drink heavily or abuse drugs. (102)
45. Is apparently abused by parents or others at home. (98)
46. Parents seem not to accept child's limitations. (104)
47. Parents become hostile or agressive when approached about child's problems. (105)
48. Parents belittle child or tell him/her that he/she is stupid. (107)
49. Parents frequently keep child out of school. (108)
50. Child reports parents do not allow him/her to play with other children. (111)
51. Using one eye more than the other. (119)
52. Frequent earaches. (122)
53. Difficulty hearing. (123)
54. Bleeding from the ear. (128)
55. Complaints of double vision. (120)
56. Complaints of ringing sounds or sensations. (126)
57. Frequent squinting. (125)
58. Red or swollen eyes. (121)
59. Has shaking, trembling hands. (132)
60. Has frequent headaches. (151)
61. Frequently wets or soils self. (154)
62. Frequently expresses the feeling that he/she is no good. (161)
63. Hears voices or sees things that are not there. (156)
64. Often thinks people are trying to hurt him/her. (162)
65. Has many unusual fears. (148)
66. Seems to feel unlovable. (165)
67. Tends to blame self for problems at home. (166)
68. Has a preoccupation with death. (159)
69. Shows frequent stuttering or stammering. (135)

70. Shows frequent shivering or shaking when it is not cold. (138)
71. Often expresses the belief that people do not like him/her. (175)
72. Usually seems to feel as if he/she is not as good as others. (140)
73. Refuses to talk. (169)
74. Has perspiring, cold, clammy hands. (134)
75. Dislikes recess for fear of being hurt. (175)
76. Frequently does not respond when others speak to him/her. (142)
77. Is preoccupied with own thoughts and fantasies. (171)
78. Shows unusual reluctance to separate from parents. (145)
79. Refuses to play with other children. (162)
80. Bleeding gums. (184)
81. Bluish tinge to lips, earlobes, or fingernails. (186)
82. Shortness of breath after slight exertion. (187)
83. Pain or burning when urinating. (189)
84. Multiple or severe burns. (190)
85. Unusual number of severe bruises. (190)
86. Cuts or scratches that do not heal. (191)
87. Reports using alcohol or drugs, or sniffing glue. (193)
88. Eats odd things like soap or paint. (195)
89. Swollen or painful joints. (192)
90. Swelling of legs or feet. (192)
91. Excessive drooling. (197)
92. Unusually overweight. (198)
93. Any signs of worms. (200)
94. Frequent, rapid, jerky movements. (209)
95. Brief or extended periods of blanking out. (210)
96. Fainting. (210)
97. Numbness of any body part. (211)
98. Weakness of one side of the body. (213)
99. Unusual staggering or lack of balance. (214)
100. Convulsions, seizures, or unusual "spells." (205)

believe, though, that no highly significant or extremely important sign or symptom has been omitted from the 450 list in
Appendix I.

A thirty-member panel of experts was surveyed for the
purpose of developing index scores for the 450 items. Specifically, this panel included: an optometrist, two general prac-
titioners of medicine, one psychiatrist, one clinical and two
school psychologists, one elementary-school superintendent,
one speech-and-hearing therapist, two registered nurses, two
school principals, three social workers, a director of a school
for the mentally retarded, a professor of education at an area
university, one dentist, two ministers, an elementary-school
physical-education teacher, and eight elementary school
teachers. (All thirty members participated directly.) Each
member was asked to rank each item in terms of severity and
frequency.

The 450 items were placed in a questionnaire, and the
respondent was asked to rate each item in terms of its significance on a scale of one through four, with one representing
"relatively insignificant" and four representing "extremely
significant." The respondent was then asked to rate each item
in terms of the frequency with which it would have to occur in
order to be significant. A rating of "1" indicated that a particular sign or symptom need only occur once to be as significant
as it would ever be; a rating of "4" meant that a sign or
symptom would have to occur more than once a day in order to
be as significant as it would ever be. For each respondent,
then, the significance and frequency scores were combined
after the frequency ratings were inverted. A severity/fre-
quency index score was then developed for each item with
a sign or symptom receiving an "8" if it would need to occur
only once to be extremely significant and a "2" if its occurrence more than once a day would be relatively insignificant.
Once the completed survey forms were returned, each item
was analyzed to develop an index score computed in terms of
the mean response from panel members.

The 100 items receiving the highest mean index scores
were then presented to a fifty-member panel for consider-

ation. This fifty-member panel was developed by adding an additional twenty panel members to the first panel. The additions included; one pediatrician, one psychiatrist, one internist, one clinical psychologist, one school psychologist, one pediatric neurologist, a director of a child-welfare agency, one speech-and-hearing therapist, two social workers, three faculty members from colleges of education, two faculty members from medical schools, a director of education from a residential program for the mentally retarded, one teacher of children with learning disorders, and three parents of young children. (This fifty-member panel was surveyed by mail, and a 68 per cent response rate was achieved.)

In general, both panels represented a highly sophisticated group of experts who deal daily either with small children or with others who are directly involved with small children. I feel strongly that these two groups of people represent the state of the art of recognizing problems in little children, although both panels may be legitimately seen as reflecting some rural midwestern bias.

The fifty-member panel of experts was presented with a 100-item questionnaire. This survey instrument contained those 100 signs and symptoms receiving the highest index score from the longer survey form. Each of the members of the second panel was asked to carefully review the 100 signs and symptoms in terms of his/her judgment of the 100 most significant signs and symptoms of early childhood difficulty observable by teachers at school. Each expert was asked to add any number of signs and symptoms to the list in line with his or her own judgment and experience. The only qualification was that in order to add a new item to the list they must mark out the item they considered least significant on the survey list of 100. When they had completed the questionnaire, their list would still contain 100 items.

The assumption was made that if five or more experts independently felt that a specific new sign or symptom should be added to the list their authority justified adding that item to the list. In order to do this, the items marked out more frequently were deleted from the list; only items marked out by ten or more experts were deleted. It required, then, the consensus of five experts to add an item to the original list and a consensus of at least ten to remove an item. This process led to the 100 signs and symptoms seen in Figure 1 and in the research instrument in Appendix II.

The 100 signs and symptoms were parceled out to volunteer graduate students working toward Master's degrees in education. These students worked with great enthusiasm and dedication. Through their efforts, each item was operationalized within the school setting, in terms of its significance or potential significance and the most appropriate response a teacher might make to it. These teachers carefully reviewed relevant literature, interviewed appropriate experts, and drew on their knowledge and experience in order to give careful, authoritative documentation to the sign or symptom's identification, significance, and to the required response. Of course, their brief presentations were not in appropriate form to provide useful information for parents and teachers. Nevertheless, the thought and energy of the students is gratefully appreciated.

Once the one hundred most significant signs of difficulty were established, the author divided the signs and symptoms into eight subgroups, each focusing on a particular area of childhood difficulty. These eight subgroups stand as chapters two through nine of this book. Once the eight chapter groupings were established, an introduction was written for each chapter that incorporated the signs and symptoms into an illustrative or classroom context. It is hoped that these introductions will help the reader recall specific signs and symptoms in groups, since it will probably be impossible to remember them all individually. For the convenience of using this book as a reference source, when questions arise relative to specific signs and symptoms, an index is included in the back of the book.

Following the introduction to each chapter, the signs and symptoms subgrouped in that chapter were systematically developed and integrated, giving the reader an overall feel for recognizing, understanding, and responding to those signs and symptoms. Hopefully, the discussion is detailed enough to offer specific suggestions, concrete patterns and policies related to dealing with particular kinds of problems and offers enough integration of signs and symptoms to allow you to recognize specific signs and symptoms and to generalize from a particular sign or symptom to other possible difficulties a child may be having. At the end of each chapter, the "most significant" signs and symptoms discussed in that chapter are organized into a "symptom profile." In addition to the uses of these profiles discussed below, they may be used as "check lists" for identifying children with particular kinds of problems, e.g., academic problems, physical problems, environmental problems, emotional problems, behavior problems, etc. As "check lists" the individual symptom profiles may be especially useful when identifying children for special programs, special class placements, special needs surveys, etc.

Once chapters two through nine were complete, the material and information included in each chapter was subjected to rigorous medical, psychological, and educational review to assure professional accuracy, completeness, and consistency. Although I prepared the final material and responsibility for it must be attributed solely to me, the individuals recognized in the acknowledgments have had substantial input and have, with care and diligence, made a real effort to be sure that you can use and rely on the content of the book with confidence.

An Exercise in How to Use This Book

As our training and experience have shown and as the following chapters demonstrate, children are multidimensional beings with physical dimensions, emotional dimensions, moral/spiritual dimensions, social dimensions, sexual dimensions, and intellectual dimensions. Seldom, if ever, do problems pervade only one dimension without some effect and influence in other dimensions. Problems of children, like the children themselves, are multidimensional and almost always reflect some "mix." More specifically, physical problems of children usually have causes and effects within their emotional and social dimensions. For example, children who do not feel very well have difficulty relating to other children, are not as happy or as enthusiastic as usual, and may tend to withdraw or become irritable. Similarly, children with serious learning difficulties usually show concomitant emotional difficulties.

The specific focus here on early elementary-age children will enhance the ability of a classroom teacher to relate to and help a specific child. We do not have thirty relationship styles for the thirty kids in a classroom. Similarly, we do not have an infinite variety of personalities and temperments to choose from for each child. We do have a few general but different ways of relating, though. Some children may need an immediate response, while others require a slower, more carefully thought-out response. Some problems you can handle yourself, while others require involvement of people from other professional disciplines. By limiting our focus in this book, we should be able to look at these kinds of things in depth. In the following chapters, we will talk about when and how to use school psychologists, school counselors, school nurses, school speech or hearing therapists, and school administrators and supervisors. We will also consider the issue of "what to do" when these resources are not available. We will talk about how you can work directly with children experiencing a wide variety of problems, how to work effectively with and help the parents of these children, and how to learn about and utilize a variety of community resources in your work with special problems and needs.

To develop a "feel for" the approach to children and their difficulties used in this book, consider the signs and symptoms seen in some specific children. As we begin to take up children with individual problems, we will want to begin to organize our thinking into categories and interrelated symptom patterns. We know that children have academic or classroom difficulties. In addition, they have physical/organic problems, usually seen as illness. Also, little children have occasional "emotional" and "social" problems. Beyond these categories, the difficulties and problems of little children occasionally relate to "environmental" conditions and circumstances. We can, then, begin to think about little children in terms of academic, physical/organic, emotional, social, and environmental problems. As already emphasized, it will be unusual to observe a problem that involves only one of these categories. Rather, the usual pattern will be that symptoms reflect a "mix" of categories.

As an exercise, let us use Figure 2 as a guide for analyzing the signs and symptoms to be seen in the two children discussed below. Under the first column (Symptoms), make note of each of the signs and symptoms seen in each child. In the academic, physical/organic, emotional, social, and environmental columns, place an "x" to indicate your judgment as to those categories involved "causally" with the particular sign or symptom. If you think a specific symptom represents both difficulty in academic performance and emotional problems, place an "x" in the "Academic" *and* "Emotional" columns. Once you have finished the chart for each child, consider the interrelatedness of the symptoms, your speculation about possible causal categories, the possible significance of the overall symptom pattern, and a tentative program for responding to that symptom pattern. (The "possible causal pattern" is reflected in the number and position of "x"s in the chart.)

Fig. 2. Categorical Symptom Profile

SYMPTOM	PHYSICAL/ ORGANIC	EMOTIONAL	SOCIAL	ENVIRONMENTAL	ACADEMIC

Ellen is in the second grade and is having difficulties. She does not do very well in any of her school work, although she seems to try hard, almost too hard at times. Ellen was physically and emotionally abused as a small child and is currently living in a foster home. When you talk with Ellen by herself, she is a pleasant child who seems fairly bright, sits in a relaxed manner, smiles a lot, seems happy, and seems to know the kinds of things you would expect from a child in the second grade. When you talk individually with Ellen, she does fairly well with numbers, simple arithmetic, spelling words, and talking about what's going on at school, and she generally seems to be having no difficulty. She appears to be very warm and responsive and gives no outward indication that she is having difficulty with her school work. However, when Ellen is asked to perform in a small group or classroom context, she is unable to read aloud, do her arithmetic problems either at her desk or at the chalkboard, participate in group discussion, or do the other things most children are able to do. It is as if being with other children seriously interferes with her ability to do those things she apparently knows how to do. Her poor classroom performance is in sharp contrast to the impressions one gets from individual discussions with her.

Fred has gotten in trouble along with another boy in his class. The two boys broke into a neighborhood church and marked up the walls, broke some objects, and generally made a mess. Since both Fred and his friend are seven, they were not taken to Juvenile Court but were returned to their families with instructions for the parents to supervise them more closely. Fred is in the second grade, lives with his mother and stepfather, has grown up in a very unstable family and environmental situation, spends most of his time with his mother and stepfather but also some time with his alcoholic, natural father. Fred has played with matches, has had oral genital sexual contact with three or four neighbor boys, has stolen money from his grandfather and given it to his friends, and seems unusually active although he is occasionally quite withdrawn.

Most of his behavior problems have occurred when Fred

was visiting his natural father, including an episode in which Fred apparently intentionally set his mattress on fire. For the last five or six weeks, Fred has not been allowed to visit his natural father. A couple of weeks ago, though, Fred became upset at home, turned things upside down in the house, and ran off for five or six hours; he finally came home, acting as if nothing had happened. There have been behavior problems at school, involving fighting with other kids, playing with matches, and one incident of glue sniffing. Fred seems to want a lot of attention and creates many disturbances in class, but he does reasonably well with his school work. At school, a series of minor problems have accumulated into a major problem. There are no outstanding incidents; Fred just frequently gets into trouble and causes confusion. Fred's mother describes him as having good days and bad days. A similar up and down pattern of behavior and adjustment has been seen at school.

As we conclude this introductory chapter, consider the signs and symptoms seen in two additional children. Develop a symptom profile for Gus; in addition you will have to consider what other "specialist" might be in a position to help Gus and what other kinds of things you will need to know about Gus—about his school adjustment and performance, about his home behavior, and about his community involvement—aside from the signs and symptoms outlined below.

Gus occasionally has temper tantrums at school but the major problem is that he soils his pants two or three times a week, sometimes on the playground and sometimes during class. He is fairly bright and very verbal. He seems quite interested in his school work and classroom activities, plays with the other children, and seems to be socially well-adjusted. Frequently, though, it seems difficult for him to pay attention and sit still, and there is some problem setting limits for him. If you approach him in a very gentle, asking way, there is usually no problem. If you are firm, abrupt, or somewhat arbitrary with him, he will react quite intensely, screaming, waving his arms, wandering about, and generally behaving rather peculiarly. For example, when his teacher took hold of his arm to slow him down one day he immediately began screaming, hitting and kicking at her, and tried to pull himself away. She tried to hold him more firmly, which only seemed to make him worse. During the episode it seemed as if Gus found it impossible to calm down. Once the episode was over, he became rather quiet and cooperative and was the best-behaved child in the classroom for a while.

Now develop a symptom profile for Helen. What additional information and/or evaluations will you require to help Helen?

Helen is a very unresponsive child who tries to avoid both verbal and visual contact. She has an extreme aversion to being touched and gets very shaky and frightened when someone tries to get close to her. Her mother reports that Helen is very spontaneous and affectionate with her and that their relationship is very healthy. At school, Helen's behavior is very controlled and all of her actions are precise. At times she has almost a mechanical quality about her as she does her work and participates in classroom activities. She seems very aware of what is going on around her and unusually alert even to minor happenings in the classroom.

As you consider the next eight chapters, keep in mind the project of developing symptom profiles [and treatment plans] for specific children and maintain focus on the children with whom you work as you consider the one hundred most significant signs and symptoms of early childhood difficulty. As you develop individual symptom profiles for specific children, be critical of your own analysis and understanding, remembering that these one hundred signs and symptoms are not all-inclusive and that specific circumstances may make other signs more significant than those on the list. For example, signs of rat or other animal bites, symptoms of malnutrition or sickle-cell anemia, cultural factors (values, beliefs, and norms) reflected in specific ethnic groups, difficulty with the English language, and other "group specific" problems may be as relevant to the children in your specific school as any of the problems seen in the one hundred signs and symptoms discussed in this book. We are talking about "all" children ages five through eight. The children with whom you work will likely have some special needs, problems, and vulnerabilities. A serious attempt has been made to point out those signs and symptoms that vary in terms of significance and causality with factors such as social class, the child's specific age, ethnicity, environmental circumstances, and where the children live. Nonetheless, it is critical that you take time to know and understand *your* children, their circumstances, and their special problems.

From the amount of time we will spend talking about serious signs and symptoms of childhood difficulty, you may come to the conclusion that most children usually have serious physical/organic, emotional, social, environmental, and academic difficulties. This conclusion would be unjustified. For example, a lot of time will be spent talking about neurological causes as a possible factor related to many of the signs and symptoms discussed. The reality is that neurological difficulty usually does not underlie the signs and symptoms seen in children. Similarly, it would be easy to come to the conclusion that a large proportion of children have serious emotional and social difficulties. The fact is that only a small proportion of children have such difficulties. Also, it is frequently the case that children who appear to have social and emotional difficulties actually have minor to serious physical problems. Children who have suspected emotional, social, academic, or environmental difficulties should always receive a thorough physical examination to evaluate the possibility that physical problems underlie the signs and symptoms.

In addition you may develop the impression that we are able to understand with a high degree of certainty almost everything that goes on with children. The opposite is true. Probably most of what is happening inside their minds and with their emotions is beyond our understanding and reach. Alice really does still spend a lot of time in Wonderland.

Nevertheless, the knowledge and understanding we do have exists at a very high level of certainty. Furthermore, that knowledge comes in a probability form. We can talk about a particular sign or symptom or about a particular group of signs and symptoms. When talking about causes and appropriate responses, though, we can talk only about the most likely causes and about responses with the highest probability of success. Nonetheless, at a very high level of certainty, we do know that effective understanding of children's difficulties and work with them requires a warm, supportive, encouraging relationship within which they can grow and develop. Sometimes, this relationship requires more permissiveness than firmness and at other times more firmness than permissiveness. Always, though, the relationship between you and a child has to be one in which he or she can sense security, caring, interest, concern, and a willingness to be involved in a positive and growth-producing manner. Each child needs to feel good about what he or she can do, has accomplished, will achieve, is able to understand, and what and who he or she is.

Hopefully, you are beginning to get a feel for the on-going and on-growing process in which kids are involved. In fact, we can see that their development reflects an interrelated and interacting set of processes. Your first inclination should be to evaluate the child in terms of how much he or she seems not to have learned and to use your wide variety of teaching skills and resources to encourage and enhance the child's learning. If this process does not lead to a reduction in the signs and symptoms, if it does not lead to the child's behaving more in line with other kids his or her age, it will be necessary to look for other causes and responses. The first causal area to consider is physical. The second causal area for consideration is the child's learning abilities and patterns. The third area to look at is the possibility of emotional difficulty or environmental difficulties interferring with the child's functioning. If a very likely explanation is developed through exploring these areas, you can follow through with the child accordingly. However, if you still don't understand what's going on with the child or what to do about it, it's time to yell loud and long for help—not for you, for the child. You will probably need to make a lot of noise and maybe rock a few boats before "the system" will respond to the child and his or her problems. Others may be inclined to think that you are either making a big deal over nothing or at least exaggerating the situation, or they may argue that if you were a better teacher you would be able to handle it. For the child's sake, don't let them get away with that nonsense. All kids can learn and will learn if we work hard enough, are clever enough, persistent enough, and learn enough ourselves to help them.

TWO

Reading, Writing, and Arithmetic

It is November and nearly time for the Thanksgiving break. The fifty-eight children in the combined first-, second-, and third-grade class at Park School are busy in their small groups working on everything from coloring to multiplication. This class has two elementary teachers and a full-time aide, plus two mothers who volunteer on Tuesday and Thursday mornings.

Once a month the school psychologist and building principal stop by to observe the class, check on the progress of children who have been having special problems, and consult with the teacher regarding several children about whom teachers are concerned.

Bobby, a usually happy and outgoing little boy, really has the teachers worried. He usually performs in the upper third of his class, always seems interested and somewhat enthusiastic about classroom assignments, and seems to enjoy school very much. During the last two weeks, though, his teachers have noticed a sudden deterioration in the quality of his work. He does not seem very interested in school, is not completing his classroom assignments, and is generally performing at a level considerably below average. The change is dramatic, and his teachers are somewhat alarmed.

Marcel presents a different kind of puzzle. She seems to feel incapable of doing her schoolwork. It's almost as if she feels defeated before starting her work. She appears not to be working up to her actual abilities, and her teachers are puzzled.

Terry is at the third-year level and still seems to be having trouble with many of the things almost all first- and second-year kids have mastered. He quite consistently reverses his numbers and letters, is unable to identify his body parts consistently, seems easily distracted by surroundings and minor noises, usually looks at pictures or books upside down, and seems unable to apply himself to a task while sitting at a desk.

Kathy sometimes makes her teachers feel as if it is extra hard for her to concentrate and learn. She seems to have real difficulty repeating three to five numbers in sequence and appears to have memory lapses where she cannot remember things her teachers think she ought to know. It is really a struggle for her to keep up with the other children, and most of the time she seems unable to. It concerns her teachers that Kathy seems to spend a lot of time rocking in her chair.

Julio is one of those really frustrating children. His work is inconsistent; he knows something really well one day but not the next. Even when he seems to know the subject matter, he seems incapable of following even the simplest directions. This is especially noticeable during classroom discussions. He will answer oral questions by completely changing the subject; his answers are sometimes not at all responsive.

Cindy has difficulty drawing and coloring. When she tries to color, she often grasps her crayon with so much pressure that she tears the paper. When her teachers ask her to draw a picture of a person, she scribbles and seems unable to give the picture any form or shape.

The nineteen signs and symptoms of childhood difficulty seen in this classroom do not represent all of the important problems that little children can have. Nevertheless, the experts agree that they are the most important or significant symptoms observed by teachers in the classroom performance of early elementary-age children. Let's look at these nineteen signs and symptoms individually and consider their identification and significance, and the most appropriate response to these difficulties. As you consider the discussion of each symptom, it is important to be alert to the appearance of the symptom in your classroom. Once any of the signs or symptoms has been recognized, individually or in combination, in a particular child, the professional challenge rests with you and your ability to respond appropriately to the problem.

Discussion

As we look at signs and symptoms of academic and classroom difficulty, *a sudden deterioration in the quality of work* is one of the most noticeable. It is usually not hard to spot. A child who generally does reasonably well in school suddenly begins performing at a markedly reduced or failing level. Over a relatively short time period a child may shift from getting most arithmetic problems, science questions, or other assignments correct to getting most of them wrong. A child who usually completes most of his assigned work may start turning in papers that are partially or totally unfinished. Sloppy, disorderly work may stand in sharp contrast to neat, orderly work done a few days before. The key to recognizing that there is a problem is noticing that the child is suddenly not doing nearly as well as he had been.

Three cautions are important to keep in mind, though. First, any child might have a bad day or come across some material that is especially difficult. Even a superior student might get a failing grade once in a while. This may reflect some particularly difficult learning challenge or perhaps more enthusiasm for playing ball or jumping rope than for the day's assignment. A frown and perhaps a little firmness from you should keep things on the right track, especially if you can remember how much fun it is to play ball or jump rope on a pretty fall morning.

Second, it is fairly easy to notice marked deterioration in

the quality of work in high-achieving, superior students. The decline from B- and C-level to D-level work, though, may not be quite so noticeable. A good way to check may be to look at your grade book every couple of weeks to see if the performance of any student seems to be falling off noticeably. If your school does not use the traditional letter-grading system, noticing a deterioration in the work of a specific student may be somewhat more difficult. Of course, you will get to know each child in your class and his or her work quite well. It will then be important to use this knowledge and awareness of each child as a "standard" for comparison purposes. As you work with the children in class and evaluate their written and oral work, it will be important to evaluate whether or not each child's work and performance reflect fairly consistent progress, in addition to evaluating the work and performance themselves. It may be convenient to keep a "performance notebook" for your class, with one page for each child in your group. Each day you can then make a note for each child who is not doing very well that day, or who is not doing as well as usual. Once each week or so you can review your performance notebook to see which children are having continuing difficulties, as well as to become aware of those children who seem not to be doing as well as they have done in the past. (Be sure to put the correct date with each note entered in the notebook so you will be able to evaluate problems in proper sequence and with an accurate understanding of their frequency.)

The third caution is to consider the possibility that you have not adequately or effectively presented specific material when a specific child or several children in your class seem not to be doing very well. Since the notes in your performance notebook will include comments about the particular subject or topic area with which the child has difficulty, you will be able to focus on problems relative to a particular child and a specific subject matter, as well as difficulties you may be having with certain subjects or topics; i.e., if several children had similar difficulties with the same topic area during a given week, it may be that you have not presented that particular material very well. At a minimum, when reviewing your performance notebook, if it suggests that specific children had similar difficulties with a specific topic you may want to go back over that material, at least with those children.

Deterioration in youngsters' school performance can be the result of a lot of things. If it lasts for more than a few days, though, you should think about what might be going on. Put possible physical problems at the top of your list. Of course, if the child is complaining about physical pain, discomfort, or other such reportable symptoms, you should check into that before a few days have passed. Nevertheless, some types of infections, glandular difficulty, sensory problems such as difficulty seeing or hearing, and so forth can begin gradually, with no dramatic or easily observable symptoms. The child may slowly become lethargic and disinterested or nervous, experience difficulties in concentration, have difficulties perceiving his world, or appear disinterested in school and things around him. The first step, then, is to talk with the child about how he or she feels, what he/she thinks about how schoolwork is going, and if he/she seems to be having any problems. You should also have the school nurse talk with the child and let the parents know that you are concerned. Unless things improve fairly quickly, or unless there is some fairly obvious alternative explanation for difficulties, the child should be taken to the family doctor. It will be important for parents to talk with the doctor about the signs and symptoms because many tests and procedures that get at this kind of difficulty would not routinely be done.

For some children and in some schools, enlisting the involvement and cooperation of parents may be considerably more easily said than done. Similarly, it may not be a simple matter to assure that a child is seen by a physician. In fact, your particular school may not have the services of a school nurse. What then? First, if your school does not have the services of a nurse or other medically trained staff member, you will need to rely on your own knowledge, judgment, and experience when deciding whether or not medical attention is required for a particular child. If you are unsure, draw on the experience and knowledge of other teachers and staff members in your school. At a minimum, share your concern about a particular child with your supervisor or building principal so that she is aware of the problem. This also gives her the opportunity to make suggestions and let you know about any relevant school policies or usual procedures.

Second, if the problem seems to justify contacting the child's parents, you will want to do this personally, but at least make sure that someone from the school gets in touch with them. On those occasions when it is difficult to get in touch with a child's parents or guardian, the difficulty of the task is not a reason for inaction or not following through. If getting in touch with the parents was initially a good idea, it continues to be a good idea even if it is difficult to do so. Most parents will follow through in a thorough way, including arranging for a physical examination, if you just let them know there is a problem. At times, though (frequently, in some school systems), parents will not follow through and are unable to arrange for a physical examination. At that point, the involvement of local health authorities and child welfare personnel is appropriate, if the child's problem continues.

Ordinarily, involving these outside resources would not be the direct responsibility of the classroom teacher. You should discuss the child and his or her problem with your supervisor and/or building principal, letting them know what steps you have taken to deal with the problem, how serious you think the problem is, and how important it is that parental involvement and medical attention be developed. At that point, your building principal and/or supervisor have the responsibility to evelute the situation and follow through. What if they do not? Keep hassling and bringing the problem to their attention—not for your sake, but for the child's.

Family and friends run a fairly close race as possible causes of academic and classroom deterioration. Usually your young students will talk with you a little bit about either of these areas if you are fairly gentle and supportive and let them know that you are not blaming or criticizing them. There probably is not a whole lot you can do about a child's problems at home other than letting the parents know that there are problems which seem to be affecting the child's schoolwork. Nevertheless, you can be especially supportive and give the children a lot of encouragement at school to compensate a little for any feelings of rejection, negativism, or futility they feel. When the deterioration reflects difficulty in peer relationships, your best bet is to leave peer problems alone. The world is divided up very nicely in terms of four-year-old problems for four-year-olds, seven-year-old problems for seven-year-olds, fifteen-year-old problems for fifteen-year-olds, and so on. Working through peer relationships is a problem suited to children of any age. Solving the problem for them only makes them less able to deal with age-level problems as they get older.

Once you have worked out for yourself an understanding of the cause of the deterioration and have responded appropriately, it is time gradually to become more firm and to insist that the child return to his previous level in classroom work. Too much attention, sympathy, and understanding can become reinforcing and can lead to the problems' continuing or getting worse instead of better. After a reasonable length of time and diagnostic certainty, the payoff for the child must again come from doing well.

A few comments are in order here about involving parents, school counselors, school psychologists, other specialized school personnel, and outside professionals and agencies. Almost all parents are interested in and concerned about their children and will willingly follow through on your suggestions and recommendations. This is true even in those families where it may cause extreme inconvenience or financial hardship. If you get the feeling that parents do not want to, or are unwilling to, follow through, consider first the possibility that you have not approached them in a friendly and concerned way, or have not adequately helped them to understand the significance of the problem. Cultural differences between you and them, difficulty with the English language on their part or yours, social class differences between you and them, and/or other factors may be operating as barriers to effective communication between you and the parents. When you are having difficulty getting parents to cooperate, consider the possibility that they may just honestly disagree with you, and then try to determine what barriers may be interfering with your efforts to communicate with them. For example, you may not be the most appropriate person to discuss a particular child's problems with his or her parents.

Next, just as your school may not have the services of a nurse, it may also not have the services of a counselor or psychologist. The role of an elementary school counselor (and sometimes school social workers) involves counseling in a supportive and interested way with little children, working with their parents, talking with you about their social and emotional problems, and either helping with or following through on arrangements for the involvement of outside agencies and professionals. In many schools, the role of the counselor is defined more in administrative than in counseling terms. If this is true in your school, probably both you and the counselor would benefit if efforts were made to change the definition of this role. If your school does not have the services of a counselor, you will frequently need to do the counseling with parents and children, as well as arranging for outside resources, if they are to be done at all. Similarly, many schools do not have the services of a psychologist readily available. Those schools which do have such services provide a valuable resource to the children with whom you work. Most school psychologists are qualified to evaluate the learning ability and achievement levels of children, in addition to evaluating possible learning disorders, neurological and visual/motor perception difficulties, emotional difficulties, and overall social/emotional adjustment. Unfortunately, the psychologists in many school systems do not have time to evaluate the large number of children needing evaluations, do not have time to consult with parents and teachers about findings and possible remedial approaches, and so on. When a time is made available for these functions, the psychologist can really help a lot. When time is not made available, or when there is no psychologist, you will need to look for resources outside of the school. (A special note should be made of the fact that most physicians are not qualified to evaluate adequately the problems noted here as the bailiwick of psychologists.)

You will need to know about resources and services available in your community. In general, most communities have a mental health center or child guidance clinic responsible for serving the residents of the area. Most communities have an active "health department" staffed by registered nurses and other personnel. Many communities have family service and social service agencies equipped to deal with the social and emotional difficulties of young children and to work with both the children and their families. All communities have some agency responsible for "child welfare" or "children's services." Even though the staff members of these agencies may not, themselves, be equipped to deal with specific children and specific problems, they should be well aware of existing resources, how to take advantage of those resources, the cost of using those resources, etc. In some communities, this "child welfare" function is handled by the public welfare or social welfare department. Most ministers are aware of community resources and church-related resources, or will at least be willing to find out how to get the resources needed by a particular child. Also, most hospitals have a "social services" department staffed by individuals who either know about or will find out about necessary resources. It is important to note that federal, state, and local financial assistance is available to pay for any resources actually needed by children when their families, in fact, cannot afford to pay for them. As you consider the needs of a specific child, keep focus on your own knowledge and resources, the resources of your school, and the resources of your community and larger geographic area. Of course, you should make every effort to involve a child's parents before involving any resources outside of the school.

With these perspectives about working with parents and involving other resources in mind, we now move to the next symptom of academic or classroom difficulty.

Sometimes a child *may seem to feel incapable of doing his or her work.* This is frequently seen in combination with a sudden deterioration in the quality of work, although this typically stands out as a pattern of response to most tasks and assignments over a long period of time. The first and most essential step is to be sure that the child actually is capable of doing his or her work. The only effective way to make this judgment adequately is to have the school psychologist or the clinical psychologist at one of your community agencies thoroughly evaluate the child's intellectual performance, academic achievement, visual/motor performance levels, and social/emotional functioning. Nothing is quite so inexcusable as not to believe a child when he tells us that he cannot do his work. For whatever reason, what he is telling us is true: he cannot do the work.

If the psychologist finds intellectual difficulties, achievement problems, learning disabilities, and so forth, special programming for the child will be required. Similarly, if the problem turns out to be the result of a very poor self-concept, significant negativism in approaching any kind of task, or other social/emotional trouble, your patience and sensitivity will be very important. If you have tried patience, sensitivity, and encouragement and the problem still persists, the next step is to talk with the child's parents to see what they think about the situation. You may want to talk to the school counselor to see if he or she will spend some time with the child, and you may want to suggest to the child's parents that some outside professional counseling for the child may be in order.

A related problem concerns the child who *seems to feel defeated before even beginning to work*. The initial response to most tasks is "I don't know how" or "I can't do that." Similarly, you may notice that the child simply sits and looks at the work without picking up a pencil or making some other gesture in the direction of starting to work. Or the child may look around, talk to neighbors, or do almost anything to avoid getting down to business.

The first step is to make sure that the task or assignment is not overwhelming. Possibly you have given the child more difficult material before she really understands the less difficult material, or the task may simply seem like too much to the child. One sheet with twenty arithmetic problems may seem like an endless task to a seven-year-old. If you are sure that the assignment really is manageable and that the child really can do the work, you should encourage her to do at least one or two problems, or the first section of the assignment. It is very important that you let the child know that the risk in doing it wrong or not getting it finished is low. You might say, "Why don't you just do three or four of them and see how that goes? If you have any trouble, I'm right here and will be ready to help." At that point, you may want to help the child with the first problem or question, gently and in a positive tone. Remember, the problem is for the child to get started. Place your emphasis, then, on her getting started instead of on getting finished. For example, it would be a mistake to try to motivate a child by saying that work must be done before she can go out for recess.

Some children perform fairly consistently with no noticeable deterioration in their work, have little difficulty starting and completing assignments, and may feel that they can do and are doing their work satisfactorily. Your concern is that they *do not seem to be working up to their ability.* Their psychological tests and past successes let you know that they can and should be doing better than they are.

The first step here is to be doubly sure that it is really true that these children are not working up to their potential or ability. Once this is ascertained, though, care should be taken to make sure that the problem does not reflect physical difficulty. For example, vision or hearing problems may be interfering with optimal performance. Also, other kinds of continuing physical problems might be present. A good vision and hearing screening, as well as a current physical examination, is in order. If all of these tests are negative, the next step is to provide extra help and support for the child, in the form of individualized tutoring, remedial help on a group basis, a special place to study with supplementary materials and equipment, or other special aids and approaches. Equally important, however, is increasing the payoff for better performance. It would probably be a mistake to punish or discipline these children, since this would tend to increase their anxiety and difficulty in dealing with the school situation. Tokens or special prizes for extra achievement or for improvement in achievement may help quite a lot, or giving them extra things to do around the classroom that the other children wish to do will probably help. Passing out papers, going to the office for supplies, and helping the teacher with special projects will serve this function. In general, the goal is to let each child know that he is fine, that people are happy with him, while at the same time letting him know that they will be even more happy if he improves classroom work.

The problem of evaluating a child's "real ability" is complex and needs special comment. In general, children with "high ability" perform and achieve relatively better than most children in relation to most activities, and children with "low ability" perform and achieve relatively less well than most children in relation to most activities. For example, a child with "high ability" would tend to perform and achieve quite well academically, socially, and in relation to most activities and assignments. If a child shows a high level of social involvement and effectiveness, demonstrates good achievement in nonclassroom activities, and generally gets along quite well, but is having a problem with classroom work, you should strongly suspect that the child probably has average or higher ability but is experiencing some special learning or academic difficulty. Similarly, if a child is experiencing academic or classroom difficulty and also experiences limited social and performance success outside the classroom, you should suspect the possibility that the child's "real ability" is somewhat less than that of most children his or her age.

More specifically, if a child experiences problems in one academic area or type of classroom assignment but not in others, you should suspect that the child has "real ability" that is somehow not being actualized in the areas in which she is having problems. It is true, though, that individual children may do quite well at almost everything and simply not have any "real talent or ability" in some specific area. This seldom is the case, though, in relation to classroom tasks and expectations. It is extremely unlikely that a child would simply not have "real ability" in arithmetic and reflect "real ability" in reading, writing, learning about science, and other academic areas. This type of problem occurs so rarely that you will be safe to assume that any child who performs well in some areas of classroom work but has difficulties in others is experiencing some "learning problem" unrelated to "real ability." Alternatively, if a child has difficulty with most areas of classroom and academic performance but shows significantly better ability in one specific area (for example, arithmetic), you may safely assume that the child's real ability is higher than reflected through most of her classroom work.

One should always start with the strong assumption that a child's real ability is solid and is at least at the level of that of most children. Coming to the conclusion that a particular child actually has low ability should only happen over time and after you have made a serious effort to help the child learn. This effort, over time, to help the child learn should be combined with other evaluations and procedures. The child should be examined by a psychologist who can evaluate his or her learning ability. One important point to be noted is that a myriad of problems can "depress" the apparent learning ability of a child. For example, serious emotional problems interfere with a child's performance and effectiveness and can occasionally give the appearance of "low ability." In addition, significant social maladjustment and environmental deprivation can result in the same depression of observable ability. Of course, some physical conditions and factors can also have this effect. An evaluation of a child's ability must, then, include your caring and careful efforts to work with and teach the child, along with evaluations of possible physical, emotional, social, and environmental factors.

It is important to note that "IQ tests" do not measure a child's "real ability." Rather, they simply measure the extent to which a child can perform certain tasks and operations at the same level as most children his or her age. The possible social and cultural biases of these tests must also be taken into consideration. For most children, standardized IQ tests reasonably approximate their actual ability. For any specific child, however, the results of the IQ test should only be used as *one indicator* among many. Further, it should be noted that intelligence and achievement tests may give us some useful information about a child's performance and achievement, and they may also suggest some possible causes and remedial strategies. It is important to keep in mind that such tests never tell us why a particular child is having a particular problem at a particular point in time.

Occasionally you will find a child who, for one reason or another, *cannot keep up with his peer group academically.* Here we are focusing on an inability as opposed to a situation where a child is simply not keeping up. The inability to compete successfully in an academic, classroom sense can be a result of severe physical problems. For example, a child would be unable to keep up with a normal peer group if he had a very severe hearing loss, a serious problem with motor control, or other seriously handicapping condition. In children with such severe physical limitations the problem is not their inability to keep up with the group but their having special needs and learning patterns that probably are not responded to adequately in the normal classroom setting. These children are quite capable of learning, but need special programs and services that usually can be combined quite nicely with a regular classroom setting.

It is sometimes less noticeable, but equally likely, that children who cannot keep up with their peer group have a serious intellectual deficiency or learning disorder. In either case, special student groupings, innovative teaching techniques, and alertness to things these children can do will help them compete more effectively. Whether the inability is a result of physical, intellectual, or learning problems, special instruction, materials related to each child's individual needs, and extra services are necessary. However, these must be carefully and caringly combined with normalizing experiences for the child. For example, these youngsters may be quite capable of participating in regular playground activities, some classroom activities, art programs, and so forth, with less handicapped children. This concept, called "mainstreaming," emphasizes the school's responsibility to involve all children with each other as much as possible.

Children who cannot keep up present the teacher with a double responsibility. First, you must be very careful that it is true that the child cannot keep up with his peer group. It is probably better to expect too much and run the risk of the child's being frustrated than to assume that he or she cannot do it. Once the "cannot" determination is made, though, it then becomes your responsibility to manipulate the school and community system in a way that permits the child to receive all of the services and special programming he needs.

So far we have been talking about general learning patterns and changes in those patterns. As experienced teachers know, though, there are many more subtle signs of academic and classroom difficulty. For example, it is typical for kindergarten, first-, and second-grade children to have some difficulty with *reversing and rotating numbers and letters;* they may write numbers and letters in the wrong sequence, upside down, or otherwise show some problem with getting things in the right order and headed in the right direction. It is not common, though, for children to continue this difficulty into the third grade with any consistency. Furthermore, it is not common for kindergarten, first-, and second-grade children to have consistent and continuing difficulty in this area. The problem usually reflects some difficulty with eye/hand coordination or with visual/motor perception. The problem is that the child does not adequately learn to process visual impressions and reproduce them. This can cause difficulty in reading, writing, arithmetic, and all other areas of school performance.

The first thing to check is whether or not the child's eyesight is adequate; this requires a professional examination. You should be aware that small children do not see very well anyway; one of the reasons for putting large print in early primary school books is that the average five- or six-year-old cannot see well enough to read the print in adult books easily. In a later chapter, we will go into detail about the possible vision and hearing problems of small children. At this point, though, let it suffice to say that, if a professional eye examination shows that the child's vision is normal, you can consider other possibilities. The first step, then, is gently to call the child's attention to the problem. Maybe he did not know it was such a big deal; if he learns it bothers you so much, he may take a little more time and be a little more careful. If this does not lead to gradual improvement, a referral to the school psychologist is in order; this professional can let you know more specifically what is involved in the problem, what its implications are for this particular child, and how you might better help this child learn the things he needs to know. For example, it may be important for much of his learning to take place orally, with less emphasis on writing and other manual tasks.

Most of what children learn at school comes "into them" through their eyes and ears. They see things, experience things visually, are asked to perform tasks that require visual processing of information, and so on. Similarly, much of what they learn is presented to them verbally, i.e., they are told things, things are explained to them, they are told about things, they hear things, etc. For most children, this works out quite nicely. If their learning difficulties relate to the processing of visual and auditory stimuli, however, there is real difficulty. Clearly, blind children must learn through hearing and touching, while deaf children must learn through seeing and touching. Most children integrate their learning and correct their "mislearning" through talking and writing about their experiences and understanding. From this, we can see that learning can involve seeing, hearing, feeling, and talking or writing, so when a child is having learning difficulties, one strategy is to put emphasis, for example, on auditory learning as opposed to visual learning, or tactile learning as opposed to auditory or visual learning.

Consider learning to read, as an example. Part of children's learning to read comes from being read to. They learn what the words sound like. Learning to read also comes through looking at and remembering words and letters. Similarly, learning to read develops through reading aloud. Also, some children need to learn to read by "feeling" letters and numbers. For example, plastic or wooden numbers or letters can be handed to these children. They can then feel them to help develop an understanding of the number or letter.

The point is that learning is a multisensory, multifunctional process; and every effort should be made to take advantage of this multiplicity when working with children who have special needs or problems. Children should be evaluated in terms of whether or not they know numbers and letters and less in terms of whether or not they can write numbers correctly or letters in the right order. With special help, a child can learn to do those things too. This general approach will almost always be effective. On rare occasions, though, there will be children whose difficulty reflects serious neurological difficulty. A careful examination by a children's neurologist should be provided for those children whose performance does not gradually improve over time.

Another sign of possible academic or classroom difficulty is seen in the child who *consistently has difficulty identifying body parts.* The child may have trouble pointing to eyes, ears, toes, or other specific body areas, or may have particular difficulty learning to tell left from right, up from down, and so on. Occasionally, this problem generalizes to difficulty in following directions about how to get from one place to another, how to arrange materials at the desk, etc. The first step is to check out whether the child is having difficulty with the concept or simply having difficulty in identification. Can he point to your nose, his toes, his neighbor's finger? Now, can he use the correct word when you point to your eye, your nose, his finger? You may also want to see if the child can draw a picture of a person, placing body parts in appropriate positions. One thing to be careful about with kindergarten and first-grade children is that you do not jump to the conclusion that they cannot do it when the problem is that they simply have not yet learned how. Most children will be able to follow simple directions, will know most of their body parts, will have some sense of up and down and front and back, will be beginning to separate right from left, and will generally show some increasing skills with these concepts and movements. If a child is having real difficulty in this area, though, it may reflect lack of learning and exposure or it may be a function of some neurological or muscular difficulty.

As with all learning processes, the key to understanding the problem is whether or not the child gradually improves, comes to understand the concepts better, and learns to perform at the same level as other children of the same age. Identifying body parts, right and left, and up and down are, of course, critical skills required in reading, writing, arithmetic, and almost all areas of classroom performance requiring visual/motor skills. If a child is not progressing at approximately the same rate as classmates, then the problem will only get worse: he or she will not adequately learn to read, write, do arithmetic, etc. The temptation, as with many problems, is to say that the child will outgrow it. That may be true. On the other hand, while the child is outgrowing it, he will gradually fall further and further behind his classmates in classroom performance. A referral to the school psychologist or to the child's physician is in order if he does not show gradual progress in developing these skills.

Distractibility, difficulty concentrating, and a short attention span are symptoms we hear a lot about in education literature. It is important to remember that young children are naturally distractible, find it difficult to concentrate, and do not have very long attention spans. Nevertheless, some children *are especially easily distracted by surroundings and minor noises.* Children with these symptoms lose track of the task at hand very easily and seem unable to sit still, stand still, or be still. They will distract other students and may wander around the classroom while their classmates are trying to work. Such children may seem to be into everything all the time. Since teachers are constantly observing groups of small children, they are usually qualified to make the judgment that a particular child is substantially more distractible and overactive than other children.

However, recognizing the problem does not automatically lead to understanding the cause. Uneven development or developmental lag is one explanation; that is, the thinking, acting, doing, feeling multidimensionality of the child develops unevenly. For example, the child's ability to concentrate and pay attention may lag behind verbal abilities, reading ability, and so on. This could lead to a child's being at a seven- or eight-year-old developmental level in most respects but still two or three years behind in terms of sitting still, being still, and paying attention. There is another school of thought which suggests that some children experience a type of neurological difficulty which makes it hard for them to filter out external stimuli. The problem is not that they do not or cannot pay attention; rather, the difficulty comes in their paying attention to everything at once, equally. For example, a child may be attending to the paper on her desk when a neighbor coughs; the child then pays as much attention to the cough as to the paper. Although it looks as if the child does not have the ability to pay attention, the problem is that she has difficulty being selective in paying attention or difficulty filtering out irrelevant or unimportant stimuli. Whether the explanation is developmental or neurological, examinations by a psychologist and physician are in order. In the meantime, you will want to place the child in a spot in your classroom where she will have as little interference as possible. For example, you might place a few of the children's desks toward a blank wall, with some type of divider between the desks to minimize the possibility of the child's distracting other students or being distracted by them.

Before jumping to the conclusion that an overly active, easily distracted child has a developmental or neurological problem, though, be sure to consider the possibility that he has not been taught to sit down, be quiet, and not bother other

children. Before making a referral to the school psychologist
or a physician, be sure to insist, gently but firmly, that the
child sit at his desk, not bother other children, get his work
finished, not speak out when others are talking or working,
etc. Be concerned about making the child mind before you
start worrying about his or her mind.

Interestingly, difficulty in concentrating and paying attention is frequently accompanied by reversing numbers and letters and *consistently looking at books or pictures upside
down.* Any sign or symptom seen by itself tends to have several possible explanations. As symptoms begin to accumulate
and group, though, it becomes more likely that a child is experiencing a particular kind of difficulty. Naturally, a child
who looks at things upside down needs to have his or her eyes
examined to make sure that the visual images are being appropriately processed.

When unusual distractibility and an inability to settle
down are combined with perceptual/motor difficulty, the likelihood of neurological difficulty increases. You will notice that
such children *seem to have difficulty applying themselves to
a task at their desk* and seem somewhat confused when given
instructions or directions, find it hard to sit still or be still, tend
to rotate or reverse numbers and letters, tend to look at things
upside down or backward, generally seem confused when trying to organize and integrate the world around them.

As with all signs and symptoms, this grouping may be seen
in any way from a very mild to a very severe form. You should
be very careful to observe these children, keep a record of
your concerns and of symptoms that seem to appear, and
watch carefully to see whether or not the children gradually
seem to be getting over the problem. If they do not, referral to
the school psychologist would be the first appropriate step.
Also, special help from a teacher qualified in learning disorders would be in order. As you work with these children,
though, it will be very important to give them short, well-
defined directions. Try to talk in very concrete rather than

abstract terms, and try to talk very calmly and clearly. Remember that they may also be having difficulty in processing auditory stimuli: they may hear well but become as confused by what they hear as by what they see.

A somewhat different type of problem is seen in children who have difficulty putting things in proper order, repeating things in sequence, or putting more than two or three things together. The extreme would be a child who has *difficulty repeating three to five numbers in sequence.* A child with this type of difficulty also may have trouble identifying a missing part in a picture, recognizing a part of a picture which does not belong in terms of context, reading out loud, putting sentences together in the usually expected order, etc. These types of symptoms can reflect a wide range of difficulty, from neurological to vision problems, from retardation to simply having not yet learned. It would be helpful to see if the child can reproduce rhythm patterns by tapping a pencil on your desk and then seeing if she can reproduce sound. It is possible that these children do not hear very well or that their auditory processing is defective. Especially with numbers, the problem may be that they simply have not yet learned the number concepts, so that putting numbers together represents a non-sense game. A way of checking this would be to see if they can reproduce word sequences. Instead of saying "three, five, seven, nine," you might say, "The elephant stuck his tail in the bathtub." If a child can repeat the sentence, he has probably just not yet learned numbers or letters. If not, the difficulty is likely to be more serious and a referral to the school psychologist and to a physician is in order. Vision and hearing examinations should be included.

In the meantime, you can help such children by being sure to speak very clearly, keeping their desks free from unnecessary materials and other distractions, being sure that they do know numbers and what they mean, etc. You may also want to help such children put two things in sequence (for example, shut the door) and gradually work up to three, four, and five things in sequence. Similarly, you might start with pictures containing only two or three objects and work up from there. Whatever the reason for the problem, start with the simplest combinations and gradually increase the complexity. As with all learning and classroom difficulties, knowing the cause of the problem will help. This does not in any way eliminate the need for teaching. Even if you understand why a child is not doing something correctly, you will still need to gradually teach him to do it appropriately.

At other times, you may see a child who usually does his or her work correctly, remembers things in sequence, follows instructions, etc., but who *appears to have occasional memory lapses*. At times, the child seems to lack the ability to recall or reproduce something that you know she has already learned or already knows. The child may be able to recall or reproduce within seconds, hours, or days; the problem is that occasionally she does not seem to have immediate recall. This type of problem could involve the entire central nervous system in its function of storing and retrieving information, or it might be a function of certain types of seizures or other physical conditions. Also, the problem frequently relates to a child's not being interested in what you are interested in when you are interested in it. From the child's point of view, there may be better things to think about or do with his or her mental energy. Also, learning tends to be a somewhat off-and-on process. Small children will remember things or understand things that amaze you, but at the same time have difficulty recalling something you talked about five minutes ago. This is part of being six or seven.

As an expert observer of small children, though, you will be able to separate the child with a real memory problem from the typical child who forgets or just does not want to remember once in a while. It is important to see that, along with possible physical and neurological causes, this type of difficulty may be related to emotional upset or anxiety. The child may become anxious and fearful in classroom situations, or may have had seriously upsetting emotional experiences that interfere with his consciousness, willingness to remember, etc. Also, this type of difficulty may be a function of other intellectual or learning problems. Once you become aware of the problem, watch it for a few days and, if it does not improve, talk with the parents and ask the school guidance counselor to talk with him. Use of memory exercises such as recorded material, flash cards, classroom games, and so on should help the child in this area. You also may want to help the child develop the habit of repeating instructions and other things to herself after first hearing them as a way of improving and reinforcing memory processes.

Children who *frequently rock in their desks or chairs* potentially present a different kind of difficulty. Little children do not sit still very well; they fidget a lot and sometimes rock in their desks or chairs. However, a child who displays this rocking motion quite frequently is behaving somewhat out of the ordinary for a child five or six years old. The behavior would, then, be somewhat more alarming for children seven or eight years old. By now you are probably aware that almost any kind of learning or classroom difficulty children have can reflect possible neurological problems. There are possible neurological causes here too, but the probability that the cause is neurological is fairly low. An explanation with a higher probability of being true is that the child has some kind of inner ear difficulty that is interfering with his balance and equilibrium. A causal possibility with an equal or higher probability is that the child is somewhat autistic. This means that the child has withdrawn into himself, is screening out or not responding to most external stimuli, and needs to rock or be in continuous motion as a way of stimulating himself. Of course, the most likely explanation is that he is a normal kid who, for some reason, likes to rock a lot. If that is the problem, you can call the behavior to the child's attention and ask him to sit still. You will find that a little effort in this direction on your part will solve the problem. In terms of probability responses, the most likely thing to work is to tell the child to stop it. If that does not work, the next best step is to have the child's parents take him to the doctor to see if there is some kind of

inner ear difficulty. The physician can also look into the possibility of neurological complications.

If these approaches do not produce any results, the next
most likely explanation is childhood autism. Your response
then becomes somewhat more complicated. You should provide as much routine for the child as possible, increasing the
structure of his school experience. Autistic children will deal
better with assigned tasks than with free time, and will not
work very well independently. As much one-to-one instruction as possible will be essential. If you have the luxury of an
aide, you might have your aide spend some special time with
this child every day. Also, it is important that you talk with the
child's parents and encourage them to get professional mental
health services for the child. You may see extreme emotional
outbursts from the child when there is no particular observable cause or precipitating event, and the child may express a
high degree of negativism. It will be important to deal with
these behaviors in a very gentle, nonpunitive way; a high degree of acceptance and reassurance is essential. If the
symptoms are extreme and continue over time, it is very likely
that the normal classroom setting is not appropriate for this
child. In all events, though, do not give up too easily. These
youngsters will surprise you from time to time by seeming to
come out of it all at once.

We hope that you are beginning to see that the types of
difficulty children have in the classroom tend to be overlap-
ping and interrelated. For example, we have talked about
children who appear to have memory lapses. A similar kind of
difficulty is experienced by a *child who works inconsistently,
who seems to know something one day but not the next.* Extreme causes for this kind of difficulty could be delirium, or a
brain abcess. Although these causes are quite unlikely, you
should watch for accompanying symptoms such as headaches,
tremors in the hands, random movement, etc. It is also important to note if the problems seem to be worse when there is a
lot of noise, confusion, or distraction. This could reflect difficulty in concentrating, in filtering out irrelevant stimuli, etc. It

would also be important to see if the child is able to recall some kinds of things more than others. The problem could actually relate to the child's not having learned specific material or concepts adequately to begin with. Or the child may also have difficulty evaluating previous experiences; for example, the child may have a lot of trouble with the same thing and may seem not to have learned much from having the problem called to her attention before. If the problem seems to pervade several dimensions of the child's life and a variety of conceptual and thinking areas, you begin to have reason for real concern. Of course, most little children tend to have better days and worse days, days when they are interested in school and days when they are not. Be careful to be sure that there really is a problem; if there is, referral for further evaluation is appropriate.

Another problem area interrelated with some of those already discussed is a child's *apparent inability to follow simple directions, or a child's answering oral questions by completely changing the subject.* Such children may sometimes seem unaware that directions are being given or totally unaware that any directions have been given. Other children may consistently seem forgetful and confused. Of course, there are a variety of possible causes, including physical and intellectual difficulties. Also, they may simply have the bad habit of not paying attention. Between these extremes lies the explanation for this type of difficulty in most children. You should make sure that they are looking at you when directions are being given, perhaps have them repeat the directions to you, ask them to recall the directions when they are behaving inappropriately, and so on. If the problem does not diminish through patience and firmness, it should be pursued further with parents and the school psychologist.

The same possible causes and responses apply to children who *grasp their pencil or crayon too tightly, occasionally tearing holes in the paper.* This is to say that these children may be reflecting neurological or physical difficulties, at one extreme, or may just simply not have learned how to hold a pencil or crayon correctly and how much pressure to apply, at the least significant extreme. As you did with children who seemed unable to follow simple directions, you will start with children who tear their papers as a result of incorrectly using pencils and crayons by first, gently and patiently, calling the problem to their attention and by letting them know that the behavior is inappropriate. If you have tried this and if the behavior persists, though, you will want to think of similar tasks that require related skills. For example, can they trace a picture with a finger without pressing on it particularly hard? Can they manipulate other small objects without being clumsy or awkward?

As you look at any of the classroom signs and symptoms, move out from the specific sign or symptom to related and interrelated skills and areas. This will help you determine whether a child is having a very specific problem or a more generalized problem. Also, the interrelatedness of signs and symptoms will lead you to look for other signs and symptoms that you may have overlooked when a particular sign or symptom became evident. It will be important to look at signs and symptoms over time, to look for possible groupings, to start with most likely causes and work back from there, and to start with most likely responses and work on from there.

Two additional signs and symptoms conclude our consideration of the most significant signs and symptoms of classroom difficulty seen in kindergarten through third-grade children. The first is seen in a child who *scribbles when asked to draw a picture of a person.* The second is seen in a child who *seems unable to draw a circle, a square, or a cross.* The first step is to be sure that the behavior is really present. Frequently the kindergarten children, and less frequently with first-graders, skills involved in using pencils and crayons have not yet been developed. They have simply not had exposure to and help with these activities. Nonetheless, even a kindergarten child should quickly get past the point of scribbling and begin to draw lines and other shapes that, from the child's point of view, approximate things in the real world. A picture of a person is a good example. Kindergarten-age children should begin to make drawings that include some indications of a head, arms and legs, and a body. If you draw a circle, square, or cross, they should be able to reproduce the figures reasonably. Be sure that all children are given a few weeks in school before coming to any conclusions relative to scribbling or an inability to reproduce figures. After a few weeks in school, though, all children should be past the point of scribbling and should show some initial ability to draw simple figures.

Consider first the child who can draw simple figures such as Xs, Os, squares, triangles, etc., but who persists in scribbling when asked to draw a picture of a person. Here, we know that the child has the necessary manual skills to do more than scribble. At an extreme, this child may be experiencing intense emotional difficulties, including self-denial, intense feelings of inferiority and inadequacy, and possible psychotic difficulties. If so, though, you would notice that the child experiences real difficulties in relating to and interacting with other children and in being involved in activities around the classroom and on the playground, and generally shows exteme difficulties in social or emotional adjustment. The likelihood of finding a child with this degree of social and emotional disturbance in your classroom, however, is fairly low. A more likely explanation is that the child is having less serious social and emotional difficulties. If so, you will notice that the scribbling behavior improves over time if you relate in a very gentle and firm way with such children, encouraging them to be more expressive both verbally and socially, giving them support and encouragement in reference to their other activities and behavior, and generally work toward making them feel more comfortable with themselves, with school, and with you. A somewhat more likely explanation is that these children are unhappy with you or with being at school, and simply do not want to cooperate. They could draw a picture of a person if they wanted to. The point is that they simply do not want to do so. Even in this situation, though, a gentle but firm approach on your part is still appropriate.

While you are working with such a child, gently but firmly encouraging better performance, be sure to notice whether or not the child has any difficulty seeing, performing other tasks and meeting other expectations, relating to other children, and so on. It would be very unlikely that the "scribbling behavior" would be the only symptom seen. Rather, with careful attention you will find that it is only one of several symptoms developed in your symptom profile for the specific child. Of course, if a child can draw a picture of a person, she can also draw a circle, square, and cross. Occasionally, you may see a child who both scribbles and seems unable to draw a circle, square, or cross. Possible physical and neurological causes should be considered. In addition, you will want to look for the possible occurrence of emotional and social adjustment difficulties. (These areas will be discussed in more detail in later chapters.) As you keep in mind these possible explanations and the responses discussed, consider the possibility that the child with these two symptoms is developmentally behind most children her age. The ability to draw pictures and reproduce figures is present in a beginning form in most children five years old. If a specific child does not have that ability, the possibility must be considered that she is developmentally behind other children of the same chronological age. If so, though, you would tend to notice that she is "behind" other children relative to other activities and behaviors. At a minimum, a psychological evaluation of the child is in order if her ability to draw and reproduce figures does not gradually improve over time. As you work with her, you should remember to utilize the multisensory approach discussed earlier.

Symptom Profile

Figure 3 shows the symptom profile format for evaluating classroom and academic difficulties. The nineteen signs and symptoms discussed in this chapter are included in the left-hand column of Figure 3. The Xs shown in the academic, physical/organic, social, emotional, and environmental columns reflect likely causal categories for the signs and symptoms. These causal categories have been discussed in this chapter. For a specific child, though, you may want to consider one of the categories in which an X does not appear. This consideration may be based on your specific knowledge of the individual child, his living circumstances, or other factors which you feel are relevant. As suggested in the introductory chapter, you must draw heavily on your knowledge of specific children, their specific needs, and their specific circumstances.

Fig. 3. Symptom Profile—Classroom Difficulties

SYMPTOM	PHYSICAL/ ORGANIC	EMOTIONAL	SOCIAL	ENVIRONMENTAL	ACADEMIC
1 Sudden deterioration in the quality of work	x	x			x
2 Seems to feel incapable of doing his/her work		x			x
3 Seems to feel defeated before even beginning to do his/her work		x			x
4 Seems not to be working up to ability		x			x
5 Cannot keep up with his/her peer group academically	x	x	x		x
6 Reverses and rotates numbers and letters	x				x
7 Consistently has difficulty identifying body parts	x				x

8	Easily distracted by surroundings and minor noises	x	x			x
9	Consistently looks at books or pictures upside down	x				x
10	Has difficulty applying him/herself	x	x			x
11	Has difficulty repeating three to five numbers in sequence	x				x
12	Appears to have occasional memory lapses	x	x			x
13	Frequently rocks in his/her desk or chair		x			x
14	Works inconsistently; seems to know something one day but not the next	x	x			x
15	Shows apparent inability to follow simple directions		x			x
16	Grasps his/her pencil or crayon too tightly, occasionally tearing holes in the paper	x	x			x
17	Scribbles when asked to draw a picture of a person		x			x
18	Shows an inability to draw a circle, square, or cross	x				x
19	Answers oral questions by completely changing the subject		x			x

THREE

Why Not Fight?

The teacher's lounge is the only safe haven from Butch. Not only does Butch have his teacher pulling out her hair, but he is also pulling out his own hair, literally. He becomes upset and his anger grows so intense that he starts pulling his hair, and occasionally succeeds in pulling some of it out by the roots. During these intense emotional spells he inflicts pain on himself in other ways, and sits there hurting himself. If he is not hurting himself, he picks at himself or his nose, bites his fingernails, or scratches. And if that were not bad enough, he frequently annoys other children to call attention to himself.

At times, all of this anger and frustration gets out of hand. Butch is frequently downright cruel to other children. He injures other children intentionally and seriously. If there is not another child around to hurt, he finds a bug or cat or some other animal to be the victim of his cruelty. This behavior is not simply limited to the halls and playground. Butch constantly gets into trouble on the school bus; and when he is made to walk to and from school, he gets into even more trouble.

Butch's temper tantrums are a regular occurrence, and occasionally he runs away from school and no one can find him. His mother says that he does the same thing at home: it is not at all unusual for Butch to run away from home and have his family and half the neighborhood in a tizzy. Somehow Butch does not seem to learn from previous experiences. He almost never follows school rules, and he frequently defies authority and acts as if no one can make him do anything. His stealing compounds the problem. It is beginning to seem as if he will take anything that isn't fastened down.

Somehow, Butch is a walking paradox. He can be totally exasperating and infuriating. At other times it is clear that he wants love and attention but does not know how to get it. He is very affectionate, in fact quite indiscriminately affectionate toward adults. It is really sad, though, because no matter whether he is angry or loving he somehow seems unlovable. His teacher cannot relate to Butch and has very mixed and confused feelings about him.

Hopefully, you do not have a Butch in your classroom. Nevertheless, all or some of these behaviors are seen in most children at times, and in a few children with some regularity. These are problems that are not easily overlooked, and the risk of their going undetected is fairly low. Nevertheless, teachers need to be alert to their appearance in milder, less overt forms. Once the difficulty is recognized, the way the problem is handled by the teacher may make a critical difference in the child's future adjustment and success, not to mention the adjustment and success of other children who happen to be in the same classroom. Special attention and creativeness is important in terms of your dealing with and responding to these children.

Discussion

The vast majority of children do not have any physical, intellectual, or learning difficulties that significantly interfere with their functioning. Nevertheless, the fact that children in the early elementary grades are growing and developing quite rapidly does lead to many complications. For example, these young children are beginning to learn to relate to and interact with each other, teachers, and the world about them. They are beginning to learn about a wide variety of things including reading and arithmetic, hopscotch and baseball, friends and other children who do not like them, getting and receiving social attention, being better at some things than at others. Their rapid physical development and the wide variations in physical development among children exaggerate many of their differences and complicate the process of relating as equals. Similarly, variations in learning patterns and abilities contribute to the difficulty children have in successfully relating and competing with one another. Finally, even children without learning disorders have difficulty learning some things at some times. Since much of their academic and social learning is new to them and they do not have a long history of success with learning in these areas, temporary and normal learning difficulty may be perceived by the child, parents, and others as an unusual problem. Even though these variables remain within typical limits for most children, variability and uneven development cause many problems for children in their efforts to negotiate a relatively new social and school world.

Hair pulling is one of those symptoms that is not particularly uncommon in little children and is more common with girls than with boys. By the time children get to school, though, hair pulling should have stopped. Of course, this problem does not include children's somewhat subconsciously tugging at their bangs or pigtails. We are talking about children who literally pull their hair out. Sometimes they pull out their eyebrows, one hair at a time, without giving any particular thought to it. In more extreme situations children may literally cause bald spots on the crown or other parts of their heads. As with other problems, it may be sufficient to call the child's attention to the problem when it first begins and let her know that it is not a very good idea to pull out one's hair. If the behavior continues, or reaches the point where the child really is causing bald spots, you are undoubtedly dealing with a child who is experiencing an unusual amount of tension and frustration. Many of these children are experiencing a physical sensation of tension in their head and scalp and are trying to reduce or relieve that tension by pulling out their hair.

Of course, the causes of the tension and stress are not physical and are far removed from the child's actual behavior. A psychological evaluation would be in order to see if the child is having some learning difficulties that are interfering with his or her functioning and with efforts to interact with his or her world. It would probably be more fruitful, though, to look within the child's home situation and school situation. The likelihood is that the child's efforts to be successful and acceptable are being frustrated. Perhaps you or the school guidance staff could talk with the child's parents to see if she is getting a lot of pressure from home, or if there is unusual turmoil at home. Similarly, you might look at the child's classroom and school situation to see what kinds of things might be causing stress, making it unusually difficult for the child to negotiate in her world. Softening school and home problems, if there are any, can be carefully combined with extra positive attention from you, opportunities for the child to be successful, and special assignments or responsibilities which the child can easily handle. These efforts, combined with a lot of patience on your part, should lead to the child's becoming more relaxed, less tense, and more competent in interacting with the world.

Sometimes the problem of hair pulling expands to the point that children *repeatedly inflict pain on themselves.* Children may not only pull out their hair but may intentionally cut themselves, stick themselves with pins, hit or bruise themselves, burn or pinch themselves, or do other things equally painful. Besides directly inflicting pain on themselves, some children want to be involved in dangerous situations, take unusual risks, and constantly perform daredevil feats. The self-infliction of pain becomes most obvious in those children who are quite consistently unsuccessful in their dangerous ventures. You may think that they would learn, but they keep doing these things even though they get hurt. Whether the pain or injury is directly or indirectly inflicted, you will wonder why they do it and why they do not quit doing it after it hurts.

When such questions occur to you, you know you are dealing with children who are responding to some other kind of problem by hurting or punishing themselves. Somehow such a child is caught in the double bind of being unable to submit to authority or pressure, on the one hand, and being unable to act out against it directly, on the other. In the extreme, such behavior is frustration at its worst. The child experiences a lot of fear, anxiety, hatred, and negativism that he cannot express directly, and finds it impossible to keep these feelings bottled up but does not have any good way of getting feelings out directly by confronting the person or situation prompting the feelings. The result is that the feelings almost come out but get turned back on the child in the process. It is important not to overlook the possibility that the child accidentally came across the behavior, got a lot of attention for it, and continues the behavior to continue getting the attention. Usually, though, the pain resulting from such behavior is not worth the little attention that comes from it. More likely, the child is experiencing fairly intense difficulty in efforts to interact with the world.

Excessive coddling is not a good idea, since the child may continue the behavior to get your attention. On the other hand, excessive punishment, especially physical punishment, is not a good idea since you are hurting the child in much the same way the child was hurting himself. Cutting the fingernails of children who scratch themselves, short haircuts for boys who pull out their hair, taking away pins or sharp objects from children who stick or cut themselves, and so forth are good temporary measures. Encouraging these children to play hard and fast will help drain off some of the angry energy, and games and activities where they can pound, kick, hit, and throw will help. Basically, though, they need better ways of directly expressing feelings and thoughts. Encouraging these children to talk about their anger, fear, guilt, and other feelings will be productive. It will also help to encourage them in those areas where they show special skill, interest, and ability. Hopefully, some of the energy and anxiety will be displaced to those activities, giving such children a healthier outlet for their feelings. What they really need are more effective ways to express themselves, relate to others, and interact within their environment. You can talk with these children about that, and give suggestions, while continuing gently but firmly to let them know that the behavior is both undesirable and unproductive.

A similar kind of difficulty is seen in children who *continually bite their fingernails, pick their noses, or scratch themselves.* These problems are more common in somewhat high-strung and especially active children; it seems as if they always have to be doing something or be into something. Even when the rest of them is not busy, or perhaps especially when the rest of them is not busy, their hands keep moving, picking, scratching. If the behavior is not too continuous, too socially unacceptable, and does not result in their hurting themselves, it will probably be sufficient to mention it to them and get them to slow down the behavior over time. For some children, though, this type of behavior is a more subtle counterpart of the more self-abusive behavior already discussed, and reflects fear, anxiety, tension, and frustration. If you have evaluated the situation and feel that the problem goes a little beyond social learning or fidgetiness, you might approach these children's difficulties in much the same way that you would if they were actually injuring themselves. Punishment will only tend to increase fear or anger. If you are vacillating somewhere between coddling and punishing, it would probably be well to lean toward coddling rather than punishing. A little more warmth and security in these children's relationships with you should go a long way in the right direction.

A few special comments should be made about possible physical causes of nail biting, nose picking, and scratching. Although there may be no direct physical cause for nail biting, a child who is physically uncomfortable is more apt to bite his nails than one who is physically comfortable. For example, a shy child may find it difficult to ask permission to go to the restroom. The discomfort of needing to use the restroom but not being able to do so may cause him to squirm, get fidgety, and possibly bite fingernails. If a usually fairly relaxed child seems to be squirming and biting his fingernails, you should privately and quietly, without calling attention to him ask if he needs to use the restroom. Similarly, minor physical illnesses that are causing a child to be uncomfortable might lead to nail biting as a result of not being able to settle down and relax. When nail biting is seen as unusual behavior for a particular child, you should check for possible physical causes by seeing if the child needs to go to the restroom or if she does not feel very well. Nonetheless, chronic nail biting is almost always a function of emotional and social adjustment difficulties.

Occasional nose picking may also have physical causes. Children with allergies or colds may experience some discomfort in the nose when the excess mucous begins to dry. Also, colds or allergies can cause a child's nose to itch. In either event, children are somewhat more likely to pick their noses than they would ordinarily be. Before trying to stop children from picking their noses, ask if the nose itches or if there seems to be something in it. The children might also benefit from some instruction as to the proper use of a tissue or handkerchief. When nose picking is a chronic problem, though, these children have either not been taught to behave more socially appropriately or are experiencing some social and/or emotional difficulties.

In addition to the social and emotional factors that may possibly be related to scratching, there are frequently "real" physical reasons for a child's feeling the need to scratch. Allergies and insect bites frequently cause fairly intense itching on the surface of the skin. Of course, you should not apply any kind of medication to the child's skin. Perhaps you or someone at school could check with the child's parents about something that could be put on the affected area. Also, not keeping the body physically clean can lead to fairly intense itching. This is especially true around the genital and anal areas. Poor toileting habits, including not cleaning properly after toileting, may be a problem. Also, not changing clothing, especially underclothing, can lead to problems with itching and skin irritation. It will be important to talk with your class about physical cleanliness. These discussions should include some discussion and specific comments about proper hygiene measures when toileting. Also, the children should begin to learn the importance of keeping their bodies and clothing relatively clean. At least, they should learn to start each day with clean clothes.

If a child in your class has a problem with scratching and itching, one of the things to keep track of is whether or not he seems to come to school clean. If the child's complaints of itching are primarily around the anal and genital areas, you or one of the other adults at school should privately look at the child's body to see if there is any obvious problem. It would be the better part of good judgment if female teachers took this responsibility for girls and male teachers took this responsibility for boys, if at all possible. Also, two adults should be present if possible. Be sure that a "big deal" is not made out of the process, though. The child complains of itching. You should ask, "Do you mind if I look?" Almost always the child will give approval. The child should then be taken to some place in the building where you can check on the problem with reasonable privacy. You might say, "I think I will have Mr. *A* or Ms. *B* look too and see what he/she thinks." In any event, nail biting, nose picking, and scratching may have physical causes that should not be overlooked. (Signs and symptoms of worms in small children are discussed in a later chapter.)

Other children do not do anything particularly harmful or dangerous to themselves but *frequently annoy other children to draw attention to themselves.* These children tend to be somewhat boisterous, impulsive, and generally disruptive within the classroom and other school settings. They frequently talk to their neighbors, poke and pinch, make faces, and say and do things to other children to upset them, tease and irritate, and generally try to get some kind of reaction from other children. This kind of behavior can reflect difficulty in the transition between home and school in that the behavior is generally acceptable at home but inappropriate at school.

Especially bright children may have these kinds of difficulties, since they get their work done much quicker than other children and are left with very little to do. Consequently, their energy, sociability, and curiosity get a little out of hand and they become disruptive. The solution is to set limits, gently but firmly letting the child know that disruptive, annoying behavior is not acceptable. These limits can be combined with special activities, special study centers, and classroom libraries, so that the child has something to do while others are busy at their desks. A variation on this type of difficulty occurs when very bright children find classroom work too easy to occupy their attention or interest; they may do a few arithmetic problems or other assignments, but the rest of the work may not be difficult enough to hold their attention. These children also tend to be quite verbally spontaneous and may give the impression that they are smart alecs or somewhat belligerent. It is important to slow down this kind of behavior without squelching the child too much.

Disrupting and annoying behavior which persists after you have set limits represents feelings of insecurity or inadequacy much of the time, and always indicates that a child is having difficulty negotiating in his or her social world. While some people say that a particular child needs more attention than other children, the reality is that all children have a nearly insatiable need for attention. Some children have learned to get attention in acceptable, effective ways, so we tend not to notice their need for attention. Other children strive for attention in awkward, inappropriate, and generally ineffective ways; and when their behavior does not bring them an acceptable amount of attention, they try a wider range of behaviors and actions which gets them into trouble: they disturb the class, annoy other children, and aggravate the teachers.

Basically, these children need to be taught how to get attention in more acceptable ways and to learn to refrain from attention-seeking behavior at certain times in order to get more attention and approval later. They need to learn the principle of delayed gratification. You might give these children special assignments, special responsibilities, and special things to do in class that bring extra status and approval from you and their peers. In time these children will gradually learn that more conformity and less disruption will get them more attention than their previous behavior. Gradually they will learn to sit still, stand still, and be still when it is appropriate, and to be active and energetic with you and the other children when that is appropriate. What to do while you are working on the problem is often a question, though. Keeping these children busy, perhaps setting up a special place in the classroom, and generally supervising them fairly closely will keep their behavior and actions at a manageable level while you are working on solving the problem.

A few children go beyond the point of teasing and foolishness and are *repeatedly cruel to other children*. It becomes apparent that these children *sometimes intentionally seriously injure* other children and delight in their suffering. At this extreme the problem represents one of the most severe childhood difficulties. These children seem to lack a conscience or inner control that keeps them from inflicting pain on others. They seem unable to empathize or sympathize with other children's suffering, and almost relate to other children as if they were objects. It is important to remember that children intentionally or unintentionally hurt each other sometimes from anger, frustration, or excessive enthusiasm. However, a few children hurt others in a fairly unemotional, self-satisfying way. Their activities should be supervised quite closely, and parents and the school psychologist should be quickly involved.

It is important for the teacher to supervise and intervene in these children's activities when necessary in a reasonably calm and matter-of-fact way. Anger generates anger; if you become angry with them you will tend to stimulate them toward more intense anger. If the behavior continues, or if the resulting injuries are serious on more than a couple of occasions, these children should be withdrawn from the classroom setting until a thorough psychiatric examination can be arranged. When they come back to school, you should work closely with the mental health professionals who are working with them. Sometimes these children express anger and aggression very directly in hitting, kicking, and similar direct physical contact. At other times they may seriously injure other children in more indirect ways, by misusing playground equipment leading to a child's being injured, doing things to desks and chairs that result in injury, putting foreign substances in other children's food, or other things a little more subtle and indirect. Whether this behavior takes a direct or indirect form, immediate psychiatric attention is indicated.

Of course, advising you to respond to the anger and hostility of these children with calmness and firmness and to avoid "reacting" with anger or hostility does not suggest that you "ignore" their behavior. You will want to call the behavior to their attention and let them know in a very direct and firm way that you disapprove of it. Also, you will want to let them know that it is upsetting to you to see other children hurt or injured. If you observe a situation where a child seems about to do something or behave in a way that will injure him or another child, and if your verbal caution does not stop the behavior or action, you will need physically to restrain the child from causing injury to someone. When you do physically restrain a child in this type of situation, you will want to be careful that you are not physically injured yourself. Such children will likely react by trying to hit, bite, scratch, or kick you. If you pick them up off the ground, be sure that you have hold of both their arms and legs. If you are simply going to hold them or prevent them from doing something, try to get hold of both of their arms, hold on firmly, and keep them out away from your body. Just remember that even five-year-olds can kick and hit rather hard. The same approach of restraining the child may be necessary if the particular child becomes destructive, tries to throw things, starts to tear up your classroom, and so on.

Children who are repeatedly cruel to animals present a similar kind of problem. They derive pleasure from hurting and seeing the animal's suffering, and from the shock and fear of adults and other children. Again, most children tease animals sometimes, and sometimes that teasing gets out of hand. However, the majority of children will stop when the animal is actually beginning to suffer. Observing suffering usually motivates a child to refrain from such behavior in the future: the child sees the suffering and feels badly about it. Children who continually torture animals are undoubtedly experiencing a lot of anxiety, hostility, and confused feelings, and are taking out this anger anywhere they can. Small animals are a good target, since they are unable to fight back. These children also tend to have strong feeling of being unloved and unappreciated. Of course, their behavior leads people to see them as even less lovable and less acceptable. Neglected and rejected children, children who have been abused under the guise of punishment, and children who are generally unloved are much more likely to exhibit this kind of behavior than most children. They need a lot of love, security, warmth, and caring. This may help them develop better ways of relating to their world and better feelings about themselves. Such prevention is highly preferable to punishment. These children need to express themselves and need to be encouraged to do so in more direct and effective ways. Also, encouraging them to work out their aggressions on inanimate objects such as dolls and other toys may help them deal more appropriately with their feelings. In addition, have the guidance staff explore the home situation, the parent/child relationships, and the child's overall environment. These professionals are equipped to evaluate the overall situation, make recommendations, and arrange for more intensive therapy if it is required.

More common than children who hurt themselves, other children, or animals, are *children who throw frequent temper tantrums*. These children stamp their feet, kick, scream, throw themselves or objects on the floor, bang their heads on the floor, thrash about, and get so worked up that they are ready to strike out at anything or anyone. At this point, they are unable and unwilling to reason things out, think things through, or settle down. This is a very normal problem with children three or four years old. By the time children get to school, though, we expect that they have for the most part gotten through their temper tantrum phase.

Some children, instead of throwing temper tantrums, are more inclined toward pouting and feeling very hurt and sorry for themselves. When children are quite small, they begin separating into tantrum throwers and pouters. Interestingly, this same kind of grouping can be seen in adults; if you think about your family members and co-workers, you will notice that some tend to clam up and pout while others become more verbal and aggressive. This reaction is set off by our wanting our own way. If we do not get it, we react in some manner. Little children are very involved in figuring out how to get what they want; temper tantrums and pouting are two of the most common approaches they try. If they do not get their own way through these behaviors, or if the consequences of these behaviors are fairly undesirable, such as getting sent to their room or being spanked, children usually come up with more effective ways of interacting. Children who are still having temper tantrums when they reach school age probably have had a history of success with that behavior and consequently have not developed any better ways of dealing with others.

As you look at a particular child and her particular temper tantrum, consider whether she could be expected to come up with any better way of dealing with things under the circumstances. For example, if two or three youngsters gang up on a child, take her toys away, or do not let her into the lunch line, a temper tantrum may be the best option at the time. With early elementary children, temper tantrums are seen as a problem only if they are a frequent, fairly habitual way of dealing with frustration.

As with other forms of aggressiveness, your responding with anger and aggression would probably be a mistake. Having a civilized, adult temper tantrum in response to a child's less civilized temper tantrum does not present a very good model and will probably not help the child's tantrum behavior. Firmness and calmness are in order when dealing with childhood temper tantrums, just as firmness and calmness are appropriate when an adult is having a temper tantrum. If possible, deal with the child by ignoring him. Simply walk away, do not respond, and, above all, be sure that the temper tantrum does not result in the child's getting what he wants. Over time, the child will have to come up with a different way of behaving to get what he wants. Isolating the child, withdrawing the opportunity to interact with peers, and generally expressing disapproval of his behavior also takes the payoff out of temper tantrums.

From your experience with small children you should also be able to see and foresee situations in which some youngsters are most likely to have temper tantrums. Perhaps some manipulation or rearrangement of the situation ahead of time can avoid the behavior altogether. Be sure, however, that the child is not getting special privileges or concessions as a disguised payoff for his behavior. The basic idea is to remain as calm and as firm as possible, and, above all, to be sure that the temper tantrum behavior has no positive payoff: for the child to get what he wants, he has to do what you want.

Of course, temper tantrum behavior may occasionally be such that the child needs to be physically restrained or contained. When this occasionally becomes necessary, as calmly, gently, and firmly as possible, follow the suggestions for physically restraining children presented earlier in this chapter.

Whereas some children attempt to deal with their confused feelings by hurting themselves or others, by being annoying or disruptive, by having temper tantrums, or by other behavior which reflects an attempt to deal with their situation, other children simply opt to run away. *Repeated running away from home or school* may possibly mean that a child has found someplace that is more fun and exciting than home or school, or may reflect an especially venturesome orientation: the child knows what is here and wants to find out what is "there." Such excursions away from the school tend to be something the child thinks about, wonders about, and plans. However, running away is usually an impulsive, unpremeditated act that is quite directly set off by some event or situation. The most frequent reason would be a situation in which a child experiences anger or resentment toward a teacher or parent, feels that he or she has been treated unfairly, or experiences other unpleasant or undesirable feelings. Instead of staying in the situation and dealing with it, the child chooses to run.

The child may fantasize that the teacher or parent is worrying about him. Of course, this is true. If we know that the child has run away, we will be worried about him. The risk to young children who run away is critically high. They are vulnerable to all sorts of accidental and intentional injury. First, they might actually get lost and not be able to find their way home or back to school. This is true in both urban and rural areas. Next, they might accidentally get hurt by running in front of a car, falling over some kind of obstruction, getting into something or someplace that is dangerous, and so on. In addition, they could become physically ill or die from exposure to the weather. Finally, we know that there are people who intentionally injure or take advantage of small children. Running away is indeed a dangerous thing to do. Children of any age should be made very aware of the dangers and risks. The problem is sufficiently important to warrant some class time talking with your children about the dangers and risks of running away or going places with strangers. Also, you should let children who are contemplating running away, or who have run away and returned, know that you really are afraid and worried. In a clear and direct way, you should let them know to what risks and dangers they may expose themselves or may have exposed themselves.

Children may become chronic runaways if their resentment and frustration generalize to authority, most people, and most situations. However, this extreme is quite unusual. More typically, from time to time a child chooses to run away as a way of dealing with a particular kind of situation or as a way of getting even with certain adults.

Even though running away is usually a function of social and emotional factors, it frequently is related to a child's physical problems. Physically handicapped children, children with observable body defects, and other physical factors that may interfere with a child's social involvement and participation can develop feelings of rejection and inferiority that contribute to a child's running away from his or her situation. "Frequency" is the issue when dealing with runaway behavior. If it happens more than once or twice, though, a physical evaluation would be in order to see whether or not the child is experiencing any physical difficulties or feelings that might be leading to his being unhappy, uncomfortable, feeling "different" from other children, and so on. Children will usually talk about or threaten running away before they do it. In this way, they are letting you know they are unhappy, feel rejected, or think they are being treated unfairly. Both adults and children usually find it easier to let us know the proposed solution to their problem than to tell us about the feelings involved in the problem. Children find it easier to tell us they are going to run away than to tell us that they feel rejected or treated unfairly. When a child lets us know about a plan to run away, we know that strong negative feelings exist. The best solution is to correct the problem, if possible. We might agree with the child about the unfairness or inequity in the situation and move to correct it. A risk is that we will give the child the message that threatening to run away is a means of changing something he or she does not like. If we correct the situation, we also need to talk with the child about better ways of letting us know what he or she feels and thinks. The child needs to learn to tell us about the problem instead of simply hitting us with the proposed solution.

Obviously, being overly critical, negativistic, or excessively punitive with children who threaten to run away only serves to reinforce their negative feelings. Children need to know that they are loved, cared about, and, most importantly, wanted. Our caring about them and their needing to face difficult situations need to be emphasized. In talking with the children about upsetting situations and their feelings, then, it is important to let them know that you will feel badly if they run away, that you do not want them to run away, and that you will find them if they do run away. At the same time, you may offer some ideas and suggestions about dealing with the problem. One possibility is playing with a different group of children or getting involved in other activities. If the children being played with do not accept a child, it may be well simply to play with other children. At a minimum, getting the child involved in some activity will divert attention from running away.

If you talk with children after they have run away or while they are in the process of running away, it is first important to let them know how scared you were, how worried you were, and how glad you are that you found them and that they are not hurt. A little anger on your part is natural, but be careful not to express only angry feelings. Let these children know you were afraid and worried. Along with this, getting them to talk about the problem, relating to their feelings, and getting them involved in other activities should begin to correct the difficulty. Whether a child is planning to run away or has run away, saying "You can run away if you want to" serves only to reinforce negative feelings within the child. If running away becomes chronic or habitual, outside guidance and counseling for the child and parents will be necessary. The guidance staff of your school is equipped to provide these services or to arrange for them.

Children who chronically run away, who continually get into social and behavioral difficulty, who *consistently fail to follow school rules,* who *do not learn from past experiences,* present a puzzling and complex problem. You may have followed through on good advice, been firm but gentle, been reasonably consistent, yet these children continue to run away, continue to disrupt the classroom, to break school rules, and generally show no improvement in behavior. Why? Infrequently, these children have an auditory or visual memory disturbance. If so, their problem spills over into classroom work and they have problems remembering such things as number sequences, assignments, procedures, and how to do things they did quite well the day before. At other times, not being able to apply past experiences may reflect excessive impulsivity, inability to slow down enough to think about what is going on, or excessive enthusiasm about everything. On the other hand, children may be so underactive, so underinvolved, and so turned into themselves that they seem to live in their own world, immersed in whatever is going on for them. Such children do not break rules; instead, they seem not to realize that there are any rules or limits. Whether a child has actual difficulty in remembering or, due to overinvolvement or underinvolvement, does not tune in to rules, procedures, and ways of doing things, there is a real problem both for the child and for you. The child does not get along very well and is not particularly successful within the school environment, and you are constantly having to deal with the child's not going along with activities and expectations in a smooth, predictable way.

When you feel that a child is having difficulty behaving and performing in an acceptable way as a result of not generalizing from previous experiences, a referral to the school psychologist will be appropriate. The psychologist will be able to tell if the child has a real memory problem in terms of visual and auditory experiences, and the evaluation will reveal whether or not the problem relates to some specific learning difficulty or intellectual deficiency. Specific recommendations and suggestions for helping children like this will be included in the evaluation. Visual memory exercises, giving both written and verbal instructions when possible, and practice in thinking about what behavior leads to what consequences, will be very useful for these children.

When the problem comes up most frequently in non-classroom activities, though, you are usually dealing with stubbornness, impulsiveness, rebelliousness, and general disobedience on the one hand, or withdrawn behavior, preoccupation, and a general lack of social involvement on the other. In either situation, gently but firmly confront the child with the rule or policy each time he or she fails to go along with usual expectations. Such children need to know that they are not following rules at the time they fail to follow them, that rules are for everyone—including themselves—all the time. Whether your goal is to get these children to slow down and think about what is going on or to be more aware of what is going on around them, confront them in a calm, firm way that will ensure your having their attention. At this point, the rules should be restated. In the case of the more enthusiastic child, you should have him go to the back of the line, not participate in part of the activity, stay in for recess, go back to the door and walk down the hall more slowly, or do other things for a few minutes that cause the child to think about what he is doing and has done. In the case of more withdrawn children, it is important to get them to talk about what they were doing or do something else that requires them to interact with you. Isolating or separating a withdrawn child from the group would only provide further opportunity to withdraw and avoid interaction.

Also, it will be well to spend some class time discussing the idea of rules, why we have rules, what would happen if there were no rules, and so on. These discussions should include focus on specific school rules, whether they are good rules or bad rules, the problem for which the rule has been developed, and so on. This group discussion will tend to reinforce the idea of rules with both overly aggressive and excessively withdrawn children. In addition, it will give the children a sense of participation in and involvement with the rules. In some situations, it may be possible to change rules, eliminate rules, make different rules, and so on, as a response to the class discussion. If the children are given an opportunity to examine the problem for which a rule seems to be necessary, they may come up with some other way of dealing with the problem than developing a rule. At a minimum, they may be able to suggest alternative rules that may be more comfortable and acceptable to them. The idea of democracy and social participation is important and these are processes in which young children both can and should become involved. To the extent possible, the rules with which they live should be their rules, rules they understand, and rules they can accept as reasonable and fair.

Of course, some children simply cannot or will not respond to rules of any kind. These children need the special attention and help discussed elsewhere in this and other chapters. For the majority of children, though, participation in and discussions of the development and implementation of rules will greatly increase their ability and willingness to follow the rules. Occasionally, most children will break a rule or will decide that a rule does not reasonably apply to a given situation. For those children, some discussion and firmness will take care of the problem, if there is one. Remember that just because a child broke a rule or did not follow a rule does not mean that he or she did anything wrong. Perhaps the rule really was silly or not applicable.

We all know that we do not respond the same way, in all situations, to all children. Here it is important to separate failure to follow the rules from what is going on with the children. We want more active children to slow down and more passive ones to interact more. Of course, the first thing to consider is the possibility that a child has not learned to follow rules very well or, at least, has not yet learned to follow the rules within your classroom or within the school. If you think this is the problem, there really is no problem. If you have first talked with the children about the rule(s) to be sure that they understand each rule and the reason for it and that they have an opportunity to discuss the rule(s) with you, you can then firmly and insistently call rule violations to their attention and let them know what is expected. For these children, the process of discussion and calling infractions to their attention will gradually resolve the difficulty over time. Also, if there is some set "penalty" for breaking the rule or not following it, a particular child may be reminded of the infraction and the penalty once or twice, but should then be subjected to the penalty when breaking or not following a particular rule. Remember, though, that he or she is a child. Do not be too rigid, too arbitrary, or too legalistic.

The problem is a little more specific and pronounced with children who *frequently defy authority*. You will notice a fairly intense pitch or quality in their voice when things do not go their way, when they do not get their own way, or when they are confronted with rules. This type of response is frequent with children who have certain kinds of brain damage, but this condition is fairly unusual. More typically you are dealing with a temper tantrum and should respond accordingly. In either event, look at the situations under which the response occurs. It will be helpful for both you and the child if such situations can be avoided. You may find that the situation or actions of other people at school are setting off the child, and you may want to deal as much with the external cause as with the defiance. It is important to realize that you will not be able to reason with the child during the defiant period. The first step is to get the child to slow down, calm down, and begin to listen. Whereas anger would generate anger, a firm, calm tone from you will help. Along with a firm verbal response and a possible physical response (possibly restraining the child), being sure that reasonable efforts are being made not to set the child off, you should be sure that there is no positive payoff for the child's behavior; defiance must not be allowed to let the child avoid the rules or the consequences of not following the rules.

Repeated stealing presents a different problem, although adults tend to think about stealing in the same terms as defiance, disobedience, and disruptiveness. It is important to keep in mind that the concept of stealing may not be applicable to young children. Whereas "stealing" has many moral and value-ladened connotations, the actual behavior of taking something that does not belong to one is a less complex issue: I want something, so I take it. Little children start at this point: if they want something, they take it. The first step for them is to learn that there is a difference between "my" things and "your" things; by the time children are in school, most of them have learned this. The second step involves developing in children a feeling about taking other people's things; we want them to feel some guilt and anxiety when they think about taking something that is not theirs. Before working with a specific child on the development of these feelings, though, you will want to spend class time talking about such things as the property rights of others and how we might feel if our things were taken. These discussions should not focus on a particular child's behavior; this would probably overdo the shame and guilt process. Also, stealing is much too common among early school-age children to single out one child in a public way. However, if the problem persists with a particular child, a private, interpersonal approach is in order.

First of all, let the child know that you really disapprove of this behavior. Since little children operate in terms of getting and keeping our approval, your disapproval may be a sufficiently negative reinforcement. At any rate, the child will feel a little guilty and apprehensive and will want to get back in your good graces; this uneasy feeling is the beginning of internalizing moral values about stealing. Also, you will probably want the child to return the object to the person from whom it was stolen; this public act tends to encourage the internalization of the nonstealing value. If the problem does not improve, it may be necessary to punish the child in some way. You also need to keep in mind that some children steal in order to get attention, to compensate for very negative feelings about themselves, and/or to deal with what they see as a fairly nonaccepting world. Children who chronically steal really need more loving, interested, concerned attention and more supportive, accepting relationships. In short, stealing is a complex behavior and requires a fairly complex response. "Taking" becomes "stealing" only when the behavior is chronic, when it does not respond to teaching and social disapproval, and when it becomes a prime way of getting things, relationships, and attention the child wants and needs.

Occasionally, you will have a child who *consistently gets into difficulty on the school bus or on the way to and from school*. You may find out about this through reports from other people at school, through overhearing conversations of the children in your class, or through complaints of bus drivers and people who live on the child's route to and from school. It would be easy to say that this is not your responsibility. The problematic behavior taking place is neither in your classroom nor in the school building. Nonetheless, the child's behavior does reflect adjustment problems.

First, you will want to evaluate whether the child is actually not having difficulty in the classroom and at school. It is fairly unlikely that a child would have consistent difficulty on the school bus and on the way to and from school but not have difficulty in the classroom and in school. You will usually come to the conclusion that the difficulty on the way to and from school is only an extension of the difficulties the child is having at school. When this is the case, you can deal with the behavior between home and school as an extension, or as a further example, of the child's difficulty at school.

Such difficulty usually involves fighting, not following rules, destroying the property of others, and so on. These problems have already been discussed; and the fact that they extend beyond the school situation is not surprising. The fact that the difficulty extends to the school bus or to the routes to and from school does suggest, however, that the problem is quite pervasive and involves a wide variety of situations in which the child finds himself. The point is that the more situations in which a particular problem occurs, the more significant the problem. Your response should be to the behavior and to the child at school. Your concern should come in terms of the fact that the problem is serious. Talking with the child, discussing the problem, letting him or her know that you are concerned about the behavior on the way to and from school, talking with the child's parents, involving the school guidance staff, etc., are appropriate and necessary parts of your "treatment plan" for this child. Also, you will want to consider the fact that the children may not be very well supervised on the school bus or that a particular child has difficulty negotiating the path to and from school. Of course, such a difficulty can involve physical factors, memory disturbances, environmental factors such as feeling that he has to follow the rules at school but does not have to behave himself at home and in the community, and so on. These other possible factors will be involved in your "symptom profile" for the child.

As with other behavior problems of children, though, consider the possibility that the adults in their world are not accepting the responsibility to supervise them, set appropriate and reasonable limits, respond to them in a fair and firm way, and so on. This possibility becomes especially likely if several children are having the same kind of behavior difficulties. You might get some clue about this by reviewing your performance notebook. If several children are having the same kind of behavior difficulties during the same time period, consider the possibility that the problem may actually be "an adult problem." This type of problem would apply to bus drivers, playground or lunchroom supervisors, hall monitors, and so on. If you suspect that this may be the difficulty, it would be appropriate to explore the problem with your supervisor and/or building principal. Let them know that several children seem to be having the same kind of difficulty when supervised by or responsible to a particular individual. Following through with this possible explanation will, then, be the responsibility of the supervisor or building principal.

Occasionally you may have a child in your class or in your school who is *excessively and indiscriminately affectionate to others*. Especially with kindergarten children, you may frequently see kids who want to be close to you, who want to sit on your lap, who want to touch and be touched, etc. This behavior lessens as children get older but can still "normally" be seen in second- and third-graders. Here we are talking about a child who excessively and indiscriminately expresses and/or asks for affection and physical contact from others. You may notice that the child is always clinging to you, is always touching you, is frequently hugging and touching the other children, frequently goes up to other adults at school and acts affectionately toward them, and so on. It is the excess and indiscriminate nature of the child's affection that is being considered here.

At the other extreme, you may occasionally see a child who really *avoids any affectionate interaction or physical contact*. This problem is seen especially in children who have been physically neglected or who have autistic tendencies. The problems of physical neglect will be discussed later. Childhood autism was briefly discussed in an earlier chapter. For those children, the need is very gently and gradually to relate to and interact with them more. Here we are talking about children who overdo it as opposed to children who underdo it.

Although these children who "overdo it" may have physical difficulties, may have been overprotected as a result of physical difficulties, etc., the cause for their excessive and indiscriminate affection is not physical. The most likely explanation is that they have grown up in a home situation where everyone is very affectionate, expresses that affection openly, spontaneously, and physically, and expects everyone else to behave in an equally open and spontaneous way. For these children, the problem is that they have not yet learned that such excessive and indiscriminate affection is inappropriate in the school and in other social situations outside the home.

For other children, the problem reflects serious emotional difficulties. They have intense unmet needs for physical contact, emotional feedback, and acceptance by others. Their behavior is "exactly what it seems to be," i.e., a somewhat awkward and overly enthusiastic effort to get love and affection from others. The behavior itself has the appearance of giving love and affection. The motivation of the child, though, is to have that love and affection reciprocated. Whether the problem reflects the child's cultural and family background or reflects serious emotional turmoil and deprivation, correcting the behavior is not an easy task. We cannot just simply tell the child to "stop it," and refuse to respond to the behavior. Why? This runs the risk of causing the child to feel unloved, unaccepted, and summarily rejected. Of course, we want to change the child's behavior but we do not want to do so by making him feel rejected and shoved away.

Our response to such children should start by reciprocal behavior. We should respond to their affection with affection. When they hug us, we should hug them back. Our affection should then be combined with verbally letting them know that they should go on to other activities, that we do not have time to talk with them now, and ever so gently let them know that such behavior is not appropriate at school. You might hug them back and then gently move their arms back from around you or remove their hands from yours, let go of them, and then talk with them for a minute or so in a very friendly and interested way. Over time, these children will gradually get the idea that you do like them, that you feel they are all right, that you do care about them and are interested in them, that you do want to talk with them, and that they should behave in a less overtly affectionate way toward you. Similarly, you might say to them, "It might be better for you not to hug and kiss the other children or other adults quite so much," while at the same time suggesting other ways that they might verbally and behaviorally interact with people. Of course, these suggestions in reference to other people should come only after you have gently and caringly begun to deal with the problem as it relates to the interaction between you and the child. The idea is to change their behavior gradually without causing feelings of rejection.

Once in a while, you will find a child in your class *who seems* to you *to be unlovable.* Here, the first step is to consider the possibility that the problem is with you. Very carefully consider to which qualities or attributes of the child you have difficulty responding. Perhaps you respond less well to boys than to girls, less well to handicapped than to nonhandicapped children, less well to members of some ethnic groups than to members of other ethnic groups, less well to overweight children than to children of "normal weight," less well to more physically unattractive children than to physically attractive children, less well to slower children than to brighter children, less well to children who are not as neat and clean as other children, less well to rude or impolite children than to polite and "well-mannered" children, and so on. All of us have prejudices and biases that may interfere with our ability to relate to a particular child.

When we find a child unlovable or difficult to respond to, the most likely reason is that our own feelings, biases, prej-

udices, and preferences are getting in the way. Part of functioning as a "professional person" involves the "conscious
use of self." This means that you need consciously to understand and be aware of your own prejudices and biases, and
avoid letting them interfere with your relationships and in-
teractions with children. For a few teachers, counseling and
therapy may be required to work through some of these difficulties. For most teachers, though, it will be sufficient to be
aware of these problems and to work them through by a process of self-examination, increasing self-awareness, and self-
developed insight.

At other times, though, it may be that a particular child is
difficult to respond to and really is not very lovable. The
"lovability" of a particular child has a good deal to do with his
past experiences with loving and being loved, responding and
being responded to, and interacting and being interacted with.
If through abuse or neglect a child has not had healthy, growing experiences in these areas, he or she may withhold affection and responsiveness, may interact in a mechanical and
artificial way, may develop body and other behavioral habits
that have the effect of "turning people off" or keeping others
at a "safe" emotional and social distance, and so on. These
children may not know how to love and be loved on the one
hand, or may avoid running the risks involved in loving and
behave in such a way as to keep others from responding in
loving ways toward them on the other hand.

A good way of deciding whether the problem has something to do with you or has something to do with a child is to
talk the problem over with your supervisor or with other
teachers at school. See if they have similar kinds of feelings in
reference to the child. Remember, though, that your peers will
tend to say those things that they think will make you feel
better and will avoid those things that they think will make
you feel worse. Don't say, "Do you find Johnnie or Sallie
unlovable?" It would be better to start the conversation by
saying, "I have been thinking about Johnnie (or Sallie) and
wonder what you think about him (her) and how you relate to
him (her)." This allows them to let you know spontaneously

whether or not they have any kind of similar feelings in their relationships with the child. If they do, the likelihood is that the child really has serious difficulties. If not, a process of self-examination is in order for you.

If the problem actually is a function of the child's behavior and adjustment, though, the difficulty is very serious. If a child has not developed effective ways of loving and being loved by the time he or she is six or seven, the damage to his personality development is permanent and may be very severe. You can begin to help by talking with these children in a quiet and interested way about their activities, interests, achievements, and so on, whether or not they respond to your comments. Also, it will be very important for you always to acknowledge their presence: say hello to them in the hall, take time to see how things are going with them, and generally create an atmosphere of interest, affection, and positive regard. Hopefully, over time they will begin to respond to you. The idea is to "make it safe" for them to relate to you.

If the problem was mild to begin with and gradually improves, the efforts you are making are sufficient. If the problem was very severe to begin with and seems not to improve, it will be important to talk with the parents in terms of the child's apparent difficulty in relating to others, his or her problems when interacting in social situations, and so on. It will be extremely important not to relate directly your sense that the child seems unlovable. First of all, the parents may simply agree with you; they may feel the same way. Your perception would only tend to reinforce their negative perceptions of their child. More likely would be a response of anger, hostility, and resentment. They would react in terms of an impression that you neither like nor are interested in their child. If you are able to get them to talk about the child's social and interpersonal difficulties, though, encouraging them to get outside counseling and guidance for the child would be appropriate. Also, it will be important for the school guidance staff to be aware of the child, your impressions of him or her, and to spend time working with the child.

The fact is that there really is a lovable little boy or girl in there somewhere. The task is to get him or her to "come out" and relate to the world. This process will be discussed in much more detail in a later chapter.

Symptom Profile

Figure 4 presents the symptom profile format for the signs and symptoms discussed in this chapter. The signs and symptoms included in this chapter are listed in the left-hand column of Figure 4. The X's in the other five columns represent the most likely causal areas related to the particular signs and symptoms. As you develop a symptom profile for a particular child, though, be sure to consider each of the five causal categories and whether or not they may apply to a particular child in your classroom.

Fig. 4. Symptom Profile–Fighting and Related Activities

	SYMPTOM	PHYSICAL/ ORGANIC	EMOTIONAL	SOCIAL	ENVIRONMENTAL	ACADEMIC
20	Pulls out hair		x			
21	Repeatedly inflicts pain on self		x			
22	Shows constant nail biting, nose picking, or scratching	x	x			
23	Frequently annoys others to draw attention to self		x	x		
24	Is repeatedly cruel to other children			x		
25	Intentionally seriously injures another child		x	x		

26	Shows repeated cruelty to animals		x			
27	Has consistent difficulty on school bus or on the way to and from school		x	x	x	
28	Has frequent temper tantrums		x		x	
29	Runs away from home or school repeatedly		x		x	
30	Seems not to learn from previous experiences	x	x			
31	Consistently fails to follow school rules			x		x
32	Frequently defies authority		x	x		
33	Steals repeatedly		x			
34	Is excessively or indiscriminately affectionate toward adults		x	x		
35	Seems unlovable		x	x	x	

FOUR

I Don't Feel Very
Well Today . . .

It's Monday morning and Mrs. Lewis knows that she can expect the usual quota of sneezes and runny noses among her twenty-nine first-graders. Mrs. Lewis has a six-year-old of her own and knows that you cannot let children stay home every time they have a sniffle or complain that their tummy doesn't feel well. Nevertheless, she is always alert to that occasional child who seems to be showing more than a normal amount of Monday morning queasiness.

The day has gotten off to a lovely start with Kindra regurgitating her breakfast and two glasses of chocolate milk in the classroom doorway. At lunchtime, Mrs. Lewis notices that Jimmy seems not to be eating. When she quietly asks him about that, Jimmy reports, "I can't swallow very good; it won't go down." Jimmy has complained about a stomachache two or three times already that day, but Mrs. Lewis knows that Jimmy complains about his stomach when he gets a little nervous. This time, though, the stomachache seems especially severe, and Jimmy appears to be in a lot of pain.

Mrs. Lewis has noticed that Aretha looks a little peaked and has an unusual quality about her today. As she looks a little closer, she notices a rash appearing on Aretha's face and on other parts of her body. Also, Mrs. Lewis is concerned about Mike's wheezing and her impression that he does it a lot. As teachers do, Mrs. Lewis makes it through the day, handling each symptom with alertness and sensitivity.

Is Tuesday any better? Ian comes to school with a wet, productive cough which sounds as if he were bringing up his whole insides. A little sniff with a couple of questions leads to the certain knowledge that Jeannie has diarrhea. Mrs. Lewis will spend the necessary amount of time teaching her class to read, write, and to learn a little science—if time allows—and she will pick out a few children for that all-important individual attention. As with all teachers of little children, though, she will spend part of her time taking care of those who do not feel very well.

These seven symptoms of childhood illness are symptoms teachers must never overlook. Recognition of the symptom becomes a matter of professional skill. Whereas a teacher would not easily overlook a child's vomiting in the classroom doorway, much more alertness and attention is required in detecting a child's wheezing or having trouble swallowing lunch. As you consider each of the symptoms, give special thought to its significance and possible importance. Perhaps the seriousness will alert you to earlier and more consistent identification. The increased difficulty in recognizing and understanding these symptoms is offset by greater simplicity in terms of response: these children need medical attention or, at least, their parents need to be made aware of the problem. However the situation is handled, your careful, prompt response may prevent fairly serious physical complications for the child.

Discussion

Like adults, children have days when they do not feel very well. They might not have as much energy as usual, might be a little preoccupied with physical aches and pains, might not tune in on what is going on around them as well as usual, might be a little more irritable and fussy and a little less cooperative than usual. Generally, this is to be expected of all children from time to time and is nothing to be particularly concerned about. A child is entitled to a bad day once in a while, as long as "bad" does not get too bad. Children get stomachaches once in a while, catch colds, do not always get enough sleep, and do not always feel top-notch. Sometimes, though, children show symptoms of more serious difficulty. Some of these symptoms almost always mean that the child is sick now, today.

Vomiting is a symptom of this type. The illness may be quite minor, although vomiting may also signal something more serious. Vomiting may be an early sign of food allergy, infectious disease, infected intestines, influenza, or even more serious problems. Fever usually accompanies vomiting associated with disease. If the vomiting merely involves the child's expelling the contents of the stomach, occurs only when the child drinks or eats, and lasts for less than eight hours or so, nothing very serious is likely to be going on, and the parents can take care of the child quite well at home. Of course, you will need to remove the child from the classroom, keep him reasonably quiet, and make arrangements for someone to take the child home. All cases of vomiting at school require that the child be taken home, since the child is probably a little too sick and woozy to walk home, and there might be no one there when he gets home. Be sure someone is at home, and have someone from school give the child a ride. Do not give the child anything to eat or drink for the first couple of hours after vomiting. If the vomiting persists beyond a six- to twelve-hour period, or if it is accompanied by severe abdominal pain, the immediate attention of a physician is necessary. Not only may the vomiting be a sign of some other, more serious physical problem, but the child may dehydrate if the vomiting goes on too long. This is potentially more serious than the problem which caused the vomiting.

Since most cases of vomiting that you see at school are short-term and associated with minor physical difficulty, you need not become overly concerned once you have worked out arrangements for the child. However, you should become concerned if the episodes of vomiting are repeated with any regularity, since even a mild problem may suggest more serious difficulty if it recurs with any unusual frequency. For example, vomiting may become a chronic condition associated with psychological and emotional problems. For some children, vomiting may occur when they are faced with a situation in which they feel extremely upset, fearful, or angry. If this happens once or twice you need not become particularly concerned, but if a child vomits frequently when upset you are beginning to see signs of a more serious problem. These children are having continuing difficulty in interacting with their world, and vomiting has become one way of dealing with that tension and stress. The children's stomach, mind, and emotions are so intimately interconnected that they may reach the point of vomiting as a spontaneous reaction to stress.

All physical possibilities must be eliminated as causes of vomiting before deciding that a child is using vomiting as a way of coping. Only a physician is qualified to make this judgment. Whether the cause of vomiting is physical or emotional, though, it is wrong to stress the unpleasantness of the mess or to make the child feel guilty about vomiting. Whatever the cause, children cannot help the behavior at the time. Of course, if the child's physician determines that vomiting is the child's way of dealing with stress, you will need to approach the problem in a firm, gentle way, removing as much stress as reasonably appropriate, helping the child develop other ways of handling stress and tension, involving him in other classroom and play activities, and generally helping the child develop ways of effectively interacting so he no longer feels undue stress and vomits.

Since *difficulty in swallowing* is another potentially serious symptom, you should be alert to children who have uncomfortable expressions on their faces, hold their throats, or who do not want to eat. Children are very suggestible so you may not want to ask them directly if they are having trouble swallowing. You might ask these children why they are holding their throats, making faces, not wanting to eat, and other questions that give them the opportunity to tell you they are having trouble swallowing. A child will probably also report having a sore throat, that it hurts, and so on. You will want to touch the child's throat lightly to see if it seems to hurt when touched and, more importantly, to see if it seems swollen. Difficulty in swallowing is probably a sign of some childhood infection. To avoid exposing other children to the possible infection, remove the child from the classroom and arrange for him to be taken home.

Difficulty in swallowing and sore throats should be treated like vomiting. The child probably is physically ill now, today. Unlike vomiting, though, difficulty in swallowing, swelling around the throat, and sore throats require immediate medical attention. The family should not wait to see if the symptoms go away in a day or so, but should take the child to the doctor that same day because of the possibility of strep throat. This kind of infection, if not detected and treated fairly quickly, can lead to rheumatic fever. Occasionally, children may have difficulty swallowing as a result of tension, nervousness, or embarrassment; they get a lump in their throat as a way of dealing with a difficult situation. In the case of these children, you will find that removing them from the situation or taking away the stress will immediately resolve the problem. Children cannot make their throats swell or become extremely painful as a result of emotional causes, though. Consequently, it is safe to say that difficulty in swallowing, especially when accompanied by swelling or soreness, always needs medical attention.

Frequent or severe stomachaches present a less clear problem. Of course, severe abdominal pain expressed by a child who has no history of stomachaches or similar symptoms represents a potentially serious problem. If the child is doubling over and cramping, you should arrange to have him taken to the doctor immediately. Legally, a parent or guardian is the only one who can give permission for medical treatment. Thus, it will be necessary to contact the child's parents and have them arrange for immediate medical attention. In emergency situations, though, most schools have legally valid permission slips signed by a parent or guardian authorizing school personnel to arrange for emergency medical treatment. If you are unable to contact the child's parents, check with the school office to be sure that an emergency medical permission is on file. If it is, you or someone else from the school can then take the child either to the physician designated on the emergency form or to the nearest hospital emergency room. If emergency permission is not on file, though, the child cannot be given medical treatment until the parent or guardian can be located and permission can be given, with the single exception that the juvenile court judge in your area ordinarily has the power to authorize emergency medical treatment for children under extraordinary circumstances.

In most situations where a child is cramping and doubling over, it will not turn out to be a serious medical emergency. Nonetheless, the fact that it could represent a problem needing medical attention or even surgery is sufficient to be sure that a physician determines the seriousness of the problem. The most common reasons for mild to moderate stomachaches are eating too much, eating the wrong foods, constipation, being a little afraid or anxious about some social situation, being upset about something, and wanting extra love and attention. Having the child go to the bathroom, slow down for a while, pass up some activity, or a similar approach should get the child through what is probably a very minor, temporary difficulty. If you try these things and the problem is not resolved in half an hour or so, have the child see the school nurse and draw on the nurse's expertise. Constipation and emotional upsets that are reflected in stomachaches are generally not accompanied by a fever elevated more than a degree above normal. If a child has a fever higher than that, she is probably physically ill. Even if the temperature is only slightly elevated, have the child slow down and rest.

Of course, stomachaches in little children can be taken too seriously; if you become too upset, accept the notion that the child is ill, and give him too much attention, you may be encouraging the child to deal with anxiety and coping difficulty by complaining of a stomachache. It is important to be careful that stomachaches do not become a way of getting out of things, avoiding situations, getting to go home, and getting all of the teacher's attention. The only way to be sure is to take the stomachache fairly seriously the first couple of times. If it goes away in a little while, was not too severe to begin with, and does not keep recurring, do not worry about it much. If the stomachaches persist, though, be sure that the child is seen by a physician. If the doctor says that the child is using the symptom, you will need to respond to the child with gentleness but firmness, being sure that the stomachache complaint does not develop a payoff for the child. Children come up with many different, generally unacceptable ways of dealing with stress, problems, and the world about them. If they can get what they want and need through stomachaches, they will continue the behavior and will not develop more healthy, acceptable ways of dealing with difficulties. If the problem is not physical, parents should send the child to school, stomachache and all, and the child should be expected to go outside for recess, to wait in the lunch line and eat with the other children, and to complete schoolwork. When physical complaints do not work the way the child wants them to work, the child will give them up.

A *rash on a child's face or on other parts of the body* represents a problem much like stomachaches. The problem almost always has a physical cause. Occasionally, though, the rash may reflect emotional and social turmoil within the child. With little children, a rash on the face or other parts of the body, especially if it itches, most likely indicates poison ivy or other allergic reactions, insect bites, or chicken pox. It will be worth your time to find a medical book you can look at so you know what these symptoms look like when you see them. It is important that you know what measles and rubella look like and that you make an active effort to be sure that all of the children in your class and school have had their vaccinations. Whatever the cause, though, the school nurse or family physician should look at the rash to be sure that it is what it seems to be. It may reflect an allergy, infectious disease, dietary deficiency, or any number of things.

Although a rash is usually not particularly serious, it does warrant medical attention. If a contagious disease is suspected, you should have the child taken home, and be sure that other children do not handle the child's belongings. If you are not sure what might account for the rash, try to make a note of what foods the child has eaten, whether or not the child has been exposed to any unusual substances at school or in the classroom, whether the child might be reacting to new clothes, or anything else that might contribute to the problem. If you transfer information to the school nurse or the child's parents, they in turn can pass it on to the child's physician. The doctor may find this a very helpful clue as to the cause of the rash.

Sometimes children have continuing difficulties that are reflected in skin discoloration or the development of a rash. If so, the child is probably aware of this and can tell you about it. Be sure not to ask in front of the other children because calling it to their attention will embarrass the child. Whatever the cause, you might ask the child if he or she takes any kind of medicine for the problem; if so, be sure that the child takes it. If the child is supposed to avoid certain foods or exposure to certain things, help him remember to do that. Little children are active and involved, and forget. Simply reminding them will usually get them to slow down and remember.

It should be rememberd that rashes and other symptoms are sometimes negative side effects of medication a child may be taking. In addition to rashes, fevers, nausea, headaches, shakiness or drowsiness, etc., can be negative side effects of medication. When talking with a child who seems not to feel well or seems to be behaving somewhat differently than usual, ask him if he is taking any kind of medicine or if he has eaten or drunk anything unusual. The negative side effects of medication are sometimes anticipated and sometimes unexpected. When talking with the child's parents or the school nurse, raise the possibility that the problem or symptom may be related to the medicine or to something the child has consumed, and strongly suggest that the child's physician be asked about this. All medicine has some negative effects, from expected to unexpected, from quite mild to very serious. Just be sure to keep the possibility of medication reactions in mind when working with children.

If the child's physician feels that the rash is a reaction to stress, tension, and being upset, it will be helpful to work with the child in an interested, supportive way. Unlike stomachaches, children cannot put on a rash. When the rash has an emotional base, it is almost always a reaction to stress and tension. Since such children probably become scared and upset fairly easily, you might gradually encourage and nudge them into activities and situations that are difficult. For example, if standing up and talking out in class is a little too difficult, they may be able to start by answering "yes or no" questions while seated at their desks. Little by little, with your help they will gradually develop more confidence and a better sense of their own ability.

Wheezing or noisy exhalation is another complicated problem. The most likely causes of this difficulty are asthma, allergies, or respiratory infection. Some children who wheeze may already be under the care of a physician. Just be sure that they are following their doctor's instructions and taking whatever medicine they are supposed to. If you have not noticed a child wheezing before, your first concern should be the possibility that a particle or other foreign body may be partially blocking the air passage. Ask the child if there is something caught in her throat. If so, look down the throat to see if there is something there.

If there appears to be no immediate danger of the child's choking, it will be better to have the school nurse or other medically trained person dislodge the object since their training and experience will make it less likely that they will accidentally cause the object to close the breathing passage further. As with all potentially serious difficulties, do not try to treat the child or administer first-aid unless the condition is likely to get worse without your actively responding to the physical problem. We will discuss the problem of breathing difficulties and blocked breathing passages more in a later chapter.

If the child does not have anything caught in her throat, you will need to consider these possibilities: the wheezing may be a reaction to some severe emotional upset, excessive exertion, or a sudden change in temperature. If the cause involves overexertion, a change in temperature, or an emotional upset, the wheezing should go away in a few minutes once the child slows down, calms down, and gets warm. If the problem persists for more than a few minutes, though, the child needs medical attention. Occasionally you will see a child who from time to time has wheezing spells for short periods of time. If you notice the problem more than once in a week, or notice it as a usual reaction to physical exertion, change in temperature, and so on, you should encourage the child's parents to have him seen by a physician. If for some reason the parents do not follow through with this recommendation, the school nurse should pursue the matter.

A frequent, wet, productive cough usually does not represent a serious difficulty but does need attention. Any cough should be taken seriously, especially if it persists for more than a few days or seems to outlive the cold with which it was originally associated. Such coughing could be a sign of allergies or chronic infection. With little children, you may need to spend some time demonstrating the proper use of a tissue or handkerchief and showing them how to blow their nose properly. Have them blow both nostrils at once in a moderately enthusiastic way. Do not teach them to blow too forcefully or to blow one nostril at a time, since they can damage their inner ear by building up too much pressure. Also, this may be a good time to talk with children about proper and extra handwashing to avoid spreading their germs around too much. If a cough recurs with any regularity or seems to continue beyond a week or two, the child should be referred to the school nurse.

Of course, if the child seems hot and feverish, he should be referred to the nurse and taken home whether or not there is a cough. Again, it should be emphasized that children should either be taken home by someone from school or arrangements should be made for their parents to come to school and get them. If a child is to be taken home by someone at school, you should be sure that there is a responsible person at home who can accept responsibility for the child and deal with his or her difficulties. If no one can be found at the child's home who can accept this responsibility, the child should be taken back to school and kept there until satisfactory arrangements can be made.

With some regularity, you will have a child in your class who has *diarrhea*. When the child is in the classroom, the unpleasant odor will be difficult to avoid. Other children will tend to make comments and gestures, such as holding their noses, that let you know a particular child is having a problem. Also, children will occasionally go to the restroom and not come back because they have had difficulty with diarrhea while there. Obviously, if a child has gone to the restroom and does not come back, you will either go yourself or send someone else to the restroom to see what the problem is. You should suspect that the child is having some kind of problem, though.

Diarrhea is a very common problem for all people, including young children. It usually reflects some minor illness such as the flu, having eaten food that upset the digestive system, other minor infections, etc. Infrequently, diarrhea is one of a set of symptoms associated with more severe gastrointestinal and other systemic illness. Usually, though, diarrhea is a symptom of a minor problem.

The first step is to let the child know that you know he has a problem. Be sure to do this in a confidential and quiet way so as not to call undue attention to the child and to avoid unnecessary embarrassment. Once you have let the child know that you are aware of his problem, the next step will be to get the child to the bathroom or other place in the school where you can (as much as possible) help him get cleaned up a little. Since the child is physically ill, there is no point in his returning to the classroom. He should be made as comfortable as possible, encouraged to lie down, and kept quiet until arrangements can be made either for his parents to come to school to take him home or for someone at school to take him home.

If the diarrhea does not continue for more than six or eight hours, and if there is no indication of blood in the discharge, there is no reason to become concerned. If the problem persists beyond eight hours or so, though, the child should be taken to a physician since diarrhea ordinarily does not persist for more than a few hours. Also, the risk of dehydration becomes significant if the diarrhea goes on too long. When diarrhea persists for more than eight hours, or when some indication of blood is noticed in the discharge, the likelihood of dehydration or some more serious medical difficulty increases and the need for immediate medical attention is present.

You may find that several children in your class have diarrhea on the same day. One possibility is that they have all simply and coincidentally become ill the same day. Also, it may be that the flu or some other contagious illness is "going around" in the school or community, with the result that several children have the problem at once. Another possible explanation, though, is that something the children have eaten or have been exposed to at school has caused the problem. This possible spread of illness as a result of exposure to food or something else at school is sufficiently alarming to justify checking with other teachers to see if children in their classes are having the same problem. Usually, if the flu or another infectious disease is "going around," the pattern will be for one or two children to become sick, with a gradual increase over a few days in the number of children involved. It would be unusual for the flu to "hit" several children in the same class or a large number of children in the same school suddenly and without a gradual increase in the number of involved children over time.

If it seems as though a lot of children have become ill all at once, the school principal should be alerted. Of course, she and the school nurse will probably be aware of the problem before you realize how widespread it is. In these circumstances, the public health department should be contacted immediately to investigate the situation. The school should have existing policies on dealing with such problems. One immediate precaution would be for no more food or beverages to be served at school until the health officials have evaluated the situation.

Symptom Profile

Figure 5 presents the symptom profile format for the signs and symptoms discussed in this chapter.

Fig. 5. Symptom Profile —Typical Childhood Illnesses

	SYMPTOM	PHYSICAL/ ORGANIC	EMOTIONAL	SOCIAL	ENVIRONMENTAL	ACADEMIC
36	Vomiting	x	x			
37	Difficulty swallowing	x				
38	Frequent or severe stomachaches	x	x			
39	Rash on face or other parts of the body	x	x			
40	Frequent wheezing	x				
41	Frequent wet, productive cough	x				
42	Diarrhea	x	x			

FIVE

What's Happening at Home?

"Parents! I don't see how some kids make it at all when you find out what they have to deal with at home." Mr. Markowski is at home talking with his wife after an upsetting day at school. One of the children in Mr. Markowski's second-grade class told him this morning that Rita, a nervous little girl, had big red and black bumps on her back and legs. Some of the other girls saw them when they were in the restroom. On the way in from recess Mr. Markowski discreetly asked Rita how she had hurt her back. She became very frightened and started crying. The guidance counselor happened to notice the situation, and after a few brief scheduling arrangements, Mr. Markowski and the counselor talked with Rita in a quiet place.

The story is not very pleasant. It started when Rita's grandfather wanted to give Rita her bath. The details are not particularly important, but this bathing apparently led to Rita's being sexually abused. Mr. Markowski knows that this kind of thing happens with little boys and girls and involves family members as well as older children and adults in the neighborhood, but it still does not go down very easily. Of course, such abuse and mistreatment occasionally occur with children who have been abducted or accosted in the neighborhood. More frequently, though, such incidents involve someone whom the child knows fairly well.

It seems that Rita was eventually able to tell her mother what was going on. Instead of trying to deal with the situation, Rita's mother did not believe her and angrily told Rita's dad about it. He apparently was drinking heavily as usual on the weekend, and the beating Rita received was the culmination of the family blowup. Somehow, the family saw the whole situation as Rita's fault. "Blaming the child" tends to be more frequent in families of lower socioeconomic status and in families in which the adults have relatively less education. Nonetheless, placing some degree of blame on the child is not uncommon.

Mrs. Markowski suggested that Rita's situation was very extreme and that things like that do not happen very often. Mr. Markowski agreed, but pointed out that this kind of thing happens more often than most people would ever believe. He went on to mention a situation of less severe, but damaging abuse involving Johnny, a friendly little boy whose learning ability is somewhat limited. Johnny's parents simply will not accept his limitations. Mr. Markowski has tried to talk with them about this, but they become hostile and aggressive toward him when he mentions any of Johnny's problems or limitations. As if this were not enough, the hostility and aggression spill over onto Johnny in that his parents then belittle him and tell him he is stupid.

Then there is Tony, who has a different kind of problem. His parents keep him out of school a day or two a week without any solid reason. When Tony does come to school, he does not care to play or interact with the other children. He says that he always plays by himself at home and that his mom does not like him to play with other children.

What can a teacher do about things like these? The signs and symptoms brought up with these children represent eight of the most significant difficulties in the family and neighborhood lives of little children. It is tempting for teachers to shy away from home and family problems and to overlook the indicators of such difficulty. As you can see, however, such problems have very serious negative implications for a child's school performance and future adjustment. Not only is a teacher's responsibility in this area professional and ethical, in many states the responsibility is legal. When we know that a child is seriously abused or neglected, the responsibility to do something is clear.

The legal obligation to report suspected child abuse and neglect deserves emphasis. In many states, professional people are legally obligated to report child abuse, child neglect, and suspected abuse and neglect. If they fail to do so, they are subject to criminal penalties. More specifically, in some jurisdictions professional people are subject to criminal penalities if they could reasonably have been expected to suspect or be aware of child abuse or child neglect but have avoided dealing with it. This means that the responsibility to report both suspected and actual situations is both professional and frequently legal. The point is that you may be subject to legal repercussions if you fail either to recognize or to report the problem. The child welfare department serving your area can advise you about the specific rules and penalties in your area.

Your innovativeness and sensitivity will be especially important in recognizing these symptoms. Understanding their significance requires little more than a warm heart and some understanding of children. Beyond trying to talk with the parents and showing special sensitivity to the child, dealing with the problem usually becomes the responsibility of outside agencies. Nevertheless, if the teacher does not first suspect and then recognize the signs and symptoms, the child may be forever the victim.

Discussion

Most children live in nice homes with good, loving parents, and have no significant social, emotional, learning, or environmental difficulty. Problems you see from time to time in these children tend to reflect normal inconsistencies and discontinuities in development, behavioral anomalies, and so on. As children grow and learn, their behavior is usualy appropriate, though sometimes inappropriate, and occasionally very inappropriate. For most children, though, good days, good relationships, and good experiences overwhelmingly overbalance those minor and major problems that come up from time to time. However, there are situations in a child's home life and experiences outside of school that clearly justify your concern and intervention, such as when a *child is apparently abused by parents or others at home.*

First, we need to clarify what is not included in child abuse. Little children occasionally do things that require a fairly severe reaction from their parents. For example, if a child persists in dashing across the street in the middle of the block or angrily throws a sharp object at a playmate, a parent may spank hard enough to leave black and blue marks on the child's bottom. Similarly, children who live in very deteriorated neighborhoods where violence and other dangerous activities such as drug abuse are prevalent need to learn very quickly where they can and cannot go, to whom they may and may not talk, what they may and may not do, etc. Parents who must "teach" young children about these things in a quick and immediate manner may "punish" them fairly severely for violations of the rules and restrictions. The risk is that the child may be hurt or damaged before milder and less severe techniques have time to work.

In the case of very fair-skinned children, a little smack on the arm or leg may leave a red spot. At other times children may get in the way while parents are doing some work and accidentally be hit by a parent or by a tool the parent is using; the injury could be fairly serious. Also, little children do fall out of trees, down stairs, and through glass windows, accidentally get burned, unintentionally scald themselves with hot water, etc. We are making two points: a parent may leave marks on a child as a result of an intentional effort to punish the child, and the child may be injured accidentally by the parent or in some other situation. Obviously, children who have been injured or bruised in these ways have not been abused, unless punishments and efforts to correct the child have given way to parental violence and extreme mistreatment. The line between punishment and violence is difficult to judge. Nonetheless, the judgment frequently needs to be made.

An associated problem is that a child might exaggerate what happened or distort the parent's intent or some other aspect of the situation. On the other hand, a child who really has been abused may minimize or misrepresent what happened in a way that allows you to conclude that the bruises or injuries were an accident when they really were not. The best guideline is to consider the possibility of child abuse in any situation where a child's bruises, burns, bumps, or other injuries are more than minor. If injuries are more than minor, ask the child such questions as how it happened, when it happened, if it happened before, if it was an accident. Even though the child's injury probably will not be the result of abuse, the possibility that it might be is enough to prompt you to ask some questions. If you have any suspicion that the child is being abused, consult with your principal or school nurse. If the suspicion still exists after conferring about it, each of you has a moral, ethical, and legal responsibility to pursue the matter further. The first step would be to talk with the parents about the problem if the injuries are not severe. This does not mean accusing them, but mentioning the injury and asking what happened, when it happened, etc. If suspicion of abuse still exists after talking with the parents, your responsibility to the child demands that you report your suspicion to local child welfare authorities.

It should be sufficient to point out that children really do get beaten with clubs, belts, and electric cords; they really are intentionally burned or scalded by adults; they really are starved for long periods of time; they really are subjected to torture and cruel treatment. Frequently, the problem goes on for a long time before a responsible adult is willing to follow through on a suspicion in a way that really gets at the problem. Of course, if you have a child in your class who has a history of neglect or abuse, and if appropriate authorities are already involved with the family, you will want to take extra care in your relationship with that child, avoiding use of physical punishment and also the trap of overprotecting the child. The child still needs firmness, guidance, encouragement, and limits. Your going to the other extreme, being excessively solicitous and protective, merely subjects the child to the opposite side of the abuse/neglect problem. You cannot make up for the child's bad experiences, but you can offer the child a good, healthy relationship and situation as he or she continues to grow and develop.

Two of the points here need further emphasis. As suggested, physical punishment should always be avoided with children who have been physically abused. Also, it will be important to avoid any substantial expressions of anger and aggravation that are expressed in an angry way. For these children, expressions of anger must come in a fairly calm and moderate form. Instead of yelling and becoming obviously angry with the child, it will be preferable to say calmly to the child, "I am quite angry with you." Of course, this approach is desirable with all children, but especially with children who have been abused. Next, it really is true that one cannot make up for the abuse and neglect that a child has experienced. Those scars are permanent and lasting. Teachers can, though, do a lot for such children by relating to them in a warm and friendly way, providing healthy relationship experiences for them, giving them a lot of encouragement and affirmation, and so on. At least, you can assure them that they have healthy adult/child relationships at school. If you are careful not to overdo the "feeling sorry for them" aspects of your relationship with them, and are careful to provide a healthy, supportive relationship for them, you will have done quite a lot to give them a positive, healthy, growing experience.

Evidence that a child has been sexually molested should be handled in much the same way as evidence that children have been beaten or abused in other ways. Physical abuse may not be easily noticeable, but sexual abuse is even more difficult to detect. Part of the recognition problem comes from the fact that little children may be relatively unaware of what has happened to them. Occasionally, sexually abused children are totally unaware that there is something wrong going on. They think they are just playing a special game with an older sibling, a parent, a neighbor, a relative, or some other older person. In this case you will probably become aware of the problem only if you take time to listen to the things these children say, the little conversations they have with their friends, etc. You may find that one of the children in your class is the group's authority on anatomy. The likelihood is that the child has open, straightforward parents who have told her anything she wants to know, or that the child has been especially observant with brothers and sisters. If you casually ask the child how she found out about a particular fact or piece of information, and the child says something that raises a little suspicion in your mind, take time to ask a few more indirect questions.

Of course, these additional, indirect questions should not be asked in front of the other children and should be pursued fairly casually, when you have an opportunity to talk with the child privately. You might start by asking, "I was wondering how you came to know so much about boys and girls," or something similar. The notion of pursuing things in a private and confidential but yet casual and informal way with children when considering the possibility of either child abuse or sexual abuse is very important.

Children who have been sexually molested may seem more withdrawn and frightened than usual, may become anxious and apprehensive when the discussion shifts to home or particular individuals, etc. As you talk with them about this (and, of course, your conversation will be private and confidential), you may want to ask, "Has anyone been bothering you?" If no inappropriate sexual activity has been going on, they will simply say no or tell you about a problem with their brother or sister; it will not occur to them that you might be asking about some sexual activity. If they have been involved in sexual activity however, they will know what you are talking about. Very gradually work up to the question, "Has someone been doing something to your body or wanting you to do something to theirs?" Be sure you work up to this gradually. If at any point you feel that there is nothing going on, do not pursue the questioning any further. Also, it is not good to ask if there has been any sexual activity with someone specific, like daddy or Uncle Joe. If there is nothing going on with that person, it has probably never occurred to the child that something might and you will have focused the child's thoughts and attention on a particular individual. Above all, avoid doing this.

If two or three questions or a particular situation still leaves you with the suspicion that the child has been sexually abused, further inquiry should be carried out by the school counselor, the school psychologist, the school nurse if these individuals are especially sensitive to the needs and feelings of small children, or a worker from the local child welfare agency. It can hardly be overemphasized that when you or anyone else talks with the child about this and other types of personal problems, a very warm, caring, sensitive, supportive relationship with the child is extremely important. The relationship must not be accusing, threatening, or in any way give the impression of anger or negative feelings. It must reflect sincere caring and interest. As with child abuse, though, a suspicion of sexual abuse is sufficient to involve your principal, guidance counselor, school psychologist, and school nurse.

With other children, you may suspect that their *parents drink heavily or abuse drugs*. These children may report that their mothers or fathers drink a lot or take something that makes them act funny. A child may add that one parent hit the other, got extremely angry, or threw something. The child may repeatedly not do homework or other assignments and, when asked, report that no one will help him, or let you know in some way that his parents are not very involved with him. You may notice that other children seem to have a workable relationship with one parent but have little or nothing to say about the other parent. At a minimum you will notice that the child's schoolwork is inconsistent in quality or that sometimes the child does his work and other times does not. You may notice that a child seems to be physically or emotionally upset some mornings more than others. Perhaps especially on Mondays. If through conversations and comments you get some direct indication that one or both of the child's parents are abusing alcohol or drugs, you can begin to think about the problem more specifically. More often, though, the indications will be fairly indirect. For example, children may seem somewhat neglected, poorly clothed, and not particularly clean, as if no one had paid much attention to them that morning. Other children may seem to have a surprisingly difficult time with reading, arithmetic, and other school skills which might lead you to suspect that something may be going on at home which is not particularly conducive to the child's feeling good about himself, about school, and so on. One possibility is excessive use of alcohol or drugs on the part of one or both parents.

In terms of your relationship with these children, you might quietly have them comb their hair, wash their faces, and make themselves a little more presentable when they get to school, and be sure that they eat lunch; possibly parents are not sending enough money to school for lunch. Also, you might find some extra time to help them with schoolwork to compensate a little for lack of attention at home. If you have an aide in your classroom, you may want her to spend some extra time with these children.

Your suspicion that there is some problem at home possibly related to misuse of alcohol or drugs will lead to your involving the school counselor. The counselor can then approach the family about the child's problems. It is important that the counselor not confront the parents directly with the suspicion of alcohol or drug abuse. Parents should be approached in terms of the child's problems, the difficulty he or she is having at school, and your concerns about the child. It is important for you to make some notes about the problems the child is having at school so that the counselor can share these observations with the parents and pursue the situation from there.

Hopefully, you are having regular conferences with the parents of all your students. Parents of those children who are having difficulty at school or who may be having difficulty at home should be at the top of your conference list. If parents will not come in for a conference, you should at least try to talk with them on the telephone. As you talk with them, be alert to whether or not these *parents seem unwilling to accept the child's limitations.* Of course, all children have limitations, including children with superior intellectual ability: there are some things they can not do and some things they have not learned to do. Whatever problems there may be at home, though, it is important that parents understand and accept their child's limitations.

There is a real caution to be kept in mind with this, however. Realistically accepting a child's limitations must be combined with an understanding of a child's real skills and abilities. To focus on the limitations may be to set up a bias or prejudice against the child, seeing him as someone who cannot learn. This can set up a "self-fulfilling prophecy" in terms of "the child has limitations" and thus he is expected to achieve in a limited way. Understanding the child's limitations should be taken as a positive understanding of "where the child is" and as a reference point from which teaching and further help for the child can be organized. "Start where the child is" and move as smoothly and as effectively with him from there as possible. "Limitations" should be understood to mean nothing more or less than those things which cause a child particular difficulty, which seem to require extra effort for him, or which seem to be getting in the way of other learning. "Limitations" are, then, only problems or difficulties that need to be taken into consideration and dealt with as learning and achievement take place for the child.

Nonetheless, if a child's performance and achievement are not acceptable when the child is doing his best, the child will be quite frustrated and may feel inferior, be unusually shy, and get quite discouraged. Other children may react by becoming aggressive or indifferent. In either event, inappropriate parental expectations are causing a reaction in the child that gets in the way of learning and growing. You should keep in mind that your failure to understand and accept a child's limitations can cause a similar reaction in the child.

In working with children who are not meeting parental expectations, it is important that you emphasize things they can do, can accomplish, can achieve. The emphasis should not be on doing better, but on doing as well as the child can. In talking with the child's parents, it will be important to emphasize what the child has learned or is able to do and to avoid reinforcing their feelings that the child is not successful. When you first meet a child's parents, it is important not to begin by discussing the child's problems or lack of achievement. If parents do not accept the child's limitations, you would be supporting what they already think—that the child needs to buckle down and shape up. If the situation does not improve after you have spent some time talking with the parents and working with the child, the school psychologist is your next resource. With most parents, though, you will find it possible to help them understand and accept the child's limitations, and to get them to focus on the child's accomplishments and achievements.

Occasionally, though, you will deal with parents who become *hostile and agressive when confronted with their child's problems and limitations.* They may become verbally aggressive, use foul language, and tell you that you obviously do not know enough to be teaching. If you are young and unmarried, they may point out that you do not have any children so what could you possibly know about children. They may also argue that they live with their child and obviously know more about the child than you do. These parents may feel that their child is lazy and needs to be whipped into shape, or they may feel that their child is fine and that you are making a big deal out of nothing.

Of course, none of the child's difficulties can be dealt with until the parents are able to calm down, slow down, and think things through. The same rule applies to you. If you get involved in their anger and hostility by becoming angry, aggressive, or defensive, nothing can be accomplished. Try your best not to be intimidated. Above all, remain as calm and even-dispositioned as you possibly can. There is no point in defending yourself, accusing them of causing the problem, or involving yourself in an argument. If nothing else, you might say nothing until they stop talking and then say, "I see you have a lot of strong feelings about this." This gives them a chance to continue ventilating and verbalizing their anger. The next time they stop talking you might say, "I surely hope I will be able to help your child. He (or she) is certainly a nice little boy (or girl)." How can they disagree with this? As you continue to let them talk until they finish, acknowledge their feelings, respond in terms of your desire to help the child, and absorb their anger without responding to it, they will gradually calm down and slow down. At this point you can begin talking with them in a more reasonable way about what is best for the child.

At times, and more frequently in some school districts than others, you may find parents who are apparently completely uncooperative and disinterested in working with you and the school. As suggested in an earlier chapter, make this analysis of the parents' attitude and intent your last conclusion. There may be a lot of reasons why they seem uncooperative. For example, they may be employed and really unable to come to school. There may be a lot of other young children or someone very ill at home, making it impossible for either the mother or father to come to school. One or both parents may have little or no formal education and, as a result, feel somewhat intimidated and as if they have nothing to say or suggest. Others may not become involved in the parent/teacher conference process because they do not have transportation or the financial resources to arrange for transportation to come to school. Perhaps the parents are not comfortable with the English language or with the "social custom" of parent/teacher conferences. In any of these situations, it is not really true that the parents are uncooperative and disinterested. The problem is that you and the school have not yet come up with a way to facilitate their being more cooperative and interested.

Your first step should be to ask the child why his mother or father did not come in for a conference. The child will probably be able to give you an explanation. The important thing is to accept the explanation as true and reasonable, and figure out some alternative way of getting the parents involved. Many parents neither come to the school nor do they have a telephone. If you are to get them involved, someone will have to go to them. Talk with your supervisor or building principal about this to see who the most appropriate person would be to make the "home visit."

Are there ever parents who simply and absolutely refuse to cooperate? Yes, but they are few and very far between. Almost always, the problem is that the teacher and other school personnel simply have not yet come up with a way of getting them to cooperate. What happens if refusal to cooperate is absolute? Keep trying; they may change their attitude. At any rate, your continuing work with and supportiveness of the child becomes even more important.

Once in a while you may find parents who express anger and hostility toward their child by *belittling the child and telling him or her that he or she is stupid.* You may observe this directly when you can watch the parents interact with the child, or you may learn about it more indirectly. The child may tell you that she is stupid. When you ask where she got that idea, the child may tell you that one or both of her parents say that all the time. With other children the clues may be a little less direct. When you feel that children have a very low impression of their own abilities and capacities, you should consider the possibility that they are being belittled and put down at home. You might ask, "How do your parents think you are doing?" During parent conferences, you may gradually come to see that the parents never have anything good or positive to say about their child.

When children are subjected to these kinds of relationships at home, it will be important for you to make an extra effort to give them credit for those things you think they do well, for example, drawing pictures, writing, reading, playing games. Negative comments and criticism from you tend to reinforce the child's self-perception perpetuated by his parents. You need to accentuate the positive. In talking with the parents, it is important to get them to look at and respond to the child's accomplishments and abilities. To do this, though, they must come to believe that the child does have some abilities and some accomplishments. Your enthusiasm about the child's performance, abilities, successes, special skills, and good points will start them thinking in that direction. Once you get them to respond to you in terms of some of the child's strengths, you can begin to mention that the child seems to feel badly about himself. When you have gotten this far in talking with the parents, it is a small step to encourage them to accentuate the positive and to slow down calling attention to the negative.

A somewhat different kind of problem is presented by the *parent who frequently keeps a child out of school*. Once in a while you should check your attendance records. When you do, you will see that most children have missed only a day or so while a few children have missed a lot of school. In most cases you will be aware of the children's reasons for missing school—illness, another kind of crisis or illness within the family, or some other situation that caused them to be absent. Usually the children show a pattern of missing several days in sequence. You may find a child, though, who consistently misses a day or two a week or sometimes two or three days in one week.

The first step would be to talk with the child about the problem. If the child does not have a reasonable explanation, you can pursue the matter further. Even if the explanation is reasonable, though, it is appropriate to call the child's parents to talk with them about ways their child might keep up with schoolwork, make up missed work, etc. Usually what you will learn from talking with the mother is that she can not get her child to go to school or that she feels her child is not well enough to go to school. The illness usually includes stomachaches and being upset or nervous. The "he won't go" complaints usually are similar in nature; parents will say that the child becomes extremely upset, refuses to go to school, works himself into a tizzy, and generally causes an uproar. In either case, it is almost always true that the child's not going to school has nothing to do with what happens when the child is at school. Parents and children will try to tell you or the principal that the problem is at school, that you are mistreating the child, or that other children are mean to their child. Almost always the reality is that the mother is unable to separate herself firmly from the child, encourage independence, and let the child grow up. This situation is typically referred to as a "school phobia," but almost always has to do with anxiety about or fear of leaving home, rather than fear of school.

Usually, however, the solution comes in making the child go to school every day. The rule of thumb should be that if the child does not have a temperature over 100 degrees, he goes to school; little children can work themselves up to the point that they have a slight elevation in temperature. The worst possible thing that can happen is that the child might get sicker at school and have to go to the doctor.

In "school phobia" situations, mother is frequently unwilling or unable to make the child go to school, but ordinarily the child's father will be willing to take the child to school if this does not interfere with work. This is an appropriate thing for the father to do, but it will possibly cause increased marital tension. Quite frequently there is fairly severe marital conflict, sometimes under the surface.

Of course, it is extremely important that you really listen to what both the children and the parents are saying to you. As we know, some schools and some classrooms really are "horrible places" for children to be. Children's fear of or aversion to being involved in the classroom or school may be both justified and real. Although this is usually not the case, be sure that you carefully and caringly consider the possibility that a child's reluctance to go to school is reasonable and justified considering the situation at school. It may really be true that other children at school are terrorizing or hurting the child. Be sure to consider the possibility that the fears and complaints of both the child and the parents are justified, and that the change needs to occur at school.

Most of the time you will conclude that school phobia is a function of home difficulty and has little if anything to do with what is going on in school. Consequently, there is almost nothing you can do about it except to talk with the parents to see if they will bring the child to school, forcibly if necessary, for two or three weeks to see what happens, and perhaps suggest to the parents that they confer with someone at a guidance or mental health clinic. It may be encouraging for both you and the parents to know that a month or six weeks of concerted professional effort is usually quite sufficient to eliminate the attendance problem. The marital and family difficulties underlying the school phobia frequently take longer to work through.

It should be kept in mind that economic conditions within a family can occasionally contribute to frequent absences from school. It may be that the family cannot afford sufficient and adequate clothing for the child, may be having some difficulty paying school fees, may not have money to send with the child for lunch or milk, and may be experiencing some "embarrassment" about sending their child to school when she is not as adequately clothed and taken care of as other children. When talking with families about attendance problems, you will want to be very sensitive to the possibility that "affording school" is a problem for them. It is true that we profess "free education" for all children, but the reality is that it costs parents a good deal to send a child to school. If the parents cannot afford this, it is a problem.

If you sensitively consider the situation and suspect that there may be an economic problem, do not say something as blatant as "Are you having money problems?" Say something more subtle, such as "Is there some difficulty in getting the things your child needs for school?" If this is the problem, you could suggest then that they might be able to get some help. They may be willing to contact the child welfare department, one of the voluntary service organizations such as the Salvation Army or Good Will Industries, or one of the federally funded poverty agencies such as Community Action. If not, suggest the possibility that you check on possible resources and have someone get in touch with them.

In any event, it will be very important not to become "heavy-handed" and insist that they send their child to school anyway. First, try to help them with what is a real problem. If you do not feel comfortable talking about these things with them yourself, think a little about why it is making you feel so uncomfortable. After that, either talk with them about it or have your school principal arrange for someone from the school or one of the community agencies to talk with the family. Also, you should arrange for the child to receive "free lunches" and get the supplies and materials she needs at school without charge to the family. Almost all schools have special arrangements that can be made for children with such economic problems.

Occasionally, you may have children in your class who come to school with regularity but do not play with the other children. When you ask them about this, you are told that their *parents do not allow them to play with the other children.* The likelihood is that the child is misrepresenting the parents' real intent. At other times, children may tell you that they do not play with the other children for fear of being hurt, because their classmates are not very nice, because they do not like to play those kinds of games, because they do not want to get dirty, or other similar things suggesting that they have a real reluctance to become involved in the active give and take of childhood play.

Whether a child reports that he is not allowed to play or demonstrates a real reluctance to play, the suspicion is that his parents are too protective and are so restricting the child that he does not socially interact in a healthy, active way. At a minimum, the problem should be discussed with the child's parents to see whether or not they are really setting such restrictions and limitations on the child. If they are, some counseling and guidance for them and the child are in order.

Frequently, though, you will find that the parents have not

intentionally set such restrictions and limitations on the child. The child has come up with the idea by himself. When this is the case, two kinds of explanations usually account for the problem. First, the child has played and interacted with the children and has had some bad experience(s). He may have gotten hurt, been rejected, embarrassed, teased, or in some way been made to feel bad. Usually, you will find that this is a very temporary state of affairs. Simply encouraging these children to go back and play, to try again, to be involved, and so on, will be enough recognition of their hurt combined with encouragement to get them to reinvolve themselves. If a little support and encouragement do not take care of the problem, though, the children are experiencing more serious social difficulties.

Occasionally, this type of problem will be seen in children who simply do not know how to play with the other children. They may have grown up in a situation where there are not many other boys or girls. If so, it is literally true that they do not know how to play. The problem may be compounded by their being somewhat embarrassed to admit that they do not know how. The way they deal with it is simply to avoid the situation. Because of this possibility, you may want to talk with the physical education teacher about the problem. She can help decide if it is really true that the child has limited social experience and limited social skills. If so, the physical education teacher can work with you and the playground supervisor on the problem.

More frequently, though, a child with this type of problem has "real difficulty" in interpersonal relationships. The school counselor, and perhaps outside mental health counseling may be needed, if things do not improve. To start working on it yourself, encourage these children to participate in and become involved in classroom games and activities. Gradually move from there to encouraging them to become involved in less active and less aggressive playground games. For example, they may be willing to swing with other children on the swings, play marbles or jump rope, climb on the playground toys, play tag if you tell the children to let them play, and so on. The idea is that they may be willing to become involved in activities and games that require individual action and effort as opposed to cooperative action and effort. Playing on the sliding board would come before "teeter-tottering" with another child.

Above all, discourage these children from isolating themselves and withdrawing. If nothing else, start by interacting with them yourself and having the playground supervisor interact with them. One additional point is to avoid putting passive, withdrawing children together. It sometimes seems like a good idea to have one shy child play with another. The result tends to be that they simply stand and look at each other. If your strategy is to pair a shy child with another child, pick a child who is more socially active and involved.

If the problem really does relate to the child's parents, though, it may relate to overprotection in a form that is infrequently seen. The parents may sincerely believe that the other children in the area are not very nice, are a bad influence, are rough and foul, and are generally the type of children to whom their child should not be exposed. Although there is not yet enough experience to confirm the impression, it is possible that this type of parental attitude is more prevalent in communities where interschool busing has been required for racial integration. It is possible that children are told that they "have to" go to that school but that they should not interact with the other children. This type of attitude would be picked up when talking with the parents. Also, it may be that the parents simply think that most other children are a bad influence on their child.

In either event, sensitivity to the parents' attitudes and feelings is important. It will probably do little good simply to argue with them and tell them that they are wrong. They will assume that you may also be a bad influence on their child. A more productive approach will be to talk with them about the need of children for social contact, social involvement, social participation, and so on. They need to understand that the "social dimension" of their child is critical to healthy development and that it must be nurtured and encouraged. Continuing work with the parents along these lines must be combined with continuing work with the child in terms of gradually increasing social involvement. The initial efforts to approach the problem both through the parents and the child may be all that you can reasonably follow through with yourself. The problem may be such that the school guidance staff or an outside community agency will need to deal with it. Nonetheless, children who will not play or who are not allowed to play need our very careful and caring attention.

Symptom Profile

Figure 6 presents the symptom profile including the most significant signs and symptoms presented in this chapter. It follows the same format developed for the symptom profiles in earlier chapters.

Fig. 6. Symptom Profile —Family and Environmental Factors

	SYMPTOM	PHYSICAL/ ORGANIC	EMOTIONAL	SOCIAL	ENVIRONMENTAL	ACADEMIC
43	Shows evidence of child's having been sexually molested		x		x	
44	Shows evidence that parents drink heavily or abuse drugs				x	
45	Is apparently abused by parents or others at home				x	
46	Parents seem not to accept child's limitations				x	
47	Parents become hostile or aggressive when approached about child's problems				x	
48	Parents belittle child or tell him/her that he/she is stupid				x	
49	Parents frequently keep child out of school	x	x		x	
50	Child reports parents do not allow him/her to play with other children		x	x	x	

SIX

Stop, Look,
and Listen

The bright-eyed enthusiasm and excitement of the children the first day they came to kindergarten was both contagious and a little overwhelming to Mrs. Reynolds. It was her first day with a real class of her very own, one of those uncommon times when everything was new for both the children and the teacher. As the first few days of the new school year settled down into something close to a routine, she became more conscious of individual children and aware of possible eye problems in a few of them.

Robin always seemed busy and involved but one of her eyes seemed less busy than the other. It was barely noticeable and rather difficult to spot, but Robin tended to use only one eye when looking at the teacher or at something on her desk. Bobby's problem was somewhat different. He used both eyes but seemed to have a special problem when trying to count things, talk about how many things he saw, or tell a story about a picture in a book. After paying a little careful attention and asking a few questions, Mrs. Reynolds concluded that Bobby was seeing double. Sally seemed to see all right and had no difficulty counting objects, telling stories about pictures in books, or looking straight at the teacher with both of her sparkling bright eyes, but during the third week of school Mrs.

Reynolds noticed that her eyes seemed a little red and swollen. Instead of her usually wide-eyed and happy expression, Sally was squinting both at things on her desk and at things off in the distance. The contrast with Sally's usual smiles and obvious enthusiasm was quite remarkable.

Mrs. Reynolds had experienced fairly painful earaches when she was a little girl, so she was quick to become concerned when Aaron talked about his ears hurting. Aaron said he had been having trouble with his ears hurting sometimes, and that they hurt more today than they ever had. Young children frequently do not pay attention very well and seem unable to hear, but Inez's problem seemed a little out of the ordinary. Even when Mrs. Reynolds had Inez's attention, Inez would occasionally get a somewhat puzzled expression on her face and act as if she either had not heard or had not understood. Mrs. Reynolds found that talking louder and addressing Inez more directly always changed the puzzled expression to one of interest and understanding. Inez seemed to be one of those very few children who really do not hear very well.

Learning about Joey's ear problems was almost an accident. Mrs. Reynolds had a bell on her desk and was talking to the children about how the ringing seemed to go on a little while after the bell was struck when Joey excitedly told Mrs. Reynolds and the other children that he hears that kind of ringing sound all of the time, usually not very loud, but once in a while quite loud. Mrs. Reynolds's curiosity led her to ask a few more questions and to learn that Joey also hears buzzing and cracking sounds sometimes. As with Joey, Danny's problem almost went unnoticed. His wavy black hair comes down to his collar and covers his ears, but one Thursday afternoon, he was tugging at his hair and accidently brushed it back from his ear and Mrs. Reynolds noticed a brownish, blotchy spot above his earlobe. Upon closer observation, the spot appeared to be dried blood. Her noticing that little patch of dried blood on Danny's ear was quite lucky for Danny.

These eight signs and symptoms are the most important indicators of difficulty in vision and hearing that teachers are likely to see in the classroom. Being sure to recognize them and equally careful not to undervalue their importance is the issue here. As you consider the discussion of these signs and symptoms, give attention to the special care which must be taken by all teachers to pick up on these problems, especially in little children. Once you have recognized the difficulty, it is essential that the child receive outside professional attention. In conjunction with that, though, your response to implications of the difficulty within the classroom is extremely important.

Discussion

The central importance of vision and hearing for children cannot be overemphasized. Almost all of their learning and life experience has a visual and/or auditory component, and most classroom learning is almost exclusively of a visual or auditory nature. Considering how delicate the eyes and ears are and how easily children's eyes or ears can be injured, it is quite surprising that it does not happen more often. When a child in your class does experience an obvious injury of either an eye or an ear, immediate medical attention is required. If the ear or the area around the ear is sufficiently injured to cause swelling or bleeding, the child needs to be taken to the doctor right away by his or her parent(s) or guardian, or other emergency arrangements need to be made following the guidelines discussed in Chapter Two.

Youngsters occasionally get black eyes. If a child is hit by a ball, another child, or some other hard object, and consequently shows swelling and irritation or "blackening" around the eye, the injury may be serious. If blurred vision lasts more than a few minutes the child should be checked by a physician. If there is any bleeding or other than watery discharge from the eye, immediate medical attention is necessary. Also, if one eye deviates or is swollen and was not in that condition before, the child should be checked by a physician. Keeping these emergency conditions in mind, let's consider some eye and ear problems that may not be quite so dramatic and noticeable.

The tendency of children to *use one eye more than the other*, or not to focus their eyes together, is a serious concern. You should be alert to children who do not look straight at you when talking with you. Similarly, children are probably having eye difficulty if they consistently tilt their heads, close one eye while looking at things, move their heads before being able to focus on something, or show other signs of being uncomfortable when looking straight at things with both eyes. Of course, all children occasionally close one eye while looking at something, do not always look directly at you when talking with you, or sometimes look around at fifteen other things before focusing on what you want them to look at. Children who really have eye difficulty do not have the problem once in a while or every other week, but fairly consistently.

Recognizing the problem may not be easy, though. If your alertness and awareness of possible difficulty leads you to suspect that a particular child may be using one eye more than the other, or may not be focusing his eyes together, you should watch him fairly closely for two or three days. If your suspicion continues, a referral to the school nurse or some discussion with parents is in order. Early recognition and treatment of eye problems is very important since they are so intimately related to a child's growth and development, and since correction of the difficulty is frequently possible if it is dealt with while the child is still young. Vision problems can be an unrecognized cause of psychological upsets, discipline problems, and school failure.

If children are having difficulty seeing, it will be important for you to learn the extent of their vision loss, what they are able to see, what kinds of things they might not be able to do. If you can find out who their eye doctor is, he will probably be happy to talk with you about the child's problems and how you can be of most help. If a child's eye problem is noticeable to almost everyone, including the other children, you will need to be sensitive to the special problems this can cause. Little children are cruel at times. They may tease or make fun of the child, and not let him be involved in their groups and activities. It will be important for you to help the child develop ways of dealing with his own feelings about the problem and with the reactions of the other children. It will also be quite appropriate for you to deal with the other children about their reactions. The momentary embarrassment and uncomfortableness the child may have over this group discussion is minimal compared with bad or nonexistent relationships with peers.

One of the problems in recognizing eye difficulty in children is that little children do not know what they are supposed to see, how they are supposed to see, or how others see. Of course, if their vision has been normal and suddenly changes, they will be aware of this and will probably tell you about it. If things have always seemed blurry or if they have always had difficulty focusing, they may not realize their problem. For example, a child with *double vision* may have gotten used to seeing two of everything, or his brain may have turned off the image from one of his eyes so that he now sees only one thing. If this is happening, you would notice that the child tends to look at things with one eye.

Less indirect clues of vision problems are occasional complaints of eyeaches or headaches. Little children rarely have headaches or sore eyes, so a complaint like this from a small child is something to become concerned about. If a particular child seems to avoid pencil-and-paper activities, has trouble buttoning clothing, has difficulty cutting neatly, writes poorly or has difficulty reading, seems to ignore lines or borders when writing or coloring, turns her body or the paper when drawing lines in different directions or changing the direction of a line, or tends to rub one eye, your first suspicion should be that the child may be having difficulty with vision. It is important to keep in mind that a routine school eye screening will not necessarily pick up some eye difficulties such as crossed eyes. If you suspect that the child is having some difficulty that may be related to vision, a professional eye examination is in order. Also, the school psychologist, if your school has one, will have special tests to further clarify the problem.

A special note should be made of the fact that allergies, sinus infections, and other pathological physical processes can cause headaches, eyeaches, tearing, blurred vision, red and swollen eyes, etc. If children have a condition of this nature that has been diagnosed by a physician, they, or at least their parents, will be able to tell you about it. Nonetheless, the existence of such a condition does not exclude the possibility of eye and vision difficulties. Children occasionally have two, three, or four basically unrelated problems that result in similar symptoms. If you suspect eye difficulty, encourage the child's parents to have a professional eye examination even if the child has other already diagnosed problems.

Red or swollen eyes are another sign of difficulty. Any redness, swelling or unusual running or tear secretion from the eye is cause for concern. The child will be uncomfortable and probably will have difficulty with many normal tasks. The problem may come from styes, allergies, foreign objects in the eye, or a variety of infections. When you notice the problem, simply ask the child, "What's wrong with your eye?" He or she may be able to tell you. Perhaps there is something in it or there is some kind of problem already being treated. If there is a possibility of something in the eye, having the child blink her eye in a glass of water filled to the brim will probably wash the foreign particle out. You may not be able to get little children to do this, though. Hopefully, excessive tearing will be enough to wash the particle out. If the problem does not clear up in a few minutes, the school nurse will probably be able to help you. In the meantime, try to get the child to avoid squinting or putting fingers in her eyes. Do not try to use your finger to remove anything from the eye; this is a job for a physician, since the eye can very easily be scratched by a fingernail or by unintentionally sliding the particle across the surface of the eye. If there is nothing in the eye, the redness and swelling should clear up in a day or two and should not get worse. If you notice red and swollen eyes for more than two or three days, or if the problem seems to get worse, talk with the child's parents to see if they are aware of the problem and what they are doing about it. The child should be taken to a doctor.

Ear problems are more common than eye problems in little children, since infections more frequently affect the ears than the eyes. For example, most little children get an *earache* once in a while. The pain is usually fairly intense, and children will usually tell you about it. If you notice children moving their heads from side to side or holding their ears as a way of dealing with pain, it will usually be sufficient to ask "What's wrong?" Through their tears they will be quite able to let you know that their ears ache. You will probably also notice that children having earaches are a little flushed and unusually warm to the touch. They probably will not have much of an appetite and will feel sick and miserable. The earache probably comes from a respiratory infection involving the inner ear. The eustachian tube gets blocked up, pressure builds, and the result is an earache.

The problem is usually not an emergency but should be taken very seriously. If the infection spreads, it could quite rapidly involve other parts of the body, and the building pressure could damage the ear. The child needs to be taken home, given a lot of mother's tender loving care, and taken to the doctor if things do not clear up in a day or so, or if they get worse. Be sure not to apply heat to the ear since heat can cause fluids within the ear to expand further. Also, do not put any kind of drops or other medicine in the ear.

It can hardly be overemphasized that you should never directly attempt to treat an injury or symptom which a child is experiencing. Above all, you should never give a child medicine or attempt to do anything other than follow minor first aid procedures. For example, if a child is bleeding, it is quite appropriate to apply a compress firmly to the bleeding area. If a child gets a scrape or minor cut, it is appropriate to wash it off with clean water and wrap it in a clean bandage. If a child gets too hot, it is appropriate to have him lie down and for you to apply a cold compress to his forehead. Similarly, it would be appropriate to give a child a cold compress to hold against the ear while waiting for the parents to come to get him. The main thing is not to give a child any medicine (including aspirin), and not to do anything to a child's injuries other than washing a minor injury with clean water, applying a clean bandage, or applying a cool, clean compress. To go beyond this is to run the risk of further complicating the child's injury or illness and subjecting yourself to legal liability for mistreatment of the child.

Occasionally you may have a child in your class who does not complain of severe earaches but does complain about her ears hurting from time to time. These complaints should be taken seriously, since a continuing minor infection could be causing the problem, and medical attention can clear it up. Also, any minor but continuing pain in the eyes or ears, or other parts of the body for that matter, is a potential problem, since children's bodies do not usually hurt on any continuing basis. Alertness to small signs of irritations, infection, or other difficulty may prevent serious problems. Perhaps a note to the child's mother, a phone call, a comment to the school nurse, or some similar action will be sufficient to get the parents to find out what the problem is. It is important to remember that almost all parents are vitally concerned about their children, will respond quickly to signs of difficulty, and are very happy to have you call any problem or potential problem to their attention so that they can take care of it.

Any feeling on your part that a child might not hear normally should be taken seriously. Of course, adults get the impression sometimes that children are stone deaf when they do not pay attention, do not respond, or get absorbed in their own activities and ignore us. Nevertheless, if you have a feeling that a child has *difficulty hearing* and that the problem is something more than finding it hard to get the child's attention, a hearing evaluation by the school's speech and hearing therapist is in order. If your school does not have the services of a speech therapist, there may be a speech and hearing service available in your community. Many universities have programs related to speech and hearing problems, and are usually willing to evaluate children from their general vicinity.

Also, public health departments frequently provide fairly good hearing evaluations. At a minimum, one of the physicians in your community should know how to get access to speech and hearing services.

You should be aware that the whisper test is not an adequate measure of a child's hearing. First of all, whispering only tests the child's hearing within the frequency of your voice. Also, when you whisper you tend to lower the pitch of your voice; the child may hear that quite nicely and still have hearing problems.

If a child complains of fullness or pressure within the ear or of strange popping or cracking sounds, or if you find yourself having to repeat instructions continually or get the impression that a student is daydreaming excessively, you should consider the possibility of hearing problems. There are many causes for hearing difficulty, including headcolds, infections, sore throats, allergies, putting objects in the ears, picking the ears with bobby pins or other sharp objects, and so on. Whatever the reason for hearing loss, a significant number of children who experience even a slight, temporary hearing loss will develop a more serious hearing loss if medical attention is not given. In addition, children who have a sudden or gradual hearing loss will tend to become somewhat confused and frustrated, and may develop other adjustment difficulties as a result of not hearing what people say or not hearing what is going on around them. Your display of concern to the school nurse, speech and hearing therapist, and parents will usually be quite sufficient to get the children all the help they need.

If an actual hearing loss is determined, it will be important to place the child in the most favorable place in the classroom so that she will be able to see your face and actions and the faces and actions of other people, and be able to hear what is going on. It will also be important to check with the child to make sure that she understands what is going on, but be sure not to generate a lot of attention from the other children when you check. You should also keep in mind that children who find it difficult to hear may become the focus of teasing and ridicule from the other children. Other children probably will not tease and ridicule the child directly, but will do it through laughing and making fun of the child with each other. As a result, the child may become the focus of the teasing and tormenting without being directly aware of it. Your calm but firm disapproval will usually be sufficient to get almost all of the children to stop doing this. There may be one or two children in your class who, for their own reasons and needs, continue the teasing and tormenting. If so, you will want to focus on what may be going on with them.

Occasionally, you may notice that a child in your class *frequently squints* when doing work at his desk or when trying to read something on the chalk board. First, you will want to keep in mind the fact that it is normal for little children to squint sometimes. They may not be particularly enjoying the assignment or activity, and the "squint" may only be part of a more general grimace, indicating their dissatisfaction or displeasure with the activity. It would not, though, be normal for a child to squint with any regularity. It could be that the squinting is related to allergies or tics (which will be discussed in a later chapter).

More likely, though, squinting represents a vision problem. Part of the eye naturally adjusts to light and dark and to other varying visual requirements. For example, the eye physically adjusts to looking at faraway things, looking at things at a medium distance, and looking at things that are closer. Squinting is occasionally an effort on the part of the child to get his eye to accommodate better to the visual task. He is trying to change the eye so that the visual image will be better processed. The physiology of this process is not important here. The point is that "squinting" may be an indication that the child is having difficulty seeing.

You will want to be especially alert to the kinds of situations in which the child squints. Does he squint more when looking at things on the chalkboard or when working at a desk? This may suggest what is commonly thought of as a difference between farsightedness and nearsightedness. In either event, the child needs an eye examination. Frequently, school nurses have some special training qualifying them to make "screening" examinations of children's vision. If your school has a nurse who is qualified to do this, have the nurse examine the child. Whether or not the child is seen by the school nurse, he should be seen by an eye specialist if the problem persists.

Calling the problem to the attention of the child's parents will usually be quite sufficient to get the necessary examination and help. If the parents do not follow through, though, the problem is sufficiently significant for both the child's development and learning that the school principal or guidance staff should assure that the necessary evaluation and corrective measures are arranged for. As with other childhood difficulties, parents may occasionally not have the financial resources for the evaluation and corrective measures. For example, glasses are fairly expensive. Child welfare authorities, private agencies, and some service organizations are quite willing to help families with these expenses. Worldwide, the Lions International (The Lions Club) helps families with eye examinations, medical procedures, glasses, etc. They are usually willing to contact a family who may need help directly. Of course, you will want to talk first with the child's parents about the problem and let them deal with it if they are able.

Two additional symptoms of ear difficulty conclude our consideration of the most significant signs and symptoms of eye and ear difficulty seen in small children. First, you will infrequently find a child who complains of a *ringing sound or sensation in the ear*. In a minor form, this symptom is neither uncommon nor particularly significant. We all occasionally experience a ringing sensation or a sense of "tightness" in the ear. Ordinarily, this is related to some change in air pressure, occasional dizziness or light-headedness that results from playing too hard or getting too hot, very minor infections or the beginning of a cold or the flu, a mild bump or bang on the side of the head, or other such minor condition. The "ringing" sensation experienced as a result of these problems is very temporary, lasting for no more than a few minutes. In addition, the "ringing" is a very annoying but relatively quiet sensation. The "sound" does not seem to be particularly loud or something that causes us to become uncomfortable. A similar sensation is also occasionally experienced as a thumping, cracking, buzzing, or humming, resulting from some unusual pressure on the ear or some unusual vibration of the mechanism in the inner ear. The key here is that the sensation, however it is experienced, is mild and temporary.

Occasionally, though, such sensations will be more chronic and/or more intense. When this is the case, the first possibility to consider is that the child may be taking some type of medication that is causing the "sensation." You should simply ask the child who reports such sensations, "Are you taking any kind of medicine?" or "Do you know what is causing the problem?" If the child is taking any kind of medication he will be able to tell you about it. Of special note, though, is the fact that some medications may cause such sensations, but are not "supposed" to do so. Also, the child may give you some other explanation for the problem that "seems to make sense." Nonetheless, you should be sure to check out the symptom(s) with the child's parents to see whether or not the child is accurately reporting the situation. If they are unaware of the problem, and if it is prolonged and fairly intense, the child should be seen by a physician and should have an evaluation by a speech and hearing therapist. Many schools provide the services of a speech and hearing therapist.

Noticing children with a ringing sensation or other similar sensation will usually be fairly easy. They will tell you about it. Other children may have experienced the sensation for so long that they are unaware of the fact that it is not normal. Still other children may not become concerned enough about the symptom to tell you about it. Listen to the discussions and comments of children about each other. Maybe you will pick up some clues in this way. Also, it will be important to be alert to those children who seem to become distracted when you are talking with them, seem to be listening to something else when you are trying to talk with them, seem to have difficulty recognizing certain notes or melodies in the music portions of your classroom activities, or give any other indication that their hearing may not be as accurate or as adequate as that of other children. Along with a lot of other possible problems, the ringing sensation may be present. In any of these situations, try to arrange for a speech and hearing evaluation as well as a medical examination.

Finally, you will want to be very alert to any sign of injury to or *bleeding from the ear*. Any number of things can cause bleeding or a bloody discharge from the ear. Primarily, the difficulty is either internal or the result of an injury or accident. One possible internal cause is an infection or other difficulty that has resulted in some rupturing of blood vessels within the ear. This results in a bloody discharge or "oozing from" the ear. This obviously represents a serious problem needing immediate medical attention. If untreated, the problem is likely only to get worse. If the bleeding is a result of an outside injury, the child will usually be able to tell you what happened. Generally, he will be very anxious to tell you because the associated pain and discomfort will be fairly intense. Other children may have developed the habit of "picking" at their ears with pencils, fingernails, pens, or other objects that injure the external surface of the ear. Whether the bleeding results from internal difficulty, an accident or injury, or a child's picking at his or her ear, some medical attention is required. Probably, it would first be advisable to have the school nurse look at the child's ear, if a nurse is available to do that. If the difficulty is quite minor and is a function of an external scratch or minor cut, the nurse will be able to advise the child's parents about how to deal with it. They may not need to take the child to a physician if the bleeding clears up fairly quickly. If you have to deal with the problem yourself, immediately advise the child's parents of the problem. If the blood has dried or if the bleeding is very minor, they should come to school, get the child, and deal with the problem. They should be encouraged to take the child to the doctor "just to be on the safe side." If the bleeding is at all extensive or profuse, emergency medical attention is required.

Part of your class time spent talking about health and health problems should focus on vision, hearing, eye, and ear difficulty. Little children should understand that their eyes and ears are very sensitive and very easily damaged. They should be made aware of the dangers involved in picking or poking at either their eyes or ears (as well as their noses). A specific child who persists in poking or scratching at her ears or eyes should have the problem discussed with her individually, insisting that she refrain from the activity. If she does not do so, the problem is potentially serious enough to warrant some disciplinary action to emphasize the problem. Perhaps you might make her stay in from recess or not participate in some activity the next time you observe her picking or scratching at herself. Of course, such action would only follow medical evaluation eliminating the possibility of allergies, infections, irritations, or some other difficulty that is causing the child to feel actually uncomfortable, to itch, etc.

Symptom Profile

Figure 7 presents the most significant signs and symptoms of difficulty related to eyes and ears and follows the symptom format developed in earlier chapters.

Fig. 7. Symptom Profile —Vision and Hearing

	SYMPTOM	PHYSICAL/ ORGANIC	EMOTIONAL	SOCIAL	ENVIRONMENTAL	ACADEMIC
51	Using one eye more than the other	x				
52	Frequent earaches	x				
53	Difficulty hearing	x				
54	Bleeding from the ear	x				
55	Complaints of double vision	x				
56	Complaints of ringing sounds or sensations	x				
57	Frequent squinting	x	x			
58	Red or swollen eyes	x	x		x	

SEVEN

Come Out, Come Out, Wherever You Are

Within all little folk there is a healthy, responsive, lovable child. However, some little folk have their healthy child so well hidden or so pushed back that he or she is not to be seen. Anne, an uptight eight-year-old, is such a child. Her hands shake and tremble much of the time, and when her teacher tries to comfort her, the message from those perspiring, cold, clammy hands sometimes seems close to terror. When Anne tries to talk, the message is sometimes lost in her frequent stuttering and stammering. On even the warmest of spring days she shivers and shakes in her desk or in the hallway. She seems to feel inferior, as if she is not as good as others, and frequently does not respond when people try to talk with her, but just stares blankly. Her mother has to bring her to school, since Anne becomes almost hysterical at the prospect of walking to school by herself. Even when they reach school, Anne shows an unusual reluctance to separate from her mother and stay in school. Will the bright, healthy little girl be able to come out from behind the fear and apprehension? Perhaps with her teacher's help she will be able to progress a little into the world of parties and playmates.

Manuel's normal, ornery self is hidden in a different sort of shell. He seems to be afraid of all kinds of things, including dust, food in the cafeteria, bugs, poison gases, buildings collapsing, airplanes, and a few other things. The odd thing is that he is afraid of things most children do not think about. He frequently complains of headaches and holds his head as if the pain were really severe. This problem child compounds his teacher's frustration by frequently wetting and soiling himself. He sometimes talks to himself and acts as if he hears voices and sees things that are not there. Almost daily he seems preoccupied with death—his death and the death of family members and people at school. Sometimes he says, "I'm going to die today, and so are you." The other children try to relate to Manuel, but he often expresses the feeling that he is no good and that nobody likes him. Sometimes he even thinks people are really trying to hurt him and he refuses to play with other children. Manuel's teacher can help if he can get past that shell.

Kim is a child who seems to feel unlovable. When she talks, she blames herself for problems at school and at home, but usually she refuses to talk. She seems preoccupied with her own thoughts and fantasies and will not go outside for recess, sometimes expressing the fear that she might get hurt. Kim keeps her lovable little girl in a box. Her teacher wants to help, but does not know how to get Kim to talk, open up, and come out of the box.

The twenty-one signs and symptoms seen in Anne, Manuel, and Kim represent the most significant signs and symptoms of emotional disturbance in frightened, withdrawn children. The symptoms shown by Manuel are sufficiently severe to suggest childhood psychosis. It would be unusual to see such a severely disturbed child in a regular classroom. Nevertheless, these same symptoms can occur in milder form, two or three at a time, often enough to cause real concern. It is important for the teacher to recognize these signs and symptoms and equally important to understand their potential significance. Once the symptoms are recognized and their significance is appreciated, the teacher will probably want some special help or consultation in order to deal with the particular problem child. Hopefully, the consultation will emphasize the fact that there really is a healthy, lovable child there somewhere. The question is how to get that child to come out.

Discussion

Children let us know a lot about what is going on with them through body clues. For example, *shaking, trembling hands* represent a body message from the child. Of course, such trembling may only reflect simple, normal weakness resulting from vigorous activity or from using the arms a lot. Transient tremors of no particular significance occasionally occur in children as a result of their being hungry, somewhat cold, or quite excited.

However, there are more significant causes of shaking. These include congenital tremors which occasionally occur in members of the same family, problems within the brain or the rest of the nervous system, thyroid difficulty, and difficulty in calcium utilization. Rarely, shaking represents the first visible symptom of muscular dystrophy. Children with these neurological and physical problems all need fairly intensive medical care. One clue that neurological and physical problems exist and that medical care is needed is shaking that does not confine itself to the hands. Considering how important the problem may be, you should observe the child with trembling hands quite closely, be able to report the frequency and duration of the trembling quite accurately, and notice whether or not there is any visible trembling or shaking elsewhere in the body. Also, you should be alert to other symptoms, such as the child's being sick at the stomach or having an elevated temperature.

You will find that trembling of the hands usually occurs in tense, shy, anxious children and that the symptom is usually not a sign of neurological or physical difficulty. Nevertheless, the possibility of a serious medical problem is enough to warrant contacting the school nurse and the child's parents so care can be taken that there are no physical complications. With shy, skittish children you may find that shaky hands are accompanied by rapid eye motion and jerkiness in arms, legs, or other parts of the body. You will find that these children tend to become apprehensive quite easily and also tend to be overly critical of their own efforts: "I'll probably do it wrong"; "I don't think I have done it right"; "I'm scared to try because I might mess it up." Shaky hands and strong self-doubt show up especially when these children are asked to do something they have not done successfully before. These children may strongly prefer continuing with familiar tasks or repeating things they have done before instead of trying new things. They tend to strive for perfection, working in a somewhat slow and extremely orderly way. Their interests tend to be fairly limited and they tend not to initiate activities requiring any responsibility on their part. At the same time, they may seem to require very little emotional support and rarely get angry. Intense feelings are there, though: you can see them in their hands.

It will be helpful to praise such children when they do things well and to relate to them in a very encouraging way. Also, you will want to help them learn skills that will bring praise from their peers, from other adults at school, and especially from their parents. Severe parental criticism, overprotectiveness, and rejection can contribute to the problems these children have, so you will want to talk with the parents to see if these kinds of things are going on. If so, the school guidance department should become involved. Your focus should be to help these children become less perfectionistic, less self-critical, and less turned into themselves. They need to be allowed to make mistakes, and especially need to be encouraged to accept their mistakes as normal and as part of learning. These children are really in competition with themselves. Structure, specific rules, and encouragement, along with a loving, supportive relationship with you, will help reduce this self-competition.

Three further points are in order here. First, parents may be placing an undue emphasis on grades and "achievement" when the emphasis should be on a child's making a sincere and fairly continuous effort to learn and achieve. Second, you may have fallen into the same trap and may actually be placing your emphasis on grades and "relative achievement" instead of on a child's learning and experiencing at his or her best pace. Third, the competition among and between children can become intense, and extremely destructive for children who are less successful competitors. Every effort should be made in your class and your school to minimize this peer competition. For example, putting lists of children's names and grades on the bulletin board only exacerbates the problem. Chastising a child in front of the other children has a similar effect. Competition will be fairly intense, despite your efforts to reduce it. Thus, your efforts to minimize competition can hardly be overdone.

Perspiring, cold, clammy hands represent a different version of the same type of difficulty. You may notice that some children keep rubbing their hands together or on their clothes. When you touch their hands, you find that they are cold and moist. It is important to keep in mind that cold, clammy hands can indicate difficulty in heart functioning. For this reason, medical attention is needed if you repeatedly notice the symptom. The likelihood, though, is that cold, moist hands are a response to stress or inner tension. Cold, clammy hands and trembling hands are a fairly universal experience in times of intense stress or extreme anxiety. Usually, however, it takes a fairly intense stress to prompt this reaction. Whatever is going on, children with cold, clammy, or trembling hands are experiencing what is for them a very bad or extremely difficult situation. When these symptoms initially occur, or if they only occur from time to time, the easiest thing to do is to try to get these children out of the stress situation. Perhaps the next time the situation comes up they will handle it fine. It will also help to encourge these children to try new activities, not to worry so much about not succeeding, and to help them be a little more realistic about what they expect from themselves. You may be surprised to find how much it will help and encourage the child if you can think of a similar experience you had in your childhood when you did not do so well: "I remember the first time I tried that; I. . . ."

Body messages in some children take the form of *frequent stuttering and stammering*. When this occurs in a mild form, the child's talking may simply be unusually slow or may be interrupted with noticeable hesitations. At other times the child may seem to make an intense effort to talk and then suddenly explode into speech. The problem may vary from speech that is mildly distracting to the listener to nearly unintelligible speech production. You will find that children have most difficulty with sounds beginning with *b, p, m,* and *w,* and that they may not have consistent difficulty with the same sounds. Such stuttering and stammering is rarely a result of some physical problem, but physical difficulties can aggravate speech problems resulting from other causes.

Speaking difficulties may appear after some extremely upsetting episode, such as the death of a family member or a serious accident. It should be pointed out that people who are naturally left-handed but trained to use their right hand tend to stutter and stammer more frequently than others, and that boys have speech production difficulties much more frequently than girls. In the least complicated situation the stuttering and stammering may result from the child's being unusually shy or bashful, or may stem from difficulty in making the mouth and tongue work as quickly and accurately as the brain. Children sometimes think faster than they can talk. Also, it is important to remember that such things as mispronunciation, stammering, and word repetition are extremely common in preschool children; there may be some noticeable difficulty in as much as one-third of their verbal productions. It may be that parents, other adults, or older children become uptight about this and respond to the child as if there is a problem. The child then becomes self-conscious, thinks there is something wrong with the way he talks, and begins to have a problem, although there was none to begin with. Most children will overcome or outgrow these problematic speech patterns if everyone takes it easy and leaves them alone.

Also, the problem will diminish as children increase their vocabulary. Children have many feelings and vaguely conceptualized ideas, but do not have enough words to describe all of these internal experiences. Consequently, as they develop a larger vocabulary, their speaking facility will improve.

As you relate to children with problems in speech production, try to minimize any unpleasantness associated with trying to talk. Be sure that other children do not make fun of them, that you do not become impatient, and that they are not allowed to withdraw or feel badly and embarrassed. Do not tell them to stop and start again, and do not emphasize the need for them to talk more slowly. You will find that if you talk slowly their speech will also gradually slow down. Children are already aware of their talking problems; our calling attention to them only makes them feel more self-conscious and aggravates the problem.

We usually find that real speech problems develop before a child is six. If children are talking clearly when they enter school, it is unlikely that they will have any speech difficulties. Little children get excited, though, and sometimes talk too fast, stammer, cannot find the right word, and have trouble getting all of their thoughts and ideas out. This in itself does not represent a speech problem. It is a problem only if there is a continuing difficulty with the flow of speech.

Two further points may help. As suggested, children are continually in the process of learning how to verbalize, articulate, and express their feelings and ideas. By the time they get to kindergarten, their speaking should have progressed to the point where they generally talk fairly clearly, do not stammer and stutter a lot, and can usually find words to express what they want to say. By the time a child is seven or eight, the flow of speech should be fairly continuous and easy to understand. (Yes, the double meaning was intended. The flow of speech will tend to be continuous. Most young children seem to like to talk all of the time.) If a child's speech production is usually clear, reasonably well articlated, and not noticeably interrupted by stammering, pauses, and stuttering, it will be good to ask him calmly to "slow down" a little as he tries to talk through his excitement and enthusiasm. You will want him to slow down a little so that you can understand what he is saying, enjoy his enthusiasm, etc. If there is any suspicion on your part that a child is having speech production difficulties, do not place any emphasis on stopping and starting again or on slowing down. Have the child evaluated by a speech and hearing therapist. If she finds difficulties, she will also have advice and suggestions for you.

Whether the problem began before or after the child entered school, you should bring it up very indirectly with the parents. The slightest suggestion from you can cause them to think that there is a problem, which will only make things worse. However, if parents think the child has speech difficulties, it will be important for you to get them to keep "hands off." Try to get them to follow your policy of being patient, not calling the child's attention to the problem, and not criticizing or ridiculing the way the child talks. Meanwhile, you can gradually expose the child to a series of increasingly more difficult speaking situations, encouraging but not pushing. For example, you might start by seeing if the child can verbally respond to yes or no questions. Then see if he or she can answer questions or tell about something in a few words, moving then to see if the child is able to give longer answers or explanations, gradually having the child stand up and discuss or explain something to the rest of the class. This process will be very gradual and must not be "pushed" or forced, but rather must be patiently encouraged.

If the speaking difficulty continues, and if your efforts and those of the parents do not gradually lead to the child's speaking more smoothly and clearly, a speech therapist is needed. Be sure that neither you nor the parents try to do therapy with the child on your own. Treatment of speech problems requires a high level of professional knowledge and skill. Trained speech and hearing therapists will let you and the parents know what you can do to help.

Body talk may become even more noticeable than trembling, cold, clammy hands and stammering or stuttering. *A child may shiver and shake all over when it is not cold* and may find it difficult or impossible to stop shaking and shivering even when she tries. This could represent a type of convulsion that does not involve loss of consciousness, though this occurs rarely. Low blood sugar or thyroid problems might cause this kind of shaking, but the most likely cause is a viral infection or other acute physical problem not particularly serious in nature. If the child has an elevated temperature, the likelihood is that she is catching a bad cold or has the flu.

If the child is a known diabetic, giving him some orange juice, a piece of candy, or a soft drink containing sugar will help. But this should only be done if you have been instructed to do so by the child's parents, after they have received instructions from a physician. It would be advisable for the parents to give you written and signed instructions as to how to handle symptoms when they occur at school. In the absence of parental instruction, you should not administer any kind of candy, orange juice, medication, etc., even if you know that the child is diabetic. Maintaining contact with the parents of the diabetic child is important so you will know how to help the child when he is hurting. Whatever the cause of the symptoms, though, try to get the school nurse to see the child immediately. If the nurse cannot, or if there is no nurse in your school, contact the child's parents and have them take the child home. If their good, loving care does not lead to the child's settling down and feeling better within a few hours, they should take him to their family doctor. If you notice over a period of two or three weeks that a child seems to be trembling and shaking a lot, or if the trembling and shaking seems fairly intense over a lesser period of time, you should strongly encourage the parents to arrange for a physical examination. Perhaps a note to the doctor would be helpful so that he would know what you have seen. School health authorities should also be involved.

A spell of shaking and trembling is most likely a very temporary response to anxiety; the child is apprehensive and uptight about something. Usually your reassurance or some specific advice will be enough to help the child calm down and relax. Like the rest of us, children occasionally need to be told that things are going to be okay, that nothing bad is going to happen, and that we think they are all right. It is very important not to ridicule, punish, or scold the child; this only reinforces fear and tension. Sometimes the problem actually stems from fear of punishment or ridicule; something has happened or the child has done something which leaves him so afraid of what you or someone else will do that he literally shakes from fear. If possible, modify the situation that is getting the child so upset or help him get out of the situation. If something is this upsetting there is no point in making the child stay in the situation. He may need to learn to deal with the situation, but the child's body is telling you that he cannot deal with it now. Perhaps some advice, suggestions, or being shown how to do or handle something will help the child gradually learn to deal with particular kinds of situations in an effective way. For now, though, the child needs to know that the world is not going to fall apart or come down on his head.

For most children, your concerned, caring attention to occasional episodes of body talk reporting intense fear and anxiety will be enough, although for some children counseling and therapy is needed. You can arrange this through your school's guidance department, or you can help the parents get in touch with a counseling service within the community. Don't forget that many ministers deal quite well with these kinds of difficulties and are a good resource for many parents and children.

You should keep in mind that a very fearful, apprehensive child may be behaving in much the same way at home. The problem may, in fact, be a function of something going on at home. Ordinarily, there is some parent/child difficulty. You should always hold the "suspicion" that the child may be being abused or mistreated at home. This will usually not be the case, but is occasionally the source of the child's difficulties. As you or the school guidance staff discuss the child's difficulties with the parents, you may quietly ask them if they have any difficulties handling the child, getting him to behave, dealing with the child's emotions and behavior, etc.

Also, you might ask how they usually deal with the child when he becomes unresponsive; they may have some ideas that you will find useful when dealing with the child at school. Additionally, this may be an opening to suggest the possibility of counseling and guidance for the child and/or for the parents. Finally, the discussion may give you some clue that something more serious, such as abuse or neglect, is occurring.

Children have other ways of letting us know what is going on with them. Most children are alert, responsive, involved, interested in what is happening now and what is going to happen, and very, very active. Those children who vary much from this norm are saying something to us about themselves. For example, most children occasionally feel left out, inferior to other children, as if they are not a part of things. *Children who usually feel that they are not as good as others* are letting us know that things are not going very well for them. You will notice that they frequently make negative self-references: "I can't do anything right"; "I'm dumb"; "I always mess things up"; "I always lose." They may show a real unwillingness to try new things and a rather sad reluctance to enter into activities. In extreme situations, these children may feel that others are always criticizing them, and may go out of their way to avoid meeting or being with others, may be quite easily embarrassed, and may even project onto others their own perceived deficiencies: *"They're* all dumb or stupid"; *"they* always mess things up for me"; "I was doing fine until *they* interfered"; I would have done it right if *they* didn't bother me."

At times these children may compensate for their feelings of inadequacy and inferiority by bullying, trying to dominate situations, or generally trying to be the center of attention. When we think about it, we can see that these children have very low self-esteem, that they really feel inferior to other kids and feel that things never work out for them. They see themselves as incompetent people and, if it goes on too long, will in fact become incompetent people. If we always think that we are going to fail or not be accepted, it will eventually turn out that way. Remember that these children might really be somewhat inadequate relative to other children. They might have some kind of learning disability or limited intellectual ability, or they may have had inadequate social experiences or limited emotional acceptance from others. When children let you know that they feel inadequate, consider the possibility that they may be relatively inadequate in some way. This possibility explains why a thorough psychological and learning evaluation is necessary when children have a strongly self-deprecating attitude. Your school psychologist or local mental health service can evaluate the possibility. If a child does have specific problems, remedial social and academic training will be very important.

Usually the inadequacy is more perceived than real. These children actually have ability; they just do not think they do. It will be very important for you to accept these children the way they are and to let them see that you do care and are interested in them: "I'm sorry you feel that way about yourself. I think you're really all right and wish I could get you to feel that way too"; or, "Some things are hard to do; but you are really good at some things, like. . . ."

Be sure that you scale the schoolwork and academic expectations to their ability and background. Start where the children are. You may even want to start a little further back than they really are in an academic sense. Focus on things these children do well and very gradually work toward more difficult tasks. It also will be helpful to allow them some self-determination as to what their assignments will be, how many problems they are to work, and which things they want to do first.

It will be important not to go too far in that direction, since they may want to do only those things that they do well. If most children are asked to do ten arithmetic problems containing a new example or to learn fifteen new spelling words, it may be well to ask these children to do two or three of the new arithmetic problems or learn to spell four or five new words. Does this mean that these children will just get further behind? Not really. If you think about it, you will see that asking these children to do ten new problems or fifteen new spelling words will lead to their not doing any of them, which will really get them further behind. What you want to do is gradually to develop their skills, success experiences, and self-confidence. This will necessitate getting these children involved in cooperative activities and learning experiences first, before involving them in competitive situations. Whereas social reward and peer approval come to children who get all ten problems right or who correctly spell all fifteen words, children who feel inadequate or inferior do not benefit from such competition. It will be much better for you to set an achievement level that these children can reach. Their success will come in pleasing you, in feeling good about having done something, and in being able to cooperate with the learning process and not having to compete with the other children.

At the extreme, low self-esteem, feelings of inferiority, and a general sense of not being a part of things can lead to a situation in which children *frequently do not respond when others speak to them.* You may notice some immobility and lack of expression along with obvious nonresponsiveness when others speak to them. Also, you may notice that these children are considerably less curious than other children, and may be almost totally uninterested in new experiences. It may also seem that these children frequently daydream instead of being mentally involved with the world around them. Be sure not to overlook the possibility of some serious hearing or visual impairment. It is possible that the nonresponsiveness is a result of eyes and ears not receiving messages or stimuli. It is also important to remember that sometimes most children do not appear to be paying attention or do not respond when you try to talk with them. When a child is unresponsive much or most of the time, aside from possible vision and hearing problems, the child may be taking some kind of medication that has somewhat dulled his or her response. There is also a possibility that the child may be having some type of quiet seizure.

Since most children behave this way once in a while, try first to get their attention, being sure that you stand squarely in front of them when you talk with them, and that you touch them or put your arm on their shoulder as you talk with them to make it less easy for them to avoid you. If their responsiveness does not increase over three or four weeks, or if you frequently have to make a special effort to get their attention, you should become concerned. Since these symptoms can reflect a fairly serious medical difficulty, a hearing and vision examination is indicated. The school nurse and speech and hearing therapist, if available, can initially deal with this quite well. Whether or not they find a problem, though, the child should be seen by a physician to determine if anything else might be going on.

Typically, children who are this nonresponsive do not have vision or hearing problems or any other physical difficulties. They are turned into themselves and are not interacting with the world around them. For some reason it is easier or more comfortable for them to avoid interaction with the world than to interact with it. Children who are this turned into themselves are very disturbed. The school guidance staff and community mental health professionals will need to become involved to give these children the specialized therapy they need.

Relating a fairly unbelievable, but true, story may serve to implant in your memory another possible explanation for a child's not responding when people try to talk to him. In a rural school system, teachers became concerned over a period of several weeks about a little boy who did not talk with anyone at school. Almost accidentally, they found out that he spoke only Spanish, but spoke it fluently and enthusiastically when given the opportunity. It could as easily have happened that a child who was mute appeared in a classroom one day, with no prior explanation or discussion.

Although these two situations are unlikely, always consider the possibility that the child cannot talk, or at least cannot talk in English. Language difficulties may appear in a different way. A child may not have good facility with the English language and periodically may not respond due to lack of English comprehension. This problem is not so likely to be overlooked. If you had a child in your class whose native language is not English, you would be aware of the fact that he would occasionally not understand. This is one of the reasons why bilingual teachers are very important in some school systems, e.g., in ethnic neighborhoods, on Indian reservations, in school systems attended by the children of migrant workers, etc. Also, children who have severe disturbances in speech production or in the flow of speech may just opt not to talk at all. The difficulty is not with language: the difficulty is with speaking. All of these possibilities, along with the possibility of significant hearing or auditory perception difficulties, should be considered anytime a child does not talk.

Your involvement and efforts are also very necessary if these children are to come out into the world. It will be very important to avoid punishing or criticizing these children for not talking or interacting. To begin with, you might ask them to write down their answers to your questions, to point to things, demonstrate certain things, and so on. They might do part of the assignment and might be willing to participate or interact with other children for short periods of time. Be sure that your emphasis is on approving and rewarding what they do instead of on emphasizing or calling attention to what they do not do. Their interaction with the world needs to be made as safe and risk-free as possible. Becoming upset or annoyed will only cause them to go back into themselves. Within their thinking, they anticipate being criticized, rejected, punished, ridiculed, and not accepted. To whatever extent possible we need to be sure that this does not happen. It is a little bit like teaching small children how to swim: they think they are going to get water in their nose, sink, or otherwise end up dead, so we begin by seeing if they will splash a little water on their faces and are very happy with them the first time they are willing to sit on the side of the pool and put their feet in the water.

An important and additional diagnostic clue related to all of these and other symptoms seen in children can be developed indirectly. Do the children relate significantly differently to you and other adults than to other children? Watch them on the playground, as they go here and there through the hallways, as they interact with other children in the classroom. Frightened, withdrawing children will tend to behave in a frightened, withdrawing manner with both adults and other children. If a child behaves in a fairly spontaneous and socially interacting way with other children but not with adults, you should strongly suspect learning problems, sociocultural problems, language and cognitive difficulties, and very serious parent/child problems. It is unusual for a child with "serious emotional problems" to express those problems with adults but not with children. Of course, your symptom profile will include consideration of all of these possible symptom areas. Physical, learning, and culturally related causes become a little more likely, though, when the problem occurs mostly with adults and in the classroom context.

A somewhat different pattern of fear and anxiety is seen in small children who show an *unusual reluctance to separate from their parents.* We usually see this in kindergarten or first-grade children early in the school year, when they seem very timid, shy, and cling to their mothers. There is usually some reluctance when children first go to school, although a few children will bolt into the classroom with enthusiasm and eagerness. However, for a few children the step from home to school is frightening. It may seem that they are afraid of going to school, but the difficulty really involves being afraid to separate themselves from their mother. Perhaps there is a new baby at home and these children have some feeling about losing their place in the family; going to school means not spending all day with mommy who, of course, will be spending all day with the new baby.

It is important to understand that not all children are equally ready to go to school. Some children have had many social experiences prior to kindergarten which prepare them for school. They may have stayed with their grandparents for a week, gone to community activities with relatives or neighbors, played with a lot of children in the neighborhood, or gone to preschool. For them, the step from home to school is not very big. Other children have had very little experience in being separated from their mother, have not been involved in many activities outside of the home, have not played a lot with other youngsters, or have no older brothers and sisters who have gone to school without negative consequences. These children are taking a big step and do not yet feel safe enough or strong enough to cope with this new experience.

It is important to see that this is mostly a parent/child problem: just as these children need to go to school, their mothers need to let them go. Usually it will be enough for these children if you are warm and supportive—talk with them in a happy way about how they are going to have a good time, show them around the classroom, introduce them to some of the other children, tell them about the activities and other things you are going to do, let them know how long they have to stay, and assure them that there are arrangements already made for going home. Your real problem will be getting the mothers to go home calmly and leave their children at school. Mothers should not stay at school for the first few days or hours to get their child over the hump. It is necessary that they go home and let you deal with their child. With the majority of children, the initial fear and reluctance will disappear in a few hours or a few days. If this does not happen, school guidance people should be asked to work on the difficulty within the parent/child relationship. Nevertheless, children should be very gently but firmly told that they have to stay in school, and mothers should be encouraged not to keep them at home.

In extreme cases, children who are reluctant to separate from their parents may develop a real school phobia. As we have already mentioned, though, the problem is less a fear of school than a fear of separation from parents. These children may develop nausea, vomiting, slight headaches, a slight elevation in temperature, and relatively mild to severe symptoms of illness. The first step is to have them examined by their family physician to make sure that they do not have a bad infection or some other physical difficulty. Once this possibility is eliminated, you should insist, and help the parents insist, that the child come to school and stay until it is time to go home. Also, it will be important to make the child stay in the classroom, to encourage participation in activities, and not to "baby" the child. You will find that other children will try to relate and generally encourage the child's social involvement. Between you and the other children, the problem will gradually improve. If not, some intensive professional mental health assistance is required within the first two or three weeks of school. The longer the problem continues, the more difficult it will be to deal with.

Although it does not specifically relate to dealing with children at school, there is an additional problem occasionally seen in all school-age children that warrants special attention. Parents may feel that they want to keep a child home since the child is complaining of stomach upset, headaches, feeling tired, or generally not feeling very well. The parent may be somewhat uncertain as to whether or not the child is really ill. The point is that if a child is ill enough to stay home from school, he should be treated as if he were ill. The child should be made to stay in bed all day, not allowed to watch television, not allowed to read or play with toys, not given a lot of opportunity to talk and interact with people at home, and so on. He should really be treated as if he were ill, needing a lot of quiet and a lot of rest. If children really are ill, this is the appropriate way to treat them. On the other hand, if they are "using" illness and minor symptoms as a way of avoiding going to school, they will not be very happy with the idea of having to stay in bed and stay quiet all day. It would have been better to have gone to school.

When you talk with parents who are keeping their children home as a result of apparent illness or minor symptoms, encourage them to follow this procedure. If the symptoms are "real" and related to illness, the quiet and rest will help. If they are "put on" and related to avoiding school, there will at least be no payoff or "good times" resulting from staying at home. This approach will be especially helpful with children in the early elementary grades who may be inclined to use "tummy-aches" or "not feeling very well" as a way of getting out of going to school.

All children have many fears, most of which are reasonable and fairly easily understood. For example, they experience some anxiety about new situations. As you know, being a little uptight in new situations is useful. We become more alert, more aware of what is going on around us, and a little sharper in our responsiveness when we feel a little more anxiety or apprehension than usual. This helps us deal with the unpredictability of new situations and our lack of experience with these situations in an effective way.

We probably all have a slight anxiety about such things as severe storms, tornadoes, strange dogs, stinging bugs, dark places we have not been in before, unusually angry people, failing, being ridiculed or rejected, and doing something socially awkward. Some things really can hurt us, some situations really hold the possibility of danger or rejection, some people really might hurt us, and something bad and unexpected really might happen. We rarely worry about these things, though. However, children with *many unusual fears* may be afraid of situations or things that objectively cannot hurt them, may frequently become anxious or apprehensive about very minor difficulties or dangers, and may be so fearful that it interferes with their day-to-day pattern of getting along. Here the danger is more imagined than real, and the expectation of danger or harm is objectively unjustified. In some situations the possibility of danger or harm exists, but the probability is so low that worrying is unwarranted. A tornado may blow the school away, but it is extremely unlikely. As children get older, they begin to consider probability in deciding whether or not to be afraid. Unusually fearful children, though, move from "might happen" to "will happen" without any consideration of probability.

For the most part, children are taught to be afraid. Aside from a possible, natural fear of falling, children are taught to fear some things and situations and not others. For example, little babies initially may be quite afraid of their father, big dogs, loud noises, and a wide variety of other things, but if their parents deal with their fears in a matter-of-fact way, give the impression that there is nothing to be afraid of, and generally ignore their fear reaction, they will gradually learn that their fear is unjustified. They will learn that being picked up by daddy does not lead to physical harm or permanent separation from mother. Gradually being encouraged to touch a particular big dog teaches them that the dog is not only harmless but can be a good playmate. If children are gently but firmly told that there is no monster in their room and that they should go back to sleep, they will gradually learn that there is nothing in the room that will hurt them. If parents become upset and agitated during thunderstorms, children will become afraid of thunder and lightning. On the other hand, if parents remain calm and talk about such things as how loud the thunder is and how pretty the lightning is, children may come to enjoy watching a storm. They will know that the storm might hurt them, but will also know that the probability of being hurt is very remote.

How do you deal with children's unusual fears after they get to school? The same way healthy parents deal with them at home. If children are afraid to do something, perhaps it will help if you or another child does it first. This can demonstrate that they are not going to be hurt, and you can teach them about the things they are afraid of. For example, if children are unusually afraid of insects, you might show them some pictures of insects, talk about different kinds of insects, and let them know that dangerous insects do not exist in your community. In other situations it may be helpful if you do something with these children. For example, if they are afraid to go to the restroom alone, you might go with them the first time. After that, though, continuing to go with them implies the need to be protected. If there is nothing to be afraid of, why do you feel that you should go with them?

Dealing with fears is a several-step proposition. First, be supportive and try to reason with the children; then encourage and assist their efforts to deal with the situation. Next, push them gently into the situation; finally, firmly insist that they involve themselves in the situation or with the thing feared: "I

know you're afraid, but you're going to have to do it anyway."
Once children have done something a few times in spite of
fear, the fear will diminish.

It is very important to keep in mind that if you are also
afraid you are not the best person to help children get over
their fear. Teachers who are afraid of insects are not well
suited to take children on field trips to observe insects in their
natural habitat.

A few children may have had life experiences that give
added credibility to specific fears. For example, children who
have been bitten by rodents or insects and who regularly live
in conditions where the likelihood of such bites is real will tend
to have fears related to small animals and insects. Children
who have been badly burned or who know someone who has
been badly burned will have an excessive fear of fire. Children who really have gotten lost for an extended period of
time will tend to have an unusual fear of getting lost, being left
alone, etc. The "probability" that their fear will be actualized
has increased for them as a function of their life experiences.
With these children, you will need first to deal with these
experiences.

When a child expresses a fear, then, ask if the feared thing
has ever happened to him. Most children will admit that it has
not. In that case, follow the pattern discussed above. For children who indicate that the feared thing has happened to them,
you must first talk with them about the difference between the
present situation at school and their home situation or past
experiences. There may be rats at home but—hopefully—
there are no rats at school. They may have gotten lost before,
but they will not get lost on the school playground. They may
have been severely injured by being hit by a ball, but it is
unlikely that it will happen again. If the prior or present experience is too negative, you may simply have to avoid or
circumvent the fear, leaving the treatment of the "phobia" to
the school guidance staff or community mental health professionals. Almost always, though, following the suggestions discussed here will "get the child" past the fear.

Frequent headaches are occasionally interpreted as a response to inner tension and anxiety in little children, although this is almost never the case. Little children rarely get headaches as a result of emotional tension or from psychogenic reasons; such headaches are primarily an adult phenomenon. By far the most likely cause of headaches in little children is an allergic reaction or hypersensitivity to something, for example, dust, pollen, bacteria, and some foods. It is important to remember that headaches caused by allergies can be unilateral, that is, more on one side of the head than the other. They also tend to occur more often behind the eyes and at the front of the head, as do adults' tension headaches. These headaches can cause children to feel tired, irritable, and generally unhappy. Fortunately, other children cannot catch an allergy or become sick from playing with children who have allergies, and there are medications to prevent or reduce most allergic reactions.

If children complain of headaches, then you should ask if they take any kind of medicine; they will probably know. It also is important that you check with the parents to see if they know about the headaches, if there has been medical treatment for them, and how their doctor wants you to deal with the headaches at school. Of course, you should not give children aspirin or any other medication for headaches unless instructed to do so by their physician. One of the main reasons for this is that the headaches might be a symptom of some serious internal difficulty. Then, too, the children might be allergic to the medicine you give them. In either event, the children will have to suffer through the headache until they can receive medical attention.

Remember that headaches are a symptom; when children have a headache, something else is going on. Although the most likely cause is some annoying but relatively minor physical problem responsive to medical treatment, another possible cause is difficulty in seeing. This is especially likely if the headaches occur most often after children have been reading for a while or after watching television for an hour or so. Their family doctor will, as a matter of routine, consider the possibility of vision problems and the possibility of an ear infection or some dental problem. You can be helpful by being alert to the situations that seem to prompt the headaches.

Occasionally, children complain of headaches after vigorous physical activity. If they sit down, slow down, and rest a while, the headache will probably go away. If this happens more than two or three times, though, be sure that the child gets medical attention. Even after vigorous physical activity little children seldom get headaches. Unless their physician has ordered otherwise, children should be encouraged to be involved in all school activities, including physical education.

Children can get headaches from being hit on the head by a ball or some other hard object, or by bumping into something or someone. If the blow on the head causes nausea, vomiting, dizziness or blurred vision that does not go away in a few minutes, or unconsciousness, the possibility of a concussion or other serious injury needs to be considered. The school nurse should see the child immediately. If the nurse is not available, the parents should make arrangements for the child to be seen by a physician. Of course, if there is severe swelling or more than minor bleeding, emergency medical attention is necessary.

In less severe situations, though, first ask children complaining of a headache if they were bumped or banged. If they were, they should lie down and rest for awhile. The pain and discomfort should go away within ten or fifteen minutes and probably was not terribly intense to begin with. (If it does not go away fairly rapidly, medical attention is required.) If the pain does disappear, the child should be encouraged to "take it easy" for at least two or three hours. Even if the bump seems minor and the pain goes away fairly quickly, the problem should be called to the parents' attention so that they can watch the child and be alert for any recurrence of symptoms. Of special importance are nausea, prolonged dizziness, blurred vision, continuation of the pain, or any change in motor function or coordination.

Although it is fairly unusual, children may develop

headaches as a result of emotional tension. Usually the cause of that tension will be fairly obvious, and related to something very unusual or unexpected within their life situation. Perhaps a family member has died, they have been in an extremely serious accident or exposed to a serious fire or other frightening event, or they might be exposed to continuing anger and rejection from their parents. It will be important for you to be especially calm, supportive, and gentle, and to make an extra effort to encourage and give approval to children having emotionally based headaches. In addition to this, professional counseling for the family is essential. Something is quite wrong in the child's life, and someone needs to do something about this. You may have to spend a lot of time and energy getting the family involved in counseling. If you do not, the child will gradually develop even more problems and difficulties.

Where to start? You will need to talk with parents about how they interact with their child, how much pressure they put on him, and how they deal with the child's successes and failures. Since most parents love and care about their children, calling attention to possible difficulties may be enough to get them started in a better direction with their child. If so, you will notice that the child's headaches become less intense and less frequent. If the headaches persist, though, something else has to be done, and you are the one to see that it happens.

What can be done when parents are either unwilling to work with you, their child, and the problem, or are simply disinterested? This situation would make your efforts and relationship with the child at school even more important. Often, too, unwilling and disinterested parents become somewhat more willing and interested when someone from the school other than the classroom teacher contacts them. Perhaps this could be someone from the guidance department, the school psychologist, or (if these services are not available) the principal of the school. Above all, the key is to be persistent and to continue to try to work with the parents, being careful that you do not generate anger or hostility that is then turned back on the child by the parents. Your skill and tactfulness in working with the parents, combined with your skill and supportiveness in working with the child, are the keys to "causing" things to improve.

Other children may have difficulty with *frequent wetting or "messing"* in their clothing. The enuretic or encopretic child has a serious problem. Remember, though, that five- and six-year-old children (and even seven- and eight-year-old children, once in a while) occasionally forget or become too involved in their activities to take time to go to the bathroom, become excited and accidentally lose control, and have problems with bowel and bladder control from time to time. Here we are talking about children who have these problems frequently and who do not gradually develop more control as they get older. Involuntary discharge of urine or poor bowel control can represent somewhat slowed physical development; muscle control and alertness to signs of an impending accident may be developing more slowly than in most children. On the other hand, this difficulty may reflect some actual physical disease or abnormality. This possibility should prompt you to be sure that the child receives medical attention if he has three or four episodes within one week, recurring episodes over two or three months, or if a child with no history of difficulty has more than one episode within a week or two. More frequently you will deal with children who have continuing or recurring problems of this type. Of course, you should let their parents know about the problem. When you talk with the parents, you will probably find that they have already gotten medical care for the child and will be able to explain to you the nature of the problem and how you should deal with it.

Most of the time, though, wetting and soiling that occurs with more than usual frequency is a sign that these children are experiencing some social or emotional difficulty. It may be that they simply are too timid or shy to ask permission to go to the bathroom. If you think this is a possibility, you can quietly talk with them about the problem, see if they sometimes need to go to the bathroom but won't ask, and perhaps work out some kind of sign or cue they can give you when they need to go. Of course, a much better situation would be one in which children could go to the bathroom without asking permission, the same as adults do. Perhaps you will be able to break with tradition enough to let your children accept this responsibility for themselves. Perhaps, rules about having to get permission to go to the bathroom are a good example of rules and traditions not necessarily equaling "good." If your children are going to be required to ask permission, be sure you let them know that it is all right to ask, that you are not going to become angry, and that you really will let them go to the bathroom.

You may also find that these children are overly conscientious and may be afraid of missing out on something important if they leave the room for a while. You can talk with them about this and assure them that you will let them know anything they missed. Of course, if the children are that conscientious, you may need to consider whether or not they are overly concerned about doing everything right, whether they are unreasonably perfectionistic.

Some children may have some difficulty in going into the bathroom. People at home may have made quite an issue about such things as strange toilets and catching diseases. It will be necessary for you to handle this problem as you would any other fear. It is also possible that children may be afraid of being harmed or injured by someone in the bathroom. This may be an unrealistic fear of strangers which will need your attention, or you may find this fear somewhat justified. Perhaps the other children are too rowdy or aggressive during restroom periods. If so, the solution would be more careful supervision of the restroom. Some children may become so engrossed in play or other activities that they do not give themselves enough time to get to the bathroom. As you talk with them, you can encourage them to go to the bathroom before they go out to play or when they first think they need to. Above all, it is important not to subject them to ridicule, criticism, or anger. It is an annoying problem for you to deal with, but communicating your annoyance to these children will not help. It is equally important that they not be subjected to teasing or ridicule from the other children. As soon as you become aware of the problem, you should quietly but quickly help them leave the classroom and find a place to clean up. It is important not to make these children feel ashamed or guilty; they will probably feel badly enough as it is.

Experienced teachers of early elementary age children know that it is a good idea to keep two or three pairs of clean underwear and a couple of pairs of clean blue jeans (big enough to fit almost all youngsters) for those occasional times when you need to help a child get cleaned up at school. Getting cleaned up may also require clean clothes. Also, you may want to help the child wash out the dirty clothes a little so they are not quite so messy when they are taken home in the very inconspicuous paper bag you have provided. Almost always, you will get the clean clothes back the next day. The occasional expense resulting from families who do not return the clothing used by the child may be covered by a special fund at school. It also may be that this is one of those "little expenses" that teachers have for which they are not reimbursed.

On rare occasions, you may deal with a child who is using soiling and wetting as an expression of hostility and anger. Such children have "accidents" to get other people upset, to annoy other children, and to demonstrate that they do not have to comply with usual behavior. When this problem comes up, specialized mental health treatment is necessary. The mental health people working with the child will have ideas and very specific suggestions about how you should deal with the problem in school. Whether the problem is developmental, physical, emotional, or social, you will want to deal with it in a very gentle, supportive, nonpunishing way to minimize embarrassment for the child and problems with other children. No matter what the cause of the problem, your pattern of response should be about the same.

Very rarely you may become aware that a child *hears voices or sees things that are not there*. These children tend to seem somewhat sullen and detached and tend to isolate themselves emotionally, especially from demanding people or situations. It is almost as if they have retreated into a shell. As you talk with them, you can almost feel the barrier between you. In some ways it seems that these children are trying to escape from a threatening and intimidating world, though their behavior is more a refusal to become involved than an attempt to escape. For some mix of reasons the real world has become untenable for them. Their efforts to cope, interact, relate, and otherwise deal with the world have been so unsuccessful, confusing, or painful that they have opted to create a world of delusion and fantasy. In that world they are able to function, although they may be quite frightened, angry, and confused.

Within these children are intense feelings and confusions, guilts and anxieties, fears and angers which are pushing and pulling them. Eventually they become so unable to cope with this that they project those feelings and ideas outside of themselves. "Voices" then tell them that they are stupid, tell them to do things they would otherwise not do, and so on. Similarly, the "visions" or things that these children see are not really there but are manifestations of this inner turmoil and projection. These children have lost touch with reality; that is, they are not dealing with reality the way it is perceived by everyone else. Through their fantasy, confusion, projection, and inner turmoil, reality has become distorted and confused and they have generally become unable to separate the real from the unreal. This may not be an all-the-time kind of thing; they may have periods during which they function more adequately and more within the framework of reality. These flights from reality represent the most extreme manifestation of their problems and difficulties.

As you try to relate to these children it will be important to touch them, put your arm around them, and let them know through physical contact that you are there and real. It is important to talk with them as calmly as possible, not to pretend that you believe their delusions, not to agree with them when they misinterpret reality, and gently but firmly to represent the real world the way it really is. Of course, a good relationship with you is not sufficient for these children. They should be under the care of a psychiatrist who can prescribe medications that can control much of the problem of seeing and hearing things. These children will also need to be involved in fairly extensive psychotherapy which includes work with their families.

In the meantime, it is very important that you relate to these children in a reality-oriented but very gentle way, touching them and letting them know that there is a healthy little boy or girl there somewhere. Be very careful not to become angry or agitated with them. Your emphasis should be less on trying to relate to them than on making it as risk-free as possible for them to relate to you. It is important for you to realize that you cannot force them out; you can only try to create a relationship in which they feel comfortable enough to come out of themselves. If you feel that these children are listening or responding to hallucinations, it will be important for you to touch them, talk to them, and otherwise relate to them so that your reality will override the unreality of the hallucinations. Above all, do not be afraid of them. These children seem a lot different from other children and sometimes scare us because of their differentness, but there is a healthy child there somewhere. Be sure that you relate to the child in a way that almost ignores or moves past the unhealthy exterior shell.

Of course, severely psychotic children are not usually placed in regular class situations. They are occasionally placed in special classes for emotionally disturbed children that may or may not be located in the "regular school" building. Nonetheless, it is occasionally important to try to deal with these children in the context of a regular school setting. This is especially true when special programs and special classes for the emotionally disturbed are not available. At other times, children who have been in such special classes and programs are "mainstreamed" back into the regular school setting. In any event, you may need to deal with a child experiencing auditory and visual hallucinations or other psychotic symptoms within your classroom. Your effort will be combined with mental health therapy for the child and consultation services for you. Be sure to follow the advice of the mental health professionals carefully, as well as following the suggestions offered here.

Little children frequently seem to have a preoccupation with death. As we watch and listen to them, though, we find that their curiosity about death is a very transient thing. Usually their questions and concerns are prompted by the death of someone they know or someone they have heard about. At other times, their questions may be prompted by things they have heard and learned about religion, for example, the concept of life after death. In either event, asking them "What got you to thinking about that?" will usually pin down what started the questions. Also, little children show a very surprising interest in metaphysical things. A six-year-old, for example, might ask many profound questions: "What was there before there was anything? Was it just black?" "If people and animals go to heaven, how does God get them there?" Usually, it is quite sufficient to say "I don't know" or to give whatever factual information we can. Most children are only briefly interested, want specific information, and are quite easily distracted from this subject by other activities and other topics of conversation.

Once in a while, though, children become *quite preoccupied with death and dying*, are not easily distracted from that preoccupation, and show what seems to be morbid curiosity or somewhat unusual fear. Their questions and feelings will recur with some regularity and surprising intensity, and they may start having nightmares about dying, being killed, or someone else's dying. When we talk with these children about their thoughts and fears, we almost always find that someone relatively close to them has recently died or is quite ill, perhaps a brother, sister, parent, or aunt. Aside from their expressed thoughts and fears about death, we usually find that they are extremely unwilling to separate from their parents and do not want to leave home for fear that someone might die while they are gone. They may also have a lot of fear about the possibility of their dying and may ask if they are going to die.

If the child's immediate death is unlikely, it will be reassuring for you to say "no" without getting bogged down in discussions of probability and possibility. If the child is going to die, though, our answer should be "yes." We can then talk with the child about the illness, what we think will happen after death, whether or not much pain or discomfort is likely. Whether children are concerned about their own or someone else's death, it is important to discuss this and to answer questions honestly and to share our sadness. Our honesty and willingness to share our own fears and sadness are extremely important for the child.

It will also be helpful for you to spend some class time discussing death, dealing with children's curiosity about death and things dying, and through your behavior letting children know that death really is a subject that one can discuss openly and honestly. If a specific child becomes preoccupied with death, it will be important to talk with his or her parents about the situation. If you find that the child really is going to die, you should find out how the parents are dealing with this issue, and follow their wishes and respect their way of dealing with it. If they are open and willing to talk with the child about his or her death, you should find out enough about the problem and what is likely to happen to enable you to talk with the child at school when the issue is brought up with you. Also, it will be important for you to understand what the child's parents feel in terms of life after death and other religious issues. Above all, your discussions with the child should be consistent with the parents' beliefs and attitudes.

If you simply cannot accept or go along with their beliefs or attitudes, you should then encourage the child to talk with his or her family about the issues. If the child presses you for your ideas and thoughts, you should honestly say, "I don't believe exactly the way your mother and father believe; and I think you should talk with them about it. I am interested in hearing what you think and feel, though. Would you like to talk with me about that?" The major point is to let the child know that he can talk with you, can express his fears and apprehensions, can let you know what he thinks or feels, etc.

In a more subtle form, children's preoccupation with death and dying may reflect real loneliness, sadness, and a limited sense of involvement and belonging. They may feel as if they are really not a part of things. Here, too, your relationship with these children remains central. Your honesty, empathy, concern, and interest will provide them with at least one relationship in which they are actively involved. The security and good feelings stemming from their relationship with you can help counteract their sense of alienation. Of course, you will want to avoid talking too much about death and dying and instead talk about fun, happy things and what is going to happen tomorrow.

If someone actually has died, it is important for children to express their grief and share their sadness and sense of emptiness. The grief process is an important part of healthy living. Also, the children may feel that their anger, hostility, or bad feelings have in some way contributed to the death of a family member, causing a deep sense of guilt. This is one more reason why it is important for us to be as honest as possible about why and how a person died. If the preoccupation with death persists for more than two or three weeks without any gradual let-up, professional counseling and therapy for the child is indicated.

Our consideration here of death has focused on the death or possible death of people. Especially with small children, it is important to keep in mind that the death of a pet hamster or puppy may be almost as upsetting to them as the death of a person would be to us. We should take their questions and concerns seriously and not minimize the significance of their feelings just because it was an animal that died. Children's pets are their "friends," and children feel very close to and involved with them. When a pet dies, children frequently feel an intense sense of loss and confusion. If they are expressing such intense feelings, we should deal with the "feeling" and not be distracted or minimize the importance because the loss was "only" of a pet.

A sense of alienation and of not being lovable sometimes comes out through a child's *frequently expressing the feeling of being no good*. Negative self-references and self-depreciation are frequently seen in these children. They say things such as "I don't like myself," "I hate myself," "I'm slow," "I'm ugly," "I'm bad," or "I'm stupid." We usually find that these children are relatively unwilling to become involved in school activities or with other children. At other times, though, they may behave belligerently, may be disruptive in the classroom and do things to call attention to themselves. They may eventually become the class clown, the class bully, or fill some other role. These behaviors point to low self-esteem, repeated failure experiences, and a real feeling of being "no good." The child's intense negative feelings may be a response to harsh remarks and criticism on a continuing basis, severe or unusually cruel physical punishment, demands too difficult for the child's abilities, a complete lack of sympathy in times of illness and stress, comments that the child is a nuisance or in the way, continuing quarreling and fighting between parents, and feelings of rejection by parents, peers, or community.

Children with severe physical handicaps, scars, or other physical problems that cause an unpleasant appearance, or children with other difficulties that set them off as different, are especially susceptible to these kinds of negative feelings. These children need frequent opportunities for success and a lot of praise and recognition for their accomplishments and achievements. It will be important for you to take a personal interest in these children and to avoid shaming them or giving any hint of ridicule or unnecessary or unreasonable criticism. You will want to encourage the development of personal skills through which they can gain increased social confidence and recognition. In severe and continuing situations, counseling for both parents and child is indicated.

Occasionally, you find a child who *frequently thinks that people are trying to hurt him,* or *refuses to play with other children.* As with children who are afraid to go to school, you should first consider that the child is realistically and accurately assessing the situation. It may really be true that someone or some group of people may actually be trying to hurt him. It may be that you have a child in your class who intentionally seriously injures other children and that this child is subjecting a classmate to that behavior. Also, other children really do sometimes, viciously and with malice, gang up on a particular child or group of children. Within the community, there are people who will hurt and injure children. Anytime children tell us something, express a feeling, or let us know what they think is happening, first consider the possibility that they are correct, that what they say is true, and that things actually are the way they say they are. Just because what they say is a little hard to believe or seems a little far-fetched does not make it false or incorrect.

Of course, all little children occasionally complain that other children pick on them and will not let them play, that people are unfair with them, and so on. However, these complaints are relatively infrequent and quite transient. Almost always it is enough for you to say, "That's a real problem that you are going to need to deal with." Do not become involved in solving these children's problems for them or in punishing other children on the strength of one child's complaints. These are problems for five-, six-, seven-, and eight-year-olds to deal with. They need to learn to negotiate and deal with their social world, so you are actually doing them a favor by refusing to become involved. If they learn how to deal with other children now, they will be effective in dealing with people when they get older. If they become used to having someone else solve their problems now, they will be much less able to deal with their world when they grow up.

Those few children who frequently seem to feel as if someone is trying to hurt them tend to exaggerate, distort, or give undue significance to everyday remarks and actions of other children. In their mind, these actions and remarks serve to reinforce their belief that someone is trying to hurt them. In general, these children tend to be unhappy, sullen, brooding children who seem to have a real problem in making close friends or being involved in continual play with other children. At other times they may seem to be stubborn, secretive, obstinate, and quite resentful of discipline. When crossed, they are likely to be sullen, peevish, and irritable, or may react with anger and unwarranted expressions of hostility. If the feeling that other people are going to hurt them becomes a continuing, repeated thing, this is a projection of their own inner insecurity, low self-esteem, and self-depreciation. These children feel so negative and punishing toward themselves that these feelings seem to be coming from other people. "I don't like myself" becomes "You don't like me."

If these symptoms are chronic and do not soften over time, children with this kind of difficulty should be placed in a special class for emotionally disturbed children. You should have the school psychologist evaluate their problems and have the school guidance staff become involved with them. In extreme situations, these children can develop very delusional thinking in which they believe that other children are continually plotting against them, that people in the cafeteria are trying to poison them, or other such bizarre notions. In rare cases, these fears and internal feelings are so intense that children compensate by believing that they are absolutely superior to other children, have magical or mysterious powers, are really not human and actually come from outer space, or have other grandiose notions. If you become aware of these rare and extremely severe symptoms, immediate psychiatric attention is indicated. It is possible that these few children cannot function within the regular school setting. They may need home instruction, residential treatment consisting of placement in a hospital or other setting for emotionally disturbed children, special class placement, or other experiences outside the regular school setting.

Before reaching the conclusion that a child is delusional, though, remember that little children do tease and plot against each other sometimes. However, they do not do this all of the time or in a continuing organized way. As with most signs and symptoms of emotional difficulty in children, it is better initially to underestimate the seriousness of the problem, to respond in terms of their really being healthy and normal, and to expect them gradually to respond and behave within the behavioral and emotional limits of most children. It is quite a disservice to children to conclude prematurely that they are emotionally disturbed. It is better to see almost all emotional, behavioral, and social problems that children have as fluctuations in their otherwise normal development and then to try to help them through the fluctuations. Only if the problem continues with no positive change over a period of several weeks is it reasonable to conclude that children are really emotionally disturbed. Of course, during those several weeks you will be making a special effort to relate honestly to these children, to talk with their parents and see what is going on. This is quite different from a "do nothing and they will outgrow it" approach. With a lot of sensitivity, effort, and patience on your part, both you and the children will most likely get through it quite nicely.

Children who feel that others are going to hurt them, that nobody likes them, and that they are not as good as other children may be generally *described as feeling unlovable.* Aside from such things as relating to these children in an honest and caring way, encouraging their accomplishments and achievements, and being sure that expectations are consistent with abilities, talking with the children's parents is very important. As you talk with them, you might ask some thought-provoking questions: "Does Mary talk much about what goes on at school?" "How does she seem to feel about herself?" "How do you think things are going with her?" "Is there anything you might be able to do at home to make her feel a little more successful and important?" "How do the other children or adults at home relate to Mary?" The point is that you want to get the parents thinking about how the child feels about herself, how they feel about her, what kind of positive experiences the child has at home, what they might be able to do to help her feel more a part of things. It is important that you not attack or accuse the parents. Instead of saying "Your child hates herself," you might ask "Do you get the feeling that Mary does not like herself very much sometimes?" Instead of bluntly telling a parent, "You are going to have to do things with your daughter that let her know you approve of her," you could ask, "Aren't there some things you might do at home that she is good at or can be successful at so you'll have more chances to let her know that you think she's okay?"

Remember that parents tend to be very involved with their children and with their feelings, have some natural ambivalence about their children and about their own parenting ability, and are quite sensitive to comments and criticisms from others. This is especially true about comments or negative notions that come from you, since the power and authority of your position and experience give added force and weight to anything you say to parents about their children. You might want to begin by overstating the positive qualities of their children to encourage parents to think more positively about them, and you might also want to understate any negative qualities or problems. Parents have a tendency to overreact a little to your negative statements anyway. Start out very tentatively, subtly, in a very low-keyed way. Listen closely to the parents' reactions and their interpretations of what you have said. As you talk, you can gradually focus your comments and make them more direct until their reactions and interpretations "fit" what you want to say. When thinking about children's parents and planning for a conference with them, be sure not to conclude in advance that you are more concerned about and interested in their children than they are. This is almost never true. If you feel that you would do better with their children than they do, you might raise some serious questions about your own motivations, your perceptions of your own abilities, and why you are prejudging the parents. This might be a good topic for discussion with your supervising teacher or in the next group meeting with fellow teachers.

One of the things that may cause you to think you might do better with children than parents is noticing that the *children blame themselves for problems at home*. Children might say, "Mom and dad don't get along with each other because my brother and I always fight," or "My dad does not come home very much because he doesn't like me." These children tend to be underachievers at school. As soon as you feel concern about their achievement level, have the school psychologist evaluate the children and give you a good notion of what their achievement level ought to be. If children are achieving significantly below that level, it will be important for you continually to encourage them to try, to support them when they do not succeed, and to acknowledge their successes with enthusiasm. Also, it might be helpful if you were to have them make a list of the things their moms and dads do not like about them or of things going on at home that they consider to be their fault. This can help children talk about the situation at home, how they feel about themselves, what they think they are doing or not doing that contributes to problems at home, and so on. Basically, you will want to relate to these children as you would to children who experience low self-esteem, think they are always messing things up, and blame themselves for things that are beyond their control.

The idea of getting children to focus on and clarify what they feel to be negative attitudes and feelings held toward them has been used with good success in counseling situations, and you can use this approach to increase focus and clarification. First, you can have your class or small groups within your class either write down or discuss "things people do and do not like about me." Even if the "game" is "played" on a verbal discussion basis, it will be best for you to write down the likes and dislikes on the chalkboard, without any reference to any particular child.

If the children write down the likes and dislikes, you should review the lists yourself and write the likes and dislikes on the chalkboard. You will then have a list of positive or desirable characteristics and a list of negative or undesirable characteristics. Then have the children decide whether or not they really think that the items in each list belong in that list. Some items may thus be excluded. They can then discuss the remaining items in terms of why the characteristics or behavior are desirable or undesirable, positive or negative. In addition, they can think about how to develop the positive characteristics and reduce the negative characteristics in themselves. Be very sure that you cross out any characteristics or behaviors over which a child has no control or which represent bias or prejudice, e.g., physical appearance, speaking patterns, qualities like "being smart," etc.

The same approach can then be used with individual children experiencing low self-concept, poor self-definition, low self-esteem, or a tendency to blame self for problems and situations. Be sure that the child verbalizes or writes down both the desirable and liked qualities as well as the undesirable and disliked qualities. Talk with them about those things over which they may have some control and about those things for which you do not realistically think they can be held responsible. Then talk with them about those things they might change, e.g., being somewhat less messy, being a little more careful with their schoolwork, trying a little harder to slow down and pay attention, not arguing so much when their parents ask them to go to bed, etc. Whether the approach is used on a classroom, group, or individual level, though, it is extremely important that your focus is only on helping the children clarify and define their likes and dislikes, helping them to think about those things which they can and cannot change, and encouraging them to think about and begin to work on those things over which they have some control. A warm, supportive, encouraging tone and relationship approach from you is also very important. Of course, you would not say it, but for a teacher to say "I have also noticed how sloppy and rude you are" does nothing to help, and much to make things worse.

When you talk with the parents you might want to say, "I've noticed that your son tends to blame himself for a lot of things. Have you noticed any tendency for him to blame himself for things that are not really his fault?" It will be important for you not to be too direct or confrontive with the parents. This could lead to their undermining your relationship with the child, could result in their directing a lot of open hostility toward you, and could generally make things worse for the child at home. If the parents are gradually able to begin talking about some of their child's feelings and ideas, it will be well for you to talk with them in a very gentle, caring way. If their openness and receptiveness to discussing the child's feelings and difficulties are not fairly immediate, though, you should stay out of it. Your next step would be to call the situation to the attention of the school guidance staff or school psychologist, who are better prepared to work with parents about such problems. Your efforts should be directed toward encouraging and continuing a warm, supportive relationship with the child.

Earlier, we talked about the child who occasionally is unresponsive or seems to refuse to respond verbally. We also briefly mentioned children who refuse to talk. Here, we want to give added emphasis to a child who *refuses to talk*. Previously, we discussed the possibility that the child is unfamiliar with or has difficulty with English, is physically unable to talk, etc. Here we are talking about children who are so withdrawn and turned into themselves that they do not communicate verbally. With such children, you would also notice that they equally tend not to communicate "nonverbally." Not only do they not speak, they also do not gesture, do not interact with other adults and children, and generally either do not respond at all or respond very minimally. They may follow directions such as "stand up" or "sit down." They may also follow your instructions to get out their books, copy things off the chalkboard, stand in line and so on. In general, though, they are extremely passive, incommunicative, withdrawn, and unresponsive. This general pattern is seen in all situations with the child.

Although it is unlikely that the cause of such extreme turning into self is caused by physical problems, children with this type of difficulty should have a thorough physical examination. In addition, they will need to have psychological evaluation and treatment. What do you do with them at school, though? You should deal with them as you deal with other withdrawing, fearful children. It will be important to touch them when you are talking with them, continue to talk to them whether or not they respond verbally, comment about the things they do participate in such as written work, and generally try to relate to them in a very quiet and "nonpushy" way.

You might say things such as "I like your shirt or dress," "It surely is a pretty day," "Do you like the pictures in the book?" and so on. You should continue making these comments and asking questions whether or not they respond. In addition, you should reciprocate any communication that comes from them. If they walk up to you as if they want something, you should smile and say hello. If they smile at you, smile back. If they act as if they are interested in something, become interested in it yourself.

Children with this kind of difficulty are usually also experiencing fairly intense difficulty at home. It may stem from things like being continuingly told to shut up or be quiet, that they are stupid, that their ideas are dumb, etc. Also, the difficulty can come from severe neglect, negligible verbal interaction at home, and generally not having any experience with people paying attention to or being interested in them. Whatever the cause, the pattern for you should be, very gradually, gently, and sensitively, to pay attention to these children, reciprocate their responses, show through your actions and behavior that you are interested, and avoid expressions of annoyance or anger. These negative expressions will only cause them to withdraw further. The hope is that you will gradually create an atmosphere and relationship within which they will feel comfortable relating, becoming involved, and so on. The process is very slow, very gradual, and very delicate.

Of course, these children also need professional counseling, which can be provided by either the school guidance staff or local community mental health center. And your symptom profile for such children will include careful consideration of learning abilities and difficulties, social abilities and difficulties, physical abilities and difficulties, and so on. It would be extremely unlikely for children with this severe withdrawing behavior not to have very noticeable difficulties in several other areas. Also, it may be that such children will do things for you other than talk. They might be willing to pass out papers, help pick up things around the room, or run errands. Anything that has the effect of getting them more involved and increasing their participation is desirable.

We have talked about children who seem unusually with-drawn and fearful as well as children who seem unresponsive. An associated difficulty is seen in *children who seem unusu-ally preoccupied with their own thoughts and fantasies.* Of course, all of us spend a lot of time indulging in our own thoughts and fantasies. We have thoughts about things that have happened, things that are happening, and things that may happen. We have fantasies about how things might have been, "if only . . ." and so on.

The same pattern is generally true for young children. They indulge in their thoughts and mental wonderings, their secrets and dreams, their fantasies and fairy tales. Like adults, though, young children are very easily brought back to the real world of things and people, places and events. For example, young children may seem to be deep in thought and "far away." Occasionally, it may take a second comment or a somewhat louder question in order to get their attention, in order to bring them out of their thoughts and fantasies into the "real world." Nonetheless, this is relatively easy to do. Also, children tend to be very involved and alert to what is going on around them and to what is happening. They seldom seem to drift off into "daydreams" or self-contemplation. In fact, chil-dren are somewhat less inclined to do this than are adults.

Occasionally, though, we will see children who seem un-usually preoccupied with their own thoughts and fantasies. They seem to be chronically daydreaming; it is difficult to get their attention; it is even more difficult to keep their attention. It is as if there were something vastly more interesting going on inside their mind than in the real world. Of course, it is occasionally true that things in the real world are quite boring and uninteresting. The point is that small children are gener-ally fairly attentive. Even if they are not paying attention to us, they tend to be paying attention to other things "in the real world" going on around them. Here we are talking about ex-cessive nonattention, something that happens with more than usual frequency, and something that will probably gradually come to be of concern to us. We will gradually get the feeling that a particular child seems to daydream more than usual, seems to have more than the usual amount of difficulty paying attention, and seems to be disinterested in what is going on much of the time. It is this excessiveness that represents the problem.

It will be helpful occasionally to bring these children back to reality by trying to get them to talk about whatever they were thinking about, to get them to imagine out loud, and to see if you can "get into" their fantasies and thoughts a little. This can only be done with their permission and cooperation, of course. If they do not want to cooperate, or withhold their permission, they will simply not tell us about what is going on inside their minds. In addition, it will be important to be sure that you have the attention of these children before trying to talk with them, that you occasionally ask them if they are still listening when you feel as though they have "drifted" off, that you try to maintain eye contact with them from time to time as you talk with them, and that you very gently keep bringing up the need to pay attention, to be involved, and to participate.

It will help to better understand why children become so preoccupied. First, there is a real possibility that the classroom activities and your presentation of material is just not very interesting, or that it is not the kind of thing young children can relate to. They make an effort to pay attention but are so disinterested or so bored that their minds wander. Perhaps your first step should be to check your performance notebook to see if several children in the class appear to be daydreaming a lot and not paying attention; if so, the problem is probably with you. This may be true even if one child is showing such symptoms consistently. You have not yet come up with an interesting and exciting way to keep his or her interest and attention. Second, many times children find it safer to stay within their own inner world. There it is safe, they have power, they can be involved and participate, people like them, etc. Within their own "made-up world" they are worthwhile and important people. These children find that kind of acceptance and involvement to be in sharp contrast to the way things are in the "real world." There they are not important, they do not have much power, they are not accepted. With any particular child, then, you should start by examining your own behavior, teaching technique, and involvement with that child. If this does not seem to be the problem, you will want gradually to start by trying to get the child to talk about what he is interested in or thinking about, gently checking to see if he is listening or paying attention, and gradually getting him more involved. You will also find that children who are physically active tend to be more mentally involved. Perhaps daydreaming children can be asked to pass out papers, help with a special project in the classroom, or do something else that would get them up and moving. Over time, your interest, attention, and approval will gradually make the world of school and reality at least as interesting (most of the time) as the world of daydreams and fantasies. Of course, if you approach the problem in this interested, "active" way and it shows no sign of improvement over time, further investigation is in order.

Start with the possibility of physical problems. Perhaps the child has some metabolic or glandular difficulty that is interfering with her ability to pay attention, be involved, etc. Also, some neurological difficulties may give the appearance of a child's occasionally turning into self and not paying attention. Other minor illnesses can also give the appearance of daydreaming, e.g., the flu and colds, other minor infections, not getting enough sleep, etc. If the physical difficulties are minor, though, the problem should only be occasional and temporary. If the problem is more persistent, a thorough physical examination is in order. If the physical examination is negative, counseling and additional support and guidance for the child and her family will be important.

Also, it will be important to note if this type of problem tends to occur more at some times in the day than at others— more after vigorous activity than after less active times, more before lunch than after lunch, etc. When the behavior occurs is potentially important. For example, it may be that there is a lot of family turmoil and difficulty that leads to the child's simply not getting enough rest. The child may be making an effort to stay awake and involved but occasionally experiences difficulty doing this. Also, children who do not eat an adequate breakfast may tend to be somewhat more lethargic and uninvolved than other children. With these children, you would notice that they seem more alert and active after having eaten a hot lunch at school.

With daydreaming behavior, it is important to remember that all little children daydream from time to time, and, once in a while, a lot. If the behavior is excessive, though, you will want to look for other possible causes, especially if it is a continuing problem. First, consider your own involvement and participation with the child; next, follow the suggestions for gradually getting the child more interested and involved; and if things do not improve, consider the need for further physical evaluation. It can hardly be overemphasized that some children live in situations where they do not get enough sleep, do not have a proper diet, do not get a good breakfast to start their day, etc. Ask these children what time they went to bed, if they slept all night, if they had breakfast, what they had for dinner the night before, and so on. Do not do this in an accusing or annoyed way, but in a friendly and interested way. Children will tell us quite a lot about what is going on with them, what is happening and not happening, if we take the time to ask.

Excessive preoccupation with thoughts and fantasies is an extremely good example of a problem that may have multiple causes, may affect multiple dimensions of a child's life, and may require multiple responses. The causes may be environmental, in terms of the way the child is being dealt with both at home and at school. The causes may be academic, in terms of the child's having learning difficulties. The problems may be physical/organic, in terms of mild to fairly serious illness. The problems may be socially or emotionally caused, in terms of the child's way of dealing with reality and relating to other people. Our symptom profile would consider all of these possibilities, with possible physical/organic and emotional difficulties at the top of the list. Similarly, your response should consider all of these areas, starting with the social/emotional response pattern of getting the child's attention, keeping the child's attention, and giving the child support and approval. If fairly immediate results are not forthcoming, the physical/ organic and environmental areas need to be pursued.

Two usually interrelated symptoms complete our consideration of the most significant signs and symptoms of withdrawing, fearful behavior. First, you will occasionally have a child in your class who *expresses a dislike of recess for fear of getting hurt.* Second, you will frequently deal with the child who *expresses the feeling that other children do not like him.* Let's consider the second problem first and then consider the two problems together.

It is a very common complaint of small children that "they don't like me." The age range from five to eight years old is a real transition period from home to school, from family to "friends." The beginning development of peer relationships is usually somewhat problematic for small children. They are in the process of deciding who they would like to have as friends, who is willing to be friends with them, and how friends interact with and relate to each other. The motivation to be involved with and accepted by other children is quite high. Thus, small children tend to interpret minor rebuffs, outright rejections, times of low acceptance, and other situations in which they do not feel comfortably involved and accepted as "not being liked." Given the honesty and openness of small children, though, the feeling of not being liked is usually true. At a given point in time, one or several of the other children do not like a particular child. When the child says to you, "They don't like me," he is probably right. The other children, for whatever reason, do not like the child very much right now. They liked him five minutes ago, and will like him again five minutes from now. At this point, though, the dislike is real.

In these situations, you will want to leave peer problems up to the child's ingenuity and developing social skill. Small children work out their own problems much more easily if adults stay out of them. Occasionally, though, you will find a child who frequently or usually feels that the other children do not like her. It may be that the perception is valid: the other children may really not like her.

If the problem is continuing with a particular child, you may want to start by getting the child to think with you about possible reasons why the other children dislike him or her. Perhaps he is too aggressive, always wants to have his own way, refuses to play cooperatively or take turns, gets upset and pouts too easily, or is in some other way not very much fun to play with. Usually, you will not want to go past this level of discussion with the child. Try to help him or her develop possible "reasons" for the nonacceptance by other children. You might conclude such a discussion by saying, "The problem may have something to do with those kinds of things. Why don't you work on it?" Then, resolving the problem should be left up to the child. At other times, it may be that the other children have consolidated their "group" with a particular child left out. When that happens there is very little that you can do about it other than suggesting that the child find someone else to play with. Ordinarily, simply encouraging a child to play with a different group of children will solve the problem.

What are you trying to do? You are trying to help the child learn about and try out new social skills, different ways of handling situations, alternatives to the friends who do not like him, and generally "teaching" the child about social skills and interaction. Just as you talk with the child about arithmetic, answer his questions and suggest ways of approaching problems without actually doing the arithmetic for the child, you approach "social teaching" in the same way.

Very occasionally, you will have a child in your class who perceives that the other children do not like her and who is also sufficiently withdrawing and fearful to make it difficult for her to work on the problem. You should begin by developing a doing, talking relationship with the child. During part of free time or recess periods, you may have the child help you with things in the classroom, talk with you a while, etc. During these times you may invite another child or two to join you. If you are working on some kind of activity such as straightening up the room, you can gradually withdraw yourself from the activity and let the children go ahead and finish. Perhaps you could put the child who feels so disliked in charge of straightening up the room. This begins to encourage social interaction. Whether your approach involves simply telling such children to work on the problem by themselves, talking with them about possible ways of working on the problem, or "contriving" situations likely to increase social interaction, your role is one of supporting and encouraging each child. There is no way that you can force any child to become more socially involved, or force the other children to respond more positively to him. In fact, your efforts to do so would only tend to make things worse. For example, you would never want to say to the other children, "You have to play with this child."

The problem of children not liking recess for fear of being hurt is a related one. For some reason the child is avoiding social involvement and participation. The child who feels that other children do not like him is reacting to an emotional "feeling" hurt. The child who avoids recess is reacting to a possible "physical" hurt. In either case, the child is avoiding or is somewhat fearful of involvement with the other children. For either child, your role is one of encouraging, teaching, and supporting. At least with those children who express a dislike of recess, you can insist that they go out to play with the other children. Even then, though, you cannot make them play with the other children.

Sometimes the two problems go together. Children avoid recess for fear of being physically hurt *and* because of a feeling that the other children do not like them. When the problems occur together, the difficulty is more significant, as with other situations where two or more important symptoms are seen in one child. Your response to the child at school is as it would be were only one of the symptoms seen. The need for a careful, "active" response is compounded. Of course, if things do not improve in a week or two with a continuing and sensitive effort on your part, other possible causal areas need to be explored. It may be that these children have physical difficulties that are interfering with their involvement with the other children. They may have difficulties with coordination, being able physically to do things other children do, being able to keep active and involved, etc. They also may have learning problems, including difficulty understanding the accepted rules for games and activities, difficulty learning the do's and don'ts of social interaction, and difficulties figuring out the subtleties and intricacies of social relationships. Remember that if a child is somewhat slower than or behind other children in one area, she will tend to be slower than or behind children in other areas. If a child is having difficulty academically, he will also tend to have difficulties socially. The idea of multiple problems and multiple responses is emphasized here again.

A special comment needs to be made about physically handicapped children. They may have special difficulties in terms of playing games usually played by other children, actively participating in playground activities, keeping up with the other youngsters, etc. It is important to see that children with these types of difficulties naturally feel less involved with and accepted by the other children. What to do? If the other children are willing to slow down, give the handicapped child extra time, change the rules just a little so that the handicapped child can play, etc., things would greatly improve for the handicapped child. It is surprising to many adults, but most young children are quite willing to make these adjustments and concessions so that the handicapped child can be involved and accepted. They will do it if only they understand how it might help. Again, it is suggested that you talk with the other children about the problem in the presence of the handicapped child. Yes, it will be embarrassing and difficult for her. Once the other children understand the problem, though, they will almost always be surprisingly accepting of the problem and the child. This acceptance and involvement far outweighs the temporary embarrassment and bad feelings the handicapped child has while you are helping the other children to understand. It is also a somewhat painful, but a good learning experience for the handicapped child. She must learn to tell other people about her difficulties, her limitations, and her abilities. The child must learn to say things like "I want to play but I can't run that fast." By dealing with the problem in an honest, open, and straightforward way, you are modeling healthy behavior both for the handicapped child and for the other children.

Symptom Profile

Figure 8 presents the most significant signs and symptoms of early childhood difficulty discussed in this chapter, using the symptom profile format.

Fig. 8. Symptom Profile —Withdrawing, Fearful Behavior

	SYMPTOM	PHYSICAL/ ORGANIC	EMOTIONAL	SOCIAL	ENVIRONMENTAL	ACADEMIC
59	Has shaking, trembling hands	x	x			
60	Has frequent headaches	x	x			
61	Frequently wets or soils self	x	x			
62	Frequently expresses the feeling that he/she is no good		x		x	
63	Hears voices or sees things that are not there		x			
64	Often thinks people are trying to hurt him/her		x	x		
65	Has many unusual fears		x		x	
66	Seems to feel unlovable		x		x	
67	Tends to blame self for problems at home		x		x	
68	Has a preoccupation with death		x			
69	Shows frequent stuttering or stammering		x		x	
70	Shows frequent shivering or shaking when it is not cold	x	x			
71	Often expresses the belief that people do not like him/her		x	x		
72	Usually seems to feel as if she/he is not as good as others		x	x	x	
73	Refuses to talk	x	x			

74	Has perspiring, cold, clammy hands		x			
75	Dislikes recess for fear of being hurt		x	x		
76	Frequently does not respond when others speak to him/her		x	x		
77	Is preoccupied with own thoughts and fantasies	x	x	x	x	x
78	Shows unusual reluctance to separate from parents		x		x	
79	Refuses to play with other children		x	x		

EIGHT

From Tooth to Toe

Susie is seven and will probably keep on going and growing for another seventy years or so if all goes well. There are a lot of things that can go wrong along the way, though. Susie's teacher is very aware of signs and symptoms of potential difficulty and is equally aware that Susie will not notice many of the signs and symptoms, or at least will not call them to anyone's attention. One such symptom of difficulty is any bleeding around her mouth or gums. Since this is a potentially serious problem, it is important that Susie be taken to her dentist or physician right away unless the bleeding is obviously the result of a minor cut or bump. Any bluish tinge to her lips, earlobes, or fingernails may be another sign of serious difficulty. If Susie is not cold and if the blueness does not go away fairly quickly, there may be something quite serious going on. Any shortness of breath or unusual tiredness after relatively little exertion is another sign of possible difficulty. Being short of breath, short of energy, or short of enthusiasm is always an indication of some kind of problem for Susie.

Although Susie forgets to go to the bathroom once in a great while, she normally has no pain or discomfort when urinating. If her comments or behavior lead you to think that she might have some pain or discomfort when going to the bathroom, you should become concerned. Similarly, any signs of worms should cause concern. Like many other children, Susie had a problem with worms once and may have it again. This requires medical attention as soon as possible, but is not usually a particularly serious problem if Susie's doctor examines her and prescribes medicine for her.

Susie gets a lot of bumps and bruises during the course of her busy days and weeks. Also, she occasionally gets a minor burn. If the bruises, bumps, and burns seem unusually frequent or severe, though, you should become concerned and find out what happened. Your experience with Susie's classmates will let you know what the normal allotment of bumps, bruises, and scratches is for seven-year-olds. Like bumps and bruises, cuts and scratches are nothing to worry about unless they do not heal fairly quickly. If Susie has any cuts or scratches that do not seem to heal within two or three days, she needs medical attention. Any swelling or soreness of her joints or swelling in her hands or feet also calls for medical attention.

Any slight indication that Susie is using alcohol or drugs is cause for immediate, serious concern. This does not include drugs given to Susie by her parents for medical reasons, nor does it include an occasional taste of beer or wine. If you have the slightest suspicion that Susie may be using alcohol or drugs, though, you should check into how much she is using, when, and under what circumstances. Similarly, it is unlikely but possible that Susie may become involved in sniffing odd things like gasoline or glue. Eating odd things like paint or soap may not be a problem unless Susie does it with some regularity. In any event, you will want to see what is going on and how often it is happening.

Also, since Susie is only seven, she may slobber once in a while and have some difficulty manipulating and controlling her lips and tongue. If you notice that she drools frequently, though, the likelihood is that there is a serious problem. Now Susie is about the same size as the other children, but if a child in your class is unusually overweight, he should be seen by a physician to check into the reason for the excessive weight.

These fourteen signs and symptoms are among the hundred most significant signs and symptoms of childhood difficulty. Teachers will need to be especially alert in order to recognize them. Their significance needs to be understood so that appropriate medical care comes quickly. A referral to the school nurse or a phone call to the child's parents will usually be the first step. Getting appropriate assistance for the growing body is essential.

Discussion

Bleeding gums may be a sign of serious difficulty. Of course, if children are bleeding from the mouth, the most likely possibility is that they have been bumped in the mouth or have accidentally bitten their cheek or lip and are not seriously injured. When this type of accident occurs, children can almost always tell us what happened and where it hurts. A quick look will reveal that there is no serious problem and the bleeding should stop fairly quickly. Occasionally, though, children's gums will be red, swollen, tender, and will bleed easily. You may also notice sores on the gums and cheeks and in the back of the throat. Poor dental hygiene may be the culprit. Children may not brush their teeth or may not brush them properly, so it will be important for you to spend some time with your class talking about dental hygiene. The school nurse will probably be happy to help you with this, or someone from your local health department will probably be willing to come and talk with your class. Even better, a local dentist may talk with the children. Although teachers are very reluctant to ask professional people to take time to talk with little children, most mental health and health professionals enjoy talking with children. It will work out especially well if you and two or three other teachers schedule classes so that they can visit two or three different classes while at the school.

Bleeding gums and other oral difficulties may also be caused by a vitamin C deficiency. The point is that children's gums are normally healthy and do not bleed, so any bleeding or unusual sores are signs of difficulty. The first step should probably be to have the school nurse examine the child's mouth to determine whether or not there is any serious problem. If so, the parents need to be encouraged to take their child to the dentist. If they are unwilling or unable to do this, your local health department will probably be willing to help the child. Since oral difficulties can result from eating dirt, chewing on rocks, and introducing other foreign substances into the mouth, be sure to ask children if they have eaten anything or have put anything in their mouths. You also should be aware that difficulties in the mouth can result from drug reactions and other allergic reactions. If you or the school nurse talk with the parents about the child's problem, they will probably know whether or not that is the source of the difficulty. Whether they know or not, they should check with their family physician or dentist about it.

Unfortunately, some families have the attitude that children are going to grow up and lose their teeth anyway and thus do not place much importance on regular dental care. Some families may not have easy access to dental care as a result of limited financial resources that need to be given over to more important things such as food and shelter. For these children and for most of the youngsters in your class, some class time should be spent on discussing the teeth, proper dental hygiene, and on developing the attitude that teeth should last a lifetime. You can encourage good dental hygiene and perhaps encourage your school to start a dental hygiene program. Children might be encouraged to brush their teeth every day at school.

A special note should be made about dealing with cuts and bleeding within the mouth. First, when you look in the child's mouth, if you can see a cut or loose skin, the injury should be checked by someone with medical training, e.g., the school nurse, a physician, or the child's dentist. Even minor cuts within the mouth occasionally require stitches, since the surface of the mouth and tongue are critical to speech production. Although minor cuts do not usually require stitches, they occasionally do. Be sure that someone with appropriate medical training makes this judgment. As a minimum, you should make a point to call the problem to the attention of the child's parents, let them know that the cut or injury may require stitches, and encourage them to have it checked. Most nurses, physicians, and dentists will not mind "taking a look just to see."

Bleeding in the mouth is a special problem. If the source of the bleeding is on the inside surface of the lips or cheek, toward the front of the tongue or on the gums, using a clean finger to press a clean piece of cold and wet gauze against the cut or source of the bleeding will usually help. If the pressure cloth is a little cold, it will help the pain some. Pressure against the injured area will tend to slow down the bleeding and encourage clotting. If the initial bleeding was more than a slight dripping or if the bleeding does not stop in five minutes or so, or if the bleeding starts again after it had once stopped, the child needs emergency medical attention. Also, if the bleeding appeared to be coming from around the teeth or if any of the teeth have loosened, the child should receive emergency dental care.

Sometimes you will notice that children have a *bluish tinge to their lips, earlobes, or fingernails.* Remember that these symptoms may be continuing or temporary. You should keep in mind that such bluish tinges are one of the first signs of heart difficulty in children. But these symptoms may also stem from anemia, heat exhaustion, insect stings, poisons, electrical shocks, prolonged illness, or being cold. If children have been playing in the snow or have gotten chilled for some other reason, have them rest quietly and be sure that they get warm. Gently rubbing chilled hands or massaging arms or shoulders will help circulation. The bluish tinge should go away quite quickly as children warm up. If you feel that the children have gotten too hot, have them lie down, elevate both feet slightly, and drink orange juice, water, or other liquids. The tinge should go away fairly quickly, and they should feel better reasonably soon. Of course, be sure that they slow down and rest for an hour or two, even if they seem to feel better.

If a child has swallowed something poisonous, contact your Poison Control Center at once for specific instructions. Take the child to the hospital emergency room immediately. If he vomits, take along some of the vomited material in case the doctor wants it analyzed. It is important to remember exactly how much and what was ingested and to take a sample along if possible.

While the child is being transported to the emergency room, someone at school should be trying to contact the child's parents, should notify the emergency room that the child is being transported, and should check school records to be sure that emergency treatment forms are on file for the child. Someone else can take the form to the emergency room, if it is to be used. Be sure not to wait around, though, while someone is trying to locate the parents or the emergency medical permission form. Nothing should delay getting the child to the emergency room. Even if the parents cannot be located and emergency medical permission is not on file, the people at the emergency room can do some things to help the child without permission. Let them deal with the legal issues. They are experts at it.

A bluish tinge may also occur during temper tantrums when children hold their breath. As soon as they start breathing again, the bluish tinge will go away. Children who intentionally hold their breath at most will pass out. As soon as they pass out, their muscles will relax and they will start breathing normally again. Whatever the circumstances, if the bluish tinge does not go away fairly rapidly, children should be taken to a physician immediately. The same response is appropriate if there is no apparent cause for the bluishness, and especially if it persists for more than a few minutes or if it recurs without any apparent cause.

Complaints of shortness of breath after slight exertion are another sign of early childhood difficulty. Remember that little children have fairly unlimited energy supplies. Brief exercise, running across the playground, or doing a little physical work is ordinarily not sufficient to cause shortness of breath. Shortness of breath after relatively little exertion is a fairly serious sign of potential problems. Difficulties are usually limited to respiratory infections or other everyday illnesses, but the child needs rest and medical attention. Occasionally, though, shortness of breath can be a sign of serious heart and circulatory disease or very significant respiratory problems. If you have not noticed the difficulty before and become aware of it some afternoon, the likelihood is that the child is coming down with something.

You may want to have the school nurse check for you, or it may be more convenient to call the parents and have them take the child home. When the child comes back to school, the problem with shortness of breath should be gone. It is more alarming, though, when children have the problem continuously or on a recurring basis. These children need to be seen by a physician fairly quickly. Also, children may not have had any noticeable difficulty breathing before but suddenly have an attack. The problem here is more than shortness of breath; the children actually seem to have difficulty breathing. This is alarming, and emergency medical treatment is necessary.

Of course, you will want to be sure that these children do not have something lodged in the throat. If they do, have them lean over and hit them fairly firmly between the shoulder blades to see if you can get them to cough it up. If the object does not immediately dislodge, rush them to the emergency room.

There is a newer method of dislodging objects from the breathing passage—the 'Heimlich maneuver'—that is somewhat safer and somewhat more effective than hitting the child firmly on the back, if this newer method is properly administered. It involves applying pressure on the diaphram and forcing air up through the breathing passage. If you are interested in finding out more about this newer method, you can do so through your local health department or Red Cross. We will not discuss it further here, since adequate space cannot be devoted to completely explaining the method, including all necessary precautions. It should be noted, with emphasis, that the Heimlich maneuver should only be used after you have taken the time to get information and instructions. (Some additional information about the 'Heimlich maneuver' is included in Appendix III.)

Pain or burning during urination is a symptom of difficulty in small children as well as in adults. In general, such pain or burning is caused by inflammation of mucous membranes in the urinary tract. Visible signs of such difficulty would be pain expressed on the face during urination, noises the child makes as a result of the stinging sensation, unusually frequent urination, complaints about stinging or burning when urinating, unusual scratching or rubbing in the genital area, or products such as blood or tissue in the urine. These signs are not easily recognizable by the teacher, primarily because of separate restrooms for boys and girls and the fact that the teacher frequently is not in the restroom when the children are. You will need to rely on direct reports of the individual child and be very alert to comments or snide remarks by other children. Remember that little children rub and pull themselves out of habit, because of difficulty getting their clothes adjusted, and for other relatively unimportant reasons. It is not normal, though, for children to complain about pain or discomfort when toileting.

The pain or discomfort can result from urinary infections, stricture of the urinary tract, worms, high acidity in the urine, along with other problems going on within the child. However you become aware of the problem, through direct reports from the children involved or in other ways, it will be important to ask these children if they are experiencing pain or discomfort, let the school nurse know about the problem, and inform the parents of the problem. As with other important signs and symptoms in small children, sending a note home with the child is not reliable enough, since children lose notes and forget to give them to their parents. These problems are important enough to warrant your calling the parents or mentioning it to them in some other direct way. Frequently, medical attention is required, especially if the pain is intense or continues for more than a day or two. If children are having some difficulty in toileting, you can save them a lot of embarrassment if you quietly arrange for them to use the restroom at times when other children are not there.

You will occasionally find a child who seems to have *an unusual number of bruises*. Whereas little children tend to get many bruises, scrapes, scratches, small cuts, and other thumps and bumps on the hands, knees, elbows, and other highly exposed parts of the body, the focus here is on unusual numbers of bruises or bruises and bumps in odd places, like the back or face, and on especially severe bruises. When they first appear bruises are bluish-purple, and gradually change to brownish-green and then yellow as they heal. You should be especially alert to bruises that do not seem to be healing. An unusual number of bruises, severe bruises, or bruises that fail to heal readily can be caused by serious blood disease, damage to or disease of the blood vessels, vitamin deficiencies, infections, diabetes, and a variety of other things. The problem is potentially serious.

Also, the possibility of child abuse cannot be overlooked. If a child's bumps and bruises are excessive, a thorough medical workup is necessary. Be sure to observe and remember exactly so that you are able to let the school nurse and/or the child's parents know what you have noticed. This is especially important if the bruises are on the head. If so, you will need to be alert to signs of dizziness, nausea, or headache. You should also ask the child or other children whether there has been an accident or severe bump on the head. As in dealing with other difficulties with little children, you will need to be a good listener and especially skilled at remembering what you see and hear.

Like bruises, *multiple or severe burns* are potentially quite serious. No matter how severe the burn, the overwhelming likelihood is that it resulted from an accident. In extreme situations the burns may leave severe scars and disfiguration. In relating to children after the burns and skin discoloration or disfiguration have occurred, you need to be very sensitive to the possible social problems these children may have. They can easily become the object of ridicule, teasing, and peer rejection. Similarly, children may develop a lot of negative, self-deprecating feelings.

When you find a child who has been burned, if the burn is not extensive or extremely serious, your immediate response should be to apply ice or cold water to the burned area to decrease the pain and possible blistering. Do not put butter or other oily substances on the burn. After you have applied ice or cold water, blot the burned area dry and loosely wrap the injured part of the body in sterile gauze from the first aid kit in your room. The school nurse should be notified to see if anything else needs to be done. If the burn is more than minor, though, medical attention is needed immediately. Since children can almost always tell us exactly how they got burned and when, you may begin to suspect neglect, abuse, or some other difficulty if they seem unable or unwilling to discuss this with you.

Along with burns and bruises, *skin cuts or scratches that do not heal* are potentially serious. A small cut or scratch should be cleaned and then covered with a bandage to keep it from getting dirty. These small cuts and scratches should begin to heal quite rapidly and be noticeably better in a day or so. The failure of a cut or scratch to heal might suggest an infection, some foreign object still remaining in the wound, or some real problem with the child's healing process. You should remember cuts and scratches that children show or tell you about, or that you find out about, so that you notice when cuts and scratches do not seem to be healing properly. If you think there may be a problem, have the school nurse take a look at the injury to determine whether or not further medical attention is needed. Also, keep in mind that physical education teachers know quite a lot about little children's bodies and are frequently with children in situations where children are wearing less clothing, are taking showers, and have more of their body surface exposed. Consequently they may notice bruises, burns, cuts, and scratches that other school staff would have no opportunity to see. In the case of bruises, burns, cuts, and scratches, you should leave the responsibility of applying medication to the school nurse, the child's parents, or the family doctor.

Very infrequently *children may complain of swollen or painful joints,* of elbows, shoulders, ankles, or other joints aching, hurting, and burning. When you touch the painful area, you may notice that it is slightly warm and possibly swollen. You may also notice that the child seems somewhat tired, restless, and generally under par. Sometimes the joint pain may be somewhat minor and vague, but you should be concerned about any sign of difficulty since rheumatic fever is one of the possible problems related to these symptoms. Joint pains should be differentiated from growing pains (children really do have growing pains, but these typically occur at night and are experienced more in the long bones of the legs). Complaints of pains in the joints are very unusual. Although the problem may be relatively minor, a physician should be the one to make that judgment. With these and other symptoms in small children, you should never conclude that the parents have noticed a problem. Your judgment will be much sharper and more objective than theirs, if for no other reason than that you have twenty or thirty other children in your class with whom you can compare the child. If the child's problems seem unusual or significantly different from those experienced by other children, this is usually a good sign that there is something wrong. Trust your judgment.

The swelling of children's feet or legs is a similar kind of difficulty. If children complain of some discomfort, pain, or of a funny feeling, you should take time to feel their feet and lower legs. If you notice any redness, tenderness, or swelling, concern is warranted. The swelling may be due to an injury such as a broken bone or a sprain, or can result from kidney difficulty, circulatory problems, and a variety of other internal problems. If the ankle seems sprained, cold compresses will make it feel better. Since it is difficult for children with swollen feet or legs to walk, you should not expect them to continue play activities or to walk home from school. Parents should be called so they can come to school and pick up their child since the pain and discomfort will prevent the accomplishment of much at school that day anyway.

If a broken bone is suspected, be sure not to move the child. Keep the child as still as possible and get help from the school nurse, another teacher, or some other adult at school. If at all possible, do not leave the child alone because he or she probably will not lie still if you do. In most communities an emergency squad, experts at moving people with broken bones or other severe injuries, is available to take the child to the doctor's office or the hospital emergency room. If no sprain, broken bone, or other injury is suspected, though, have the child lie down and elevate both legs somewhat. Cold compresses will help reduce the pain and discomfort. As with breaks and sprains, the child's parents need to be notified immediately so that they can deal with the problem. They may already be aware of the difficulty and may let you know how to deal with it. If not, medical attention is necessary.

One thing you will find is that little children are inclined to introduce all sorts of substances into their bodies. Their *reports of using alcohol, taking unprescribed drugs, or sniffing glue* or other substances should therefore be taken quite seriously. The unsupervised use of drugs or *intentional and repeated inhaling of fumes* from gasoline or other substances is reason for extreme alarm. The seriousness of reports of using alcohol is less clear. Children may be given a drink of beer, wine, or other liquor by parents, relatives, or by some other adult. Whether you approve or disapprove of this, occasional ingestion of small quantities of alcohol is not alarming from a medical standpoint. Of course, if a child reports consuming substantial quantities of alcohol, or even small quantities on any regular basis, there is reason for real concern. As you listen closely to the child's conversations with you and with friends, or when friends talk about the child, you may pick up a clue that something is going on. Gently and somewhat casually, you should pursue this with the child. You should also be alert to any unusual mood or behavior changes in the child, any changes in physical appearance, especially around the eyes and face, or unusual odor coming from the child's clothing or body.

If you have even slight reason to suspect that the child has been using alcohol, misusing drugs, or is involved in fume sniffing, immediate involvement of the school principal and guidance staff is necessary. In the event that these resources are not available at your school, check with the child's parents to see if they are aware of any problem. Almost always parents will become concerned, will take the problem seriously, and will make every effort to deal with it. If they do not, or if the signs of these difficulties continue, you have a clear responsibility to let the local child welfare authorities know of your suspicions. They will investigate the situation without involving you or revealing your identity. Also, keep in mind that substance abuse is usually associated with other behavioral, attitudinal, and social problems, so a child using such substances will ordinarily have other noticeable problems.

Of course, you will want to be sure that children are not keeping drugs or other dangerous substances in their desks, pockets, or elsewhere. It is generally not advisable for little children to be responsible for any kind of medication or pills, though some children who take medication regularly may be able to accept some responsibility for this. Even so, you should know what the medication is, how much they are supposed to take, when they are supposed to take it, and what the medicine looks like. In addition to these precautions, you will want to spend class time discussing material related to making value judgments, the importance of being able to say no to other children, the necessity of taking responsibility for one's own behavior and actions, and drug and alcohol information. With little children, factual information combined with a focus on values clarification and formation is quite useful. Little children will tend to reflect their parents' values and attitudes about most things. In addition to reinforcing most parental values, part of your responsibility is to help children begin looking at alternative ideas, attitudes, and values.

Occasionally, a child's use of or positive attitude toward alcohol and other drugs may in fact be a direct reflection of positive parental attitudes and values toward these substances. Nonetheless, it will be important for you to help the children consider other attitudes and values, placing your emphasis on the especially negative physiological and social implications of such substance "abuse" for young children and adolescents, particularly in reference to drug and alcohol abuse. For example, the physiological susceptibility to alcoholism is thought to be substantially higher with children and adolescents than with adults. Similarly, the potentially negative effects of drug and alcohol use and abuse are much higher with children and adolescents than with adults, i.e., the negative physiological effects and negative socio-emotional effects are more pronounced much more quickly. Most mental health centers and many health departments either have or have access to staff members especially trained in the area of alcohol and substance abuse who will be quite willing and eager to talk with you and the children in your class. Frequently, these individuals have programs prepared that can be as short as half an hour and may include as much as an hour a week for eight or ten weeks. The problem is potentially serious enough to warrant your seriously considering an eight- or ten-week unit devoted to the subject. Similarly, cigarette smoking is a serious problem. Your local lung association can provide information and programs related to cigarette smoking.

You may find that a child in your class *eats odd things like paint or soap.* You may observe this directly, or pick it up from other children or from things the child says. These children may look thin and pale and may have stomach and digestive problems. They may also tend to withdraw, show considerable fluctuation in mood and behavior, seem somewhat physically and emotionally weak, and generally seem unhealthy. Of course, ingesting such things as paint, soap, chalk, dirt, and paper can lead to many physical complications, poisoning, and general bad health. Children who eat these kinds of things with any regularity may either be experiencing some vitamin, mineral, or other deficiency, or may be fairly seriously disturbed in an emotional sense. Children who put almost anything in their mouth after the age of four or five have not successfully moved from infantile behavior to behavior appropriate to older boys and girls.

Since lead poisoning is common in some geographic areas, especially in older parts of cities, a few special comments are in order. Children can get it from eating paint chips or flakes or from chewing on things painted with lead based paint. Also, lead poisoning can result from using water from plumbing systems with lead pipes, as well as from a few other less usual sources. Severe stomach cramping, headaches, unusual sleepiness, unusual aggressiveness, delirium, weakness or coordination difficulties in the arms or legs, difficulty sitting or standing, extreme paleness, and a black line where the teeth and gums meet are all symptoms of lead poisoning. When these symptoms occur individually or in combination, and especially when children live in older homes or neighborhoods, lead poisoning should be suspected. Of course, any of these symptoms is, by itself, sufficient to warrant medical concern and attention. In combination, though, they are alarming and require a fairly immediate medical response.

You will first need to talk with the child, and possibly with the parents, to be sure that the child is getting a proper diet. If some deficiency is contributing to the behavior, proper diet with adequate supervision of eating will remedy the problem fairly quickly. If there is no dietary problem or if changing the child's diet does not remove the behavior, you have reason to suspect more serious emotional difficulty. To understand what is going on and what to do about it, the help of the school psychologist and school guidance staff is needed. Usually though, it will be enough to have the child's parents watch for the behavior and deal with it as they would any other behavior they want to eliminate.

You can deal with the problem in the same way at school. If a child is behaving improperly, it is quite likely that he or she simply has not learned to behave in the usual, expected way.

The solution is to teach the child the new behavior just as you would teach anything else. First, call the behavior to the child's attention and talk with her about the fact that the behavior is undesirable and about why it is undesirable. In the case of eating odd things, the child should understand that he is likely to get sick and could possibly die from eating some things, or even from just putting them in his mouth. Also, talk with him about the fact that neither you nor he wants him to get sick. "I don't want you to get sick or hurt; and you don't want to either, do you?" Yes, the child might indicate that he wants to get sick and die. If so, that is a problem really needing professional attention, probably through your local mental health center or family service agency. Generally, though, the child will agree that he does not want to get sick. Next, firmly insist that the child "stop" the behavior. If the behavior persists, you may want to keep the child in from recess or not let him participate in some activity in an effort to stop the behavior at school. Parents may want to make the child go to bed a half hour or so earlier than usual, not let him watch a favorite television program, etc, as a way of dealing with the problem at home.

These approaches should be followed through with a physical examination of the child to see if there is any physiological basis for the problem. If there is no noticeable improvement within two or three weeks, the child should be evaluated by the school psychologist or at the area mental health service to see if other emotional and social factors may be contributing to the problem.

Some children have a problem with *excessive drooling*. This can reflect a problem in slow development of the saliva glands, problems with the mouth or teeth, or poor control of the mouth and tongue, or it may be that children are hungry and want to eat, especially if the problem occurs only occasionally. You should notice if the problem occurs at the same time each day, and, if it occurs daily, what is going on in the classroom when the problem occurs, and what happens after you quietly discuss the problem with the child. You might develop a signal to let children know when they are drooling so they can gradually learn to control the saliva once they become aware of what they are doing. If a more significant problem is suspected, you should discuss your concern with the child's parents and the school nurse. Since the school's speech and hearing therapist works with children who have problems with the mouth and tongue, he may have some very helpful suggestions. If your school does not have a speech and hearing therapist, you should keep in mind that such resources are usually available through large universities and children's hospitals. Both of these types of facilities ordinarily operate outpatient programs for children in the area.

A *child who is unusually overweight* has many special problems. Here we are not concerned about children who are a little chubby or who have not yet started developing the body shape of older children, but children who are excessively overweight or extremely fat. You will find that these children are slower in their movements and tend to tire more easily than other children, and that they tend to be less agile and less skilled at things requiring balance than are other children. You will probably find that these youngsters are under a lot of emotional strain at school and probably also at home. They tend not to be accepted as readily by their peers, may become a focus for teasing and ridicule, and often find it difficult to negotiate their social world. The problem may not be so pronounced at home, since an unusually overweight child may have parents who are quite fat.

Whether or not the parents of an obese child are overweight themselves, real progress for the child will usually only come in terms of significant changes in eating patterns and habits. Some work with the child at school will be helpful; but since most of the eating undoubtedly takes place at home, significant change will need to occur there for any planned program to be successful. This program should be supervised by a physician and will probably require the involvement of outside counseling or support. Sometimes there are community groups organized to help with problems of being overweight.

Perhaps the parents and child could start with that type of program. If it is not successful, though, they may need to become involved with their local mental health service or some other professional counseling service. However, you and the parents will want to keep in mind that changing eating patterns and habits within a family is extremely difficult, and that it frequently is unresponsive to outside counseling efforts. Emphasizing the potential health hazards to both the child and adult seems to have about as much positive effect as anything else. Of course, this type of emphasis should be made by a physician or other qualified individual. You will be on safe grounds, though, if you emphasize that extreme obesity in children is a potential health hazard as well as a real social liability.

Most frequently the problem has no physical origin but relates to taking in more food than the body can use up. Children may be accustomed to eating starchy foods, candy, and other fattening things rather than meats, fruits, and vegetables, and they may snack a lot. Occasionally, such obesity is caused by a malfunctioning gland or other physical difficulty. In order to determine whether the problem is physical or socio-environmental, excessively overweight children should be checked by a physician. At school you will want to see that they get recognition for their accomplishments, encourage them to become involved in physical activities, and to the extent possible, keep other children from teasing or shunning them. (Nutrition programs and discussions should be developed for the whole class to encourage good eating habits.) Helping the child will also involve working with the family. The school nurse would be an appropriate person to help parents help the child develop new eating patterns.

You will also want to keep in mind that some trauma within the child's world can cause him to feel unloved, rejected, unhappy, or despondent and to turn to food for consolation. The death of a relative, a severe failure experience, or other losses can lead to a child's using food as a source of love, security, and warm feelings, and as an alternative to involvement with other people. This pattern is very difficult to break, so it is important for you to be alert to any child who may be starting this kind of pattern. If the child is already into this pattern, relationships with people, social involvement, and good feelings between you and the child need to be encouraged to turn the child's orientation away from food and toward other sources of gratification. Your emphasis should be on these other sources of gratification and not on turning away from food. Punishment, ridicule, and other negative responses to children's eating will reinforce their sense of rejection and of not being lovable. Do not tell them that it is all right to be fat, that fat people are usually jolly and happy, or offer them false reassurances. You know and they know that it is better to be normal. If your relationship with these children cannot tolerate honesty, it is not a helpful one.

Also, you may have been exposed to the myth that poor children naturally tend to be fat because they do not have a lot of protein in their diet and tend to eat a lot of starchy foods. Just keep in mind that being fat almost always is caused by "eating too much." Although a diet including a lot of vegetables, fresh fruits, meat, and so on is preferable to one that does not include adequate quantities of these foods, being fat usually has to do with nothing other than eating too much. This problem is not related to socioeconomic factors.

Also, it would not be advisable to single out a child for special comments or rules at snacktime at school. This would only tend to subject the child to increased negative attention and probably to negative comments from his or her peers. The few calories saved by a child's eating one cookie instead of two represents a negligible contribution to the overall problem. In most situations, the risk of negative attention and negative peer comments is not worth the slight savings in calories. Besides, simply changing the child's eating habits at snacktime at school will probably do little or nothing to change the overall eating habits at home.

Any sign of worms is a serious problem with little children, including children from good, clean homes. Scratching or rubbing around the anal area, problems with constipation, severe anemia or paleness, loss of appetite, loss of weight, sensitivities somewhat like those with allergies, a slight fever, loss of interest in activities, and dull, lusterless hair, can be signs of worms. Generally, children with worms will not seem quite up to par. Sometimes the worms can actually be seen around the genital or anal area or other places on the child's body. Of course, if you see a worm or suspect that what you see might be a worm, the child should receive immediate medical attention. Similarly, if the child is showing signs and symptoms that might be caused by worms, medical attention is necessary.

Worms are potentially a very serious problem. Some kinds of worms move to the mouth and nose, block the appendix or obstruct the intestines, and in extreme cases cause permanent damage to the child's body, or even death. Since the eggs of worms might be widely distributed in bed clothing, furniture, and other places in the child's home, the whole family might become infected. Fortunately, the initial appearance of worms is not particularly serious. They are fairly easily treated by a physician and present no real problem to the child's health if treated. However, children might be effectively treated for worms today, get them again several months from now, and need to be treated again.

(As an aside, you may want to note that ringworm is actually a parasitic fungus condition that usually appears as a round sore on the surface of the skin and develops a scaly, scab-like surface. This condition also requires medical treatment and should be viewed by you and the child's parents as a potentially serious condition.)

To prevent worms, you can insist that all children in your class wash their hands before eating and after going to the restroom, and encourage them to keep hands, pencils, and other objects out of their mouths. Also, you should encourage children to avoid kissing or putting their mouths on pets and other animals, avoid letting their pets lick them around the mouth and face, and wash their hands after they have played with an animal.

If you feel that a student may have worms, it will be important to let the parents know about that right away, and to be tactful, since there are many myths that worms are related to filthy housekeeping and poor parenting. When you tell the parents that you suspect worms, be sure to let them know that worms are a common childhood problem, that many children get them, and that the problem has very little to do with housekeeping. Mothers may need a lot of reassurance that it probably is not their fault, that no one thinks it is, and that it is possible to be a good mother and housekeeper and still have a child with worms. Parents will need to take their child to the family doctor, get some medicine for the child and possibly for other family members, be sure that everyone takes the medicine, and not worry about it.

Symptom Profile

Figure 9 presents the most significant signs and symptoms of early childhood difficulty discussed in this chapter, using the symptom profile format.

Fig. 9. Symptom Profile–Less Frequent Health Problems

	SYMPTOM	PHYSICAL/ ORGANIC	EMOTIONAL	SOCIAL	ENVIRONMENTAL	ACADEMIC
80	Bleeding gums	x				
81	Bluish tinge to lips, earlobes, or fingernails	x				
82	Shortness of breath after slight exertion	x				
83	Pain or burning when urinating	x				
84	Multiple or severe burns	x			x	
85	Unusual number of severe bruises	x			x	
86	Cuts or scratches that do not heal	x				
87	Reports using alcohol or drugs, or sniffing glue		x	x	x	
88	Eats odd things like soap or paint	x	x			
89	Swollen or painful joints	x				
90	Swelling of legs or feet	x				
91	Excessive drooling	x	x			
92	Unusually overweight	x	x		x	
93	Any signs of worms	x				

NINE

It's Somewhat Unusual

Sometimes we see symptoms in children that seem unusual and really puzzle us. We know that children occasionally have seizures or convulsions, but most of us have probably not seen a child have a spell of this type. If you have a child in your class who is seizure-prone, you must be sure that he or she takes the appropriate medication and you will need to know what to do if the child has a seizure at school. Many things that happen to children, though, may appear to reflect neurological difficulty or may cause you to think of epilepsy when the symptom really reflects a very different kind of physiological or emotional difficulty. For example, José is one of those children people refer to as "high-strung" or "nervous." His head appears to jerk and he flinches from time to time. If you observe him closely sitting at his desk, you will notice a lot of rapid, jerky movements involving his arms and legs and sometimes his whole body, as if he were shivering or shuddering. This type of apparently involuntary, jerky motion can reflect any of a variety of emotional and/or physiological difficulties.

Only rarely may you have a child in your class who experiences brief or extended periods of blanking out, who temporarily loses conscious awareness. This may have something to do with epilepsy but also may be a function of difficulty with blood sugar levels or a result of intense emotional stress. When Nicole, a perky eight-year-old, fell to the floor while waiting in line for lunch, she seemed to have fainted, but her fall could reflect anything from a touch of flu to quite serious psychogenic problems. Similarly, when children complain of numbness of some part of the body, the numbness can be due to anything from sitting in one position too long to a severe neurological problem.

There are other things that automatically suggest more serious complications. Pronounced weakness on one side of the body relative to the other should cause immediate concern. Likewise, any unusual staggering or apparent loss of balance is cause for some alarm. As you consider these seven signs and symptoms, it is important to realize that their occurrence is not necessarily reason for great alarm. Their potential seriousness, though, underlines the importance of your alertness and sensitivity to comments of children and to somewhat unusual behaviors. When the signs occur, it is always important to be sure that the child receives appropriate medical attention. The task for you is to recognize the symptom when it occurs and to understand its potential significance, especially since you may be the one who needs to encourage the child's parents to follow up on the problem. One thing you will especially want to keep in mind is that these signs and symptoms may come and go; they may occur once or twice at school and not occur at home at all. This gives you at least equal responsibility with the child's parents for recognizing the problem.

Discussion

Infrequently you may have a child in your class who experiences *convulsions, seizures, or unusual spells.* Since it is uncommon for a child to have the first major (grand mal) convulsion at school, the child's parents will probably have made you aware of his or her difficulties and will let you know what you might expect. If the child is epileptic and the parents are already aware of that fact, the child will be under medical treatment and will be taking medication for the problem.

Lesser seizures present a different sort of problem, though, since a child may briefly lose consciousness or awareness of surroundings without any particularly noticeable symptoms. These small seizures can be recognized by brief periods of nearly complete inattentiveness, episodes of blank staring, or short periods during which the child stops participating or being involved in whatever is going on. At first these spells are not easily noticeable. Nevertheless, if you are alert to them, you will probably become vaguely aware that the child has turned off for a few seconds or a few minutes. The child's behavior will seem rather strange in that he or she momentarily seems to be paying no attention to anything. If you become vaguely aware that this is happening, you should suspect that the child may be having little seizures.

As you consider children who appear to have brief periods of blanking out, you will also want to consider the discussion in earlier chapters related to frightened withdrawn children and children who tend at times to be fairly unresponsive. These problems are much more likely than small seizures. As suggested here and in earlier chapters, the specific diagnosis of the condition needs to be made by a physician. The important thing is for you to be aware of the possibility that brief periods of blanking out may relate to small seizures and may be barely noticeable. Your alertness and ability to describe what the child is or is not doing is the important skill to develop. Be sure to keep careful notes about such behavior in your performance notebook.

At this point you need to become much more alert to the child's pattern of interacting, participating, and responding, to see if there are any gaps in awareness or consciousness. Be careful to keep written or mental notes about your observations. If you feel that the child may be losing awareness on several occasions, it will be important to share your observations with the school nurse, the child's parents, and with the child's physician when you are contacted about what you have observed. Also, if you are very sure that the child has lost awareness for a brief or extended period of time, even once, your concern should be conveyed to these same people. Several suspected episodes or one fairly certain episode is sufficient to have further tests and observations made. Remember that the most common time for the onset of petit mal epilepsy is between the ages of four and eight. After all seizures, whether major or small, the child will tend to be somewhat disoriented, somewhat drowsy, and will have little or no recollection of the episode. In the case of a little seizure, the child will be unaware of the lapse in consciousness whereas the child will probably be aware of grand mal seizures.

During a grand mal seizure the child will probably fall to the floor. There is nothing you can do to stop, slow down, or minimize the seizure; the only thing you can do is to be sure that the child does not injure himself while thrashing around, moving and jerking, and behaving in a convulsive way. If you have an opportunity while the child's mouth is open, put a long, solid object in the mouth to keep the child from biting the tongue and cheeks. The object should not be small enough for the child to be able to swallow it; for example, a pencil should not be used because the child could very easily bite it in two and accidentally swallow part of it. If you know that a child in your class may have a seizure, keep a tongue depressor wrapped in adhesive tape to place in the child's mouth during a seizure. It should be emphasized that an object should be placed in the child's mouth while it is open; forcing an object into the mouth during a seizure can do more damage than would result if the child bit himself. During a seizure you should loosen the clothing around the child's neck and move furniture and other objects away to minimize the likelihood of the child's hurting himself.

If you are aware that a child may have a seizure, ask the parents how to deal with it. It will also be helpful to talk with the child in a quiet sort of way so that he knows you are aware of the problem, that you know he cannot help it, and that he need not worry since you will help if problems develop. If it seems likely that the child might have a seizure because medication cannot completely control the problem, it will be very helpful if you let other children in the class know what might happen. They will have many questions, will need to know a little about what causes the problem and a little about what the seizure might look like. This will keep them from becoming frightened, will help them relate more positively to the child after the seizure, and will smooth the situation for everyone. If children do not know what another child's problem is, why the problem exists, or what its significance is, they can be cruel, rejecting, and generally "bratty" about it. However, when they know about the problem, they tend to deal with the child and the problem as if it were no big deal. When explaining to children why another child is having or has had a seizure, it will usually be quite sufficient to tell them that all of us have very small amounts of electricity in our brains. Sometimes, this electrical activity is a little irregular or is not quite the way it is supposed to be. When this happens, people occasionally have seizures.

Very infrequently children experience a condition known as psychomotor epilepsy. These episodes look a lot like rage or temper tantrums. When you deal with these episodes in the same way you would normally deal with severe temper tantrums, your efforts will not eliminate or reduce the behavior. When you refer a child with continuing or severe temper tantrums to the school guidance staff or school psychologist, this possibility will automatically be considered and checked, although psychomotor epilspsy is only rarely a factor in even very severe temper tantrums. If there is no school psychologist or guidance staff, you should encourage the child's parents to have their physician consider the possibility that the temper tantrums may have a neurological or physiological basis.

Regardless of the type of seizure children have, they will probably be taking medication for it once the condition is diagnosed. You should be aware of what the medication is, know what it looks like and how often it is to be taken, and accept some of the responsibility for being sure that it is taken properly. Your efforts will pay off for the child and for you in terms of not having as much disruption in your class. Of course, the child should be treated like the other children except during those rare seizures. After a seizure, a child should be encouraged to rest, slow down, and be given some time to get back together again. Overprotection, oversolicitousness, or discouraging these children from involvement in activities with their classmates is a danger.

Some children may not have seizures and may not experience any loss of consciousness, but you may notice that they seem to have some kind of problem with movement and coordination. You may notice this through *frequent, rapid, jerky movements.* These children may seem momentarily to lose control of their arms or legs, and you may notice jerkiness and rather random, purposeless motion. Here we are talking about unusual or especially jerky movement, not about little children squirming and moving around a lot, tapping their fingers, swinging their feet, rocking in their chairs, and generally finding it difficult to stand still, sit still, or be still. Various conditions can cause this kind of problem, including convulsions as already discussed. Without a loss of consciousness, though, the most likely cause is muscle spasms or cramping. This is probably a temporary condition resulting from the way a child was standing, too much physical exertion, getting too cold or hot, or some other such reason. In these situations, the problem is very temporary and does not occur with any regularity. Once in a while, though, this problem can be caused by abnormal nerve impulses from the brain. In extreme cases, the child loses consciousness. This may also be a symptom of rheumatic fever, serious infection, or other physical problem.

Rapid, jerky movements, including facial movement, may also reflect emotional difficulty. When the cause is socioemotional, the problem is known as tics. These occur in fairly nervous, high-strung children and usually do not present a serious problem. Making children aware of the motion, gently calling their attention to it when they jerk or move spontaneously, and giving them opportunities to get their emotions and energy out in other ways is usually sufficient to eliminate the problem. The tics ordinarily go away with gentle reminders and encouragement. If they do not, however, there is a possibility of serious physical or emotional difficulty. Of course, a physical examination is the first order of business. Probably the cruelest thing one can do to children is to attribute problems to emotional causes when they are physically based. Always evaluate the possibility of a physical cause before concluding that the cause is social or emotional. If physical causes are ruled out, then counseling and guidance is indicated for these children.

During this process it will be important for you to maintain a warm, supportive relationship with these children, to look for any tendency on their part to be excessively perfectionistic, to help them feel good about what they have accomplished and can do. The idea is to let them know that you find them lovable the way they are and assume that they will continue to be lovable and successful. They do not have to prove anything to you or fear punishment or rejection for not being more successful than they are. You may want to keep in mind that tics are most common in youngsters from seven to twelve years of age, are somewhat more frequent with boys than with girls, and are somewhat more prevalent among slower children than among brighter children. Overambitiousness and over-conscientiousness contribute to the problem; it is the excess that you need to respond to.

Some children experience *brief or extended periods of blanking (blacking) out.* Of course, these spells could reflect little seizures. Here, though, we are talking about something more than momentary loss of awareness. These children seem to faint or pass out; they become somewhat disoriented, perhaps dizzy, and have a general sense of faintness. These feelings in themselves are not necessarily very significant. They may come from getting too tired or too hot, from a cold, or from a variety of other day-to-day kinds of things. We have all had the experience of momentary dizziness and disorientation, but these dizzy spells do not usually lead to *fainting* or passing out. In these situations the child usually loses muscle tone, becomes limp, and slumps to the floor if not supported. These symptoms could be caused by a variety of things, such as a high fever, infections including meningitis, problems with the blood sugar levels, or problems with the body's metabolism.

If children feel dizzy, have them lie down so they will not hurt themselves by falling, or if they might be getting dizzy, have them at least sit down. If they do faint or pass out, it is important to remember that the symptom in itself is not particularly dangerous. If you wipe the children's face with a cool, damp washcloth, they will probably come back to consciousness gradually. Consciousness will probably return fairly quickly whether you do anything or not. The important thing is that fainting or passing out may be a sign of quite serious difficulty within the child. Unless you know that the child is diabetic and is supposed to have some candy or orange juice, or unless you know that she is supposed to have some medication, be sure not to administer any medicine or try to treat the spell yourself. Even if the child regains consciousness fairly quickly and feels fine, she needs to see the school nurse and probably the family doctor. A medical evaluation is important, especially if the child does not resume consciousness quickly or if the spell recurs. As with all childhood difficulties, it is better to overrespond, to get too much help, or to send a child to the doctor too quickly than it is to wait too long, do too little, and express too little concern. If you overrespond, people have been inconvenienced; if you underrespond, the child may be the ultimate victim of your reluctance.

Numbness of any body part is another cause for concern. This temporary lack of sensation is most likely to occur in the hands and feet or in the arms and legs. We have all experienced temporary loss of sensation and usually describe it as numbness or a feeling that the particular body part is "asleep." Ordinarily, the problem comes from getting too cold. We may experience some numbness or lack of sensation in the ears, the nose, or other areas of the body that have been exposed to the cold. Normally this does not present an emergency situation, and it is sufficient to go where it is warm, cover the numbed part with a blanket or warm clothing, and take a few minutes to warm up. The possibility of frostbite or other tissue damage makes it important not to be exposed to cold too long. You will want to watch little children rather closely since they may be inclined to stay out in the cold too long and are also apt to play in the snow, rub ice on their hands or face, or do other things that intensify the exposure. Do not let them stay out too long during cold weather, and encourage them to stay dry. Once they are inside, though, it should be sufficient to be sure that they get warm. The numbness should go away in a few minutes. Because of the possibility of frostbite or other injury from the cold, you should watch for any complaints of itching or burning in the numb or exposed area. This burning or itching sensation should go away as sensation returns. If it does not, more careful medical attention is needed. The school nurse will be well equipped to deal with this.

If there is no school nurse, the child should be seen by a physician if the numbness, burning, or itching persists for more than fifteen minutes or so after you have made an effort to get the child warm, have gently massaged the numb or burning area, and have either blown warm air on the area or placed a warm, damp cloth on it. Blowing gently on the area will help to warm it up, since your breath will be considerably warmer than the cold skin surface.

In addition to coldness, temporary numbness or loss of sensation can come from sitting or lying too long in one position, or in a way that cramps the circulation of some body part, or doing something else that temporarily interferes with good circulation. Usually there will be a tingling sensation when temporary numbness is caused by these conditions. As when numbness is caused by exposure to the cold, sensation should return fairly quickly. When the surface of the skin is "asleep" it will also help to massage the area.When numbness continues beyond a few minutes or if it occurs with unusual regularity or for no apparent reason, further medical attention is necessary, particularly if the numbness does not disappear fairly quickly. The symptom becomes especially significant if the numbness involves the trunk of the body or a limited area of other parts of the body. Of course, if numbness follows an accident or injury, you might suspect the possibility of nerve damage or some other serious difficulty, and the child should be seen by a physician. If the numbness occurs for no apparent reason, or includes atypical body areas or does not go away in a few minutes, the possibility of some neurological or other physical difficulty should not be overlooked. The child's complaint should be taken seriously.

As we think about taking children's complaints seriously, you should consider the possibility that the child is copying the behavior of some other child. It is not very likely that you would have more than one child in your class at a time who has a serious medical problem involving numbness. If one child shows the symptom, gets attention for it, and seems to get some social payoff from having the problem, other children may decide that it would be good if they had the problem also. Just keep this in mind without automatically relying on it as a basis for decision making. Two children may show signs of possible neurological difficulty almost simultaneously. If the second child does not get much attention for it but is still complaining about the symptom later on that day or again two or three days later, the safe course is to check it out. He may be "putting you on," or he may really have a problem.

A relatively uncommon but serious symptom is *weakness of one side of the body* relative to the other. This weakness will probably be quite noticeable to you, and may even be noticeable to other children. One of the first signs of difficulty may be some unusual body posture. For example, children may stand more on one foot than the other, may not walk or sit perpendicular to the ground, may have an unusual walk, may seem to go out of the way to support themselves or catch their balance with one arm instead of the other. You may also notice short, jerky movements or other unusual body motions. This weakness can be caused by a mild form of cerebral palsy or may be the precursor of future, more serious muscular disease. The likelihood is that the child's family will already be aware of the problem, though it is possible that they have not noticed it. You should mention to them the things you have noticed, see if they are already aware of the problem, and find out how it is to be dealt with at school. For example, should the child's activities be restricted in any way? Does the child take any special medications? Are there any special teaching approaches that will be more effective than others? If symptoms have not occurred before and you are the first to observe them, it is likely that the problem has resulted from a recent injury or reflects some new difficulty in the child's brain functioning that has not come up before. If the child's parents are unaware of the problem or can recall no previous symptoms, immediate medical attention is required. Also, if a child in your class has not shown such symptoms before but suddenly appears weaker on one side of the body than the other, fairly immediate medical attention is necessary.

Staggering or an apparent lack of balance is a related cause for concern. The child may not show any particular weakness on one side of the body or the other, but may not be able to walk, run, sit, stand, or be involved in activities in the same smooth and reasonably well-controlled way that other children are. You may notice this in a milder form in that the child has difficulty moving from a sitting to a standing position, climbing stairs, or actively participating in running, jumping, and other moving activities. Remember that the problem may be minor or serious, so do not minimize your mild concern. Be sure to keep mental or written notes about all the symptoms or problems you have noticed since they may be signs of a potentially serious disease process.

As with other problems with children, the first step is to talk with the child's parents about it. They may be aware of the problem and will be quite happy to see that you are interested and observant. If they are unaware of the problem, though, medical attention is the next step. They may have noticed but have not wanted to admit the possibility that there is a problem. They somehow think that if they ignore the problem it will go away. This does not reflect a lack of love or concern; we are all this way to some extent. Of course, real problems in little children seldom go away by themselves. They need our caring, concerned attention.

Symptom Profile

Figure 10 presents the most significant signs and symptoms of early childhood difficulty discussed in this chapter, using the symptom profile format.

Fig. 10. Symptom Profile —Particularly Unusual Symptoms

	SYMPTOM	PHYSICAL/ ORGANIC	EMOTIONAL	SOCIAL	ENVIRONMENTAL	ACADEMIC
94	Frequent, rapid, jerky movements	x	x			
95	Brief or extended periods of blanking out	x				
96	Fainting	x	x			
97	Numbness of any body part	x				
98	Weakness of one side of the body	x				
99	Unusual staggering or lack of balance	x				
100	Convulsions, seizures, or unusual "spells"	x	x			

APPENDIX I

450 Signs and Symptoms of Early Childhood Difficulty

The 450 signs and symptoms included in this Appendix are those presented to the first (the thirty-member) panel of experts in the process of selecting the one hundred most significant signs and symptoms of early childhood difficulty. These have been roughly organized into smaller groupings, each preceded by general comments about all of the signs and symptoms included in the grouping. For example, the comments preceding the PHYSICAL/ORGANIC grouping apply to all of the signs and symptoms in that section. More specific comments relative to a particular sign or symptom follow the item. As you use this Appendix, try first to think in general about the *kinds of* signs and symptoms in each grouping. Next, think about other possible signs and symptoms that might have been included. Once you have done this, consider the specific comments about particular items. Try to become familiar enough with this Appendix so that you will be able to locate easily a particular sign or symptom as you work with children. Once again, any sign or symptom of difficulty in young children may have physical causes or implications. Any child about whom you are concerned should be evaluated by a physician.

I. Physical/Organic

The signs and symptoms in this section usually reflect some
physical illness or difficulty and need the attention of a physician if the sign or symptom is severe or continuing. As a
minimum, the parents of the child and the school nurse or
building principal should be notified whenever any of these
are observed. If it is not productive for the child to remain at
school, he should be taken home either by a parent or by a
school staff person. If someone from school takes the child
home, she should be certain that there is a responsible adult at
home willing and able to accept responsibility for the child.
Children should never be sent home or left at home alone. If
the child's parent or other responsible adult cannot be located
and the problem is more than minor, the school nurse or principal should contact the child's doctor or the physician "on
call" to the school for advice.

The signs and symptoms in this section are unrelated to a
child's age and represent potentially very serious problems
(unless specific note to the contrary is made).

Difficulty in seeing. Professional eye examination needed; medical
     emergency if it occurs in a normally seeing child.
Red or swollen eyes. Possibly related to excessive crying, allergy or
     eye strain.
Frequent sties. Glandular infection.
Watery or runny eyes. If other than watery discharge, needs im-
     mediate medical attention.
Crossed eyes. Watch for a few days and check with parents.
Use of one eye more than the other. Watch for a few days and then
     check with parents.
Squinting. Watch for a few days and then check with parents.
Excessive blinking. Possible object in eye; possible nervous reaction.
Eyes differing in color. No problem unless one eye red, black, yel-
     lowish, irritated, etc.
Pupils of eyes differing in color. Not a problem if present at birth. If
     difference develops after birth, then potentially serious and
     needs medical attention.

Protruding eyes. May reflect thyroid or other physical difficulty or may be physical characteristic. Needs checking by physician.

Drooping eyelids. Can reflect muscle difficulty or may be normal physical characteristic. Needs checking by physician.

Frequently encrusted eyes. Needs medical attention. If more than minor, needs immediate attention.

Loss of hair. Possible reaction to medication; possible serious physical illness.

Excessive dandruff. Possible poor personal hygiene; possible skin problem. Usually responds to treatment; may need medical treatment.

Lack of sense of smell. May result from cold or allergies.

Runny nose. Very common; teach use of handkerchief. Problem if excessive or continuing for more than two weeks.

Constant sniffing. Fairly common; teach use of handkerchief. Possible problem if continues more than two weeks with regularity.

Frequent nose bleeds. Medical emergency if quite profuse or does not stop in 10 minutes.

Dark circles under the eyes. Probably excessive fatigue, but can reflect physical problems, e.g., iron deficiency.

Swelling of the lips. Possible allergic reaction or reaction to insect sting; possibly from accident. Medical attention needed if more than a little swelling.

Running sores around the mouth or nose. Possible viral infection; problem if continues. Needs medical attention.

Bleeding gums. Possible injury; needs to be checked by physician or dentist.

Dental cavities. Poor dental hygiene. Discuss with parents if excessive.

Missing teeth other than baby teeth. Ask the child and parent privately what happened; suspect child abuse.

Dry, cracked tongue. Needs medical attention.

Swollen tongue. Needs medical attention.

Red tongue. May result from food coloring in candy, etc.

Lack of sense of taste. Usually associated with cold or minor illness; may suggest more serious illness. Needs medical attention if it outlasts cold or minor illness or if it occurs without other minor physical symptoms. Look at tongue and ask child about possibility of injury or foreign substance in mouth.

Frequent clearing of throat. May be a nervous habit.

Pale skin. Not a problem unless extreme or atypical for specific child.

Flushed appearance. May result from getting too hot, too cold, or embarrassed; may be normal coloring.

Rash on the face. Ask school nurse to check; may need medical attention.

Frequent earaches. Apply ice; never apply heat or put anything in ear.

Trouble hearing. Requires professional hearing examination; usually child just not listening.

Bleeding from the ear. Always needs medical attention.

Odor from the ear. May reflect infection; may need medical attention.

Frequent sore throats. Child with sore throats needs to be seen by physician for possible strep infection.

Holding head to one side. Possible vision or hearing problem; other possible physical problems.

Dry, hacking cough. Medical attention if intense or continues for more than a week; suspect foreign object in throat.

Wet, productive cough. Problem if lasts for more than a week.

Blue tinge to lips, earlobes, and fingernails. Temporary reaction to getting too hot or too cold; if recurrent or does not decrease in ten minutes, possible serious physical problem.

Shortness of breath after slight exertion. Problem if occurs more than once in a month.

Squatting or sitting after short period of exercise. Not unusual; watch for other symptoms.

Asthma. Get written instructions from parents on how to treat an asthmatic attack at school, any activity or other restrictions, etc.

Barrel chest, large rib cage. Probably normal characteristic. Should be checked by physician if out of proportion to rest of body. Needs immediate medical attention if apparent change from usual size.

Holding one shoulder higher than the other. Should be checked by a physician.

Frequent stomach aches. May reflect emotional problems; medical emergency if pain is intense or prolonged.

Frequent vomiting. May reflect emotional difficulties; can be symptomatic of severe physical illness. Medical attention if no improvement in eight hours.

Excessively protruding belly. Possible malnutrition; other possible physical causes.

Appearing too fat. Possible emotional difficulty; generally results from eating too much.

Appearing too thin. Common in young children; physical problems or possible child neglect if extreme.

Gagging frequently. Possible emotional reaction.

Frequent diarrhea. Medical attention needed if any episode exceeds eight hours.

Frequent urination. Probably normal for child; may reflect emotional difficulties or physical problems.

Pain or burning during urination. Possible infection or more serious problem; needs medical attention.

Deformity of arms, hands, or fingers. Requires your sensitivity and can lead to social and emotional problems.

Missing arm, hand, or finger. Requires your sensitivity and can lead to emotional and social problems.

Missing leg, foot, or toe. Requires your sensitivity and can lead to social and emotional problems.

Cuts. May require stitches; wash clean; do not apply any medication. Apply a sterile bandage.

Burns. Medical attention needed if other than minor; apply ice or very cold water; do not apply any substance to burn, e.g., butter, commercial preparations, etc.

Excessive number of bruises. Suspect child abuse.

Lumps. Should be checked by physician unless directly resulting from minor bump or fall.

Swelling of joints. Potentially quite serious; needs medical attention.

Painful joints. Potentially quite serious; needs medical attention.

Curvature of the spine. Needs medical attention even if apparently minor.

Walking with a limp. Needs medical attention if it continues for more than a day or if it is not obviously a direct result of a minor accident.

Walking pigeon-toed. First, privately call to child's attention to see if he can stop. Needs to be checked by physician if child usually walks pigeon-toed.

Blisters on the feet. Shoes probably too small; needs medical attention if more than two or three small blisters, or if one quite large blister, or if blisters do not begin to heal in three days.

Ingrown or painful toenails. Encourage parents to see physician; they may not think it is necessary.

Rapid, jerky movements. May reflect emotional difficulty.

Frequent headaches. Headaches very uncommon in young children.

Scaly patches on the skin. Should be checked by doctor.

Rash on the skin. Should be checked by school nurse or doctor.

Boils or abscesses. Sign of infection; needs medical attention.

Frequent itching. Possible poor personal hygiene; possible nervous habit or allergy.

Unusual body odor. May reflect poor personal hygiene; can reflect physical illness. If chemical smell, suspect inhalation of fumes—child may have gotten into something potentially harmful. If cause not obviously minor, then medical attention required.

Twitching of any body part. Possible emotional difficulty; potentially serious if more than minor, occasional, and temporary.

Brief periods of blanking out. Always needs medical attention.

Complaints of double vision. First occurrence should be seen as serious.

Complaints of ringing sounds. Needs medical attention if recurring.

Deformity of the face or body. Needs your sensitivity; can cause social and emotional problems.

Paralysis of any body part. Extremely serious if it occurs in normal child and is more than temporarily a result of getting too cold.

Excessive tallness. Needs medical attention if extreme.

Excessive smallness. Some children normally quite small, but can reflect serious growing problems.

Broken Teeth. Ask child and parents privately what happened; suspect accident or child abuse.

Crooked teeth. Should be checked by a dentist.

Clumsiness. Be sure not to call the problem directly to the attention of the child or to the attention of other children.

Excessive drooling. Check with speech therapist and physician.

One leg longer than the other. May interfere with play and other activities; can cause other physical problems.

Rubbing of the eyes. Only a problem if very frequent or intense; could reflect nervous habit or emotional difficulty.

Hoarseness. A problem if extreme or frequent.

Numbness of any body part. Potentially serious if other than temporary reaction to getting too cold.

Weakness of one side of the body relative to the other. Emergency if occurs in a normally functioning child.

Fruity breath odor. May be from food or chewing gum; could be related to diabetes or other serious illness. Needs medical attention if cause not minor and obvious.

Cleft lip or palate. Can interfere with speech; can cause social and emotional problems.

Staggering. Serious if not associated with very temporary dizziness, brief minor illness, or if it occurs more frequently than seen in other children.

Convulsions or seizures. Be sure you know how to handle them when they occur.

Allergies. Be sure you supervise any medication or special "do's and don'ts" in terms of the child's activities, eating, etc.

Difficulty in swallowing. Suspect foreign object in throat.

Poor gross motor control. Many possible causes; needs medical attention.

Poor fine motor control. Many possible causes; needs medical attention.

Poor eye/hand coordination. Consult with psychologist or physical education teacher.

Congenital heart disease. Be sure to follow "do's and don'ts" for child's activities, need for rest, etc., in the written instructions from the child's physician.

Cut or scratches that don't heal. Several possible causes; needs medical attention.

Frequent broken bones. Suspect child abuse; never move a child when a broken bone is suspected or possible.

Wearing leg braces. Requires your sensitivity; may cause social and emotional problems.

Infected cuts. Needs medical attention.

Bald areas on the head. Can reflect emotional problems resulting in child pulling out hair.

Dribbling urine. Little boys without fathers or older brothers at home sometimes need to be taught how to be sure that the urine flow and dribbling are stopped after urinating. May need medical attention.

Strong odor of urine. May suggest digestive difficulties or mild to serious illness. Needs medical attention if extreme or continuing for a week or more.

Swelling of feet and/or legs. Possible injury; needs medical attention.

Excessive hair on face and arms. Can cause social and emotional difficulties.

Excessive sweating. Needs medical attention if extreme or if occurring after little or no exertion.

Change in the color of a mole. Potentially serious.

Many warts. Possible infection; should be checked by physician.

Birthmarks. Can cause social and emotional problems if very notice-able.

Change in skin color in spots. Should be checked by school nurse or doctor.

Blinking one eye independently of the other. Usually not significant unless one eye blinks excessively or other eye does not blink at all.

Left/right confusion. Common in kindergarten and first grade children; only an occasional problem by third grade.

Front/back confusion. Not common in school age children.

Talking incoherently. Other than talking too fast, a medical emergency when seen in normally coherent child; frequently accompanies severe blow to head.

Talking louder than necessary. Probably not a problem; can reflect hearing difficulty. Initially handle as a behavior problem.

Sleeping in class. Perhaps too little sleep the night before; may reflect boredom or family problems at home; a potential sign of physical illness.

History of high fever. May be related to neurological and other physical difficulties or infectious disease.

Shivering or shaking. Probably a reaction to being cold, having a cold, flu, or other minor illnesses; can be related to emotional difficulties or other serious physical problems.

Loss of balance—tripping or falling frequently. Potentially quite serious; should be checked by physician.

Sudden bursts of energy or activity. Not usually significant.

Difficulty waking up in the morning. Probably not going to bed early enough. Five and six year olds need about eleven hours sleep per night, and seven and eight year olds need about ten hours.

Drinking excessive amounts of water. Usually not significant, but needs medical attention to be sure.

Eyes that work independently. Watch for two or three weeks. If still present, professional eye examination indicated.

Extremely small hands or feet. Usually not significant; may cause problems in school activities, including classroom activities.

Constipation. Not uncommon; needs medical attention if child does not have a bowel movement in 48 hours, or if accompanied by continuing pain. Encourage parents to refrain from giving the child laxatives.

Child does not urinate. Potentially quite serious if continues for more than 24 hours. Needs medical attention.

Taking prescription medicine. Always supervise carefully children and the medicine prescribed for them by their physician; never allow child to take medication unless you are sure it was prescribed for him.

Eating odd things like paint or soap. Possible poisoning, dietary problem, physical difficulties, or emotional problems.

No right–left dominance. Not necessarily significant. Most people are right or left dominant, but some have mixed dominance.

Flat feet. School nurse should check.

Ring worm. Contagious; needs medical attention.

Straggling, dull hair. Probably reflects poor grooming and personal hygiene; can reflect physical difficulties or poor diet.

Knock-knees. Should be checked by physician.

Hard blow to the head. If swelling is noticeable, apply ice; do not allow child to walk at all. Should be checked by school nurse or physician.

Vomiting blood. Some degree of internal bleeding. Needs medical attention.

Blood in stool. Some degree of internal bleeding. Needs medical attention.

Inability to crawl. Some type of physical/developmental problem.

Cerebral Palsy. Needs your sensitivity; may cause social and emotional problems; may need special assistance and instruction.

Many burn scars. If obvious, may cause social and emotional problems; ask child and parents what happened; suspect child abuse.

Lack of depth perception. Needs professional eye examination.

Not recognizing an object by touch. Possible developmental difficulties; child may not know name for object; may reflect difficulties in sense of touch.

Inability to follow object with eyes. Needs professional eye examination.

Inability to move around or through objects. Possible developmental, vision, hearing, or other physical difficulties; perhaps child does not immediately understand what is expected.

Inability to recognize sound direction. Possible hearing loss in one or both ears; needs professional hearing examination.

Inability to sleep. Excitement about some coming event, not being tired, emotional difficulties, or possible physical problems.

Head lice. Contact school nurse and parent for follow-up; can spread to others.

Hard blow to back or stomach. Potentially quite serious; needs medical attention if pain or breathing difficulty does not diminish quite rapidly.

Dry, cracked lips. Reaction to fever or medication; other illness.

Breathing too fast. Possibly serious respiratory problem. Child may be extremely frightened or upset or quite excited. Needs immediate medical attention if increases or does not decrease in three minutes.

Deformed leg, foot, or toe. Requires your sensitivity; can lead to social and emotional problems.

Fainting. Minor to serious physical illness, being too hot, hunger; infrequently an emotional reaction. Child should be kept quiet and carefully observed for twenty–four hours.

Wheezing. Possible allergies or minor illness; possible symptom of serious illness. May have foreign object in throat; if so, try to get child to cough loose; if not successful, have physician or nurse dislodge object. Potentially quite dangerous.

Color blindness. Probably not significant; may interfere with some activities or assignments; may be a problem crossing streets at traffic lights.

Chronic disease. Consult with child's physician about implications.

Terminal disease. Be honest with child, be available to talk, and don't respond by overprotecting.

Passing large amounts of gas. A game children play; usually not significant. May reflect mild to serious physical problem if continues for more than one day.

Frequent burping. A game children sometimes play; may reflect difficulty breathing; potentially serious if extreme or continuous for more than one day.

II. Emotional/Social

The signs and symptoms in this section most commonly represent social and/or emotional difficulties in young children. With all of them, however, remember that the possibility of physical causes or significant physical implications should be thoroughly explored before any are interpreted as socially or emotionally based. Similarly, all of the signs and symptoms in this section can directly or indirectly reflect serious learning or developmental problems manifesting themselves through social and emotional problems. After the possibility of physical problems is excluded and any learning and developmental difficulties have been thoroughly explored, all of these signs and symptoms should be dealt with within the context of your relationship with the child and in terms of your understanding of his behavior. Children manifesting problematic behavior need to experience firm but gentle limits in the context of a caring and concerned relationship. If the behavior needs to be contained, the child must experience negative consequences as a direct result of the behavior. When certain behavior is to be encouraged, the child must experience a desirable payoff for behaving in the desired way. These positive and negative consequences come through your awareness of and control of both the child's school environment and your relationship with him or her.

As you consider these signs and symptoms, think first in terms of whether you want to limit particular behavior through firmness, disapproval, and negative consequences or to encourage behavior through approval and positive consequences. Next, think in terms of whether the child needs more emotional closeness or more emotional distance. Finally, develop a consistent plan for relating to the child and dealing with his behavior which you can, in fact, pursue for several weeks or months if necessary. In addition, consider how you will counsel the child's parents to deal with him at home. Once you and the parents have begun to work cooperatively and consistently with the child, consider what other school or community resources might be useful. You will also want to discuss the child's symptoms with the school counselor or psychologist, if available. If parental cooperation cannot be elicited, you can still think about what school and community resources might be useful.

The signs and symptoms are followed by comments which should be added to these general comments as you consider the specific symptom. Also, think beyond this list to other difficulties children may have which might reflect social or emotional problems. The signs and symptoms in this section generally tend to be somewhat more significant in first graders than in kindergarten-age children, more significant in second graders than in first graders, etc. Generally, the younger the child is when the teacher starts consistent work on the difficulty, the easier it will be to help him, and the more quickly improvement will be seen.

Shaking, trembling hands. Often suggests anxiety, more rarely a central nervous system disorder; may reflect minor to serious physical illness.

— *Very slow movement.* May reflect emotional withdrawal and a lack of social and emotional involvement.

Biting of fingernails. Not uncommon; start by telling child to stop it. Consider fearfulness or overemphasis on achievement.

— *Picking at, scratching, or pinching self.* Not uncommon; consider restlessness, boredom, learning problems, overemphasis on achievement.

Pulling out hair. Consider anger, frustration, learning problems, social problems.

Thumb sucking. Not uncommon; try telling child to stop it; possible uncertainty of child about relationship with you or other children.

— *Lack of facial expression.* May reflect a lack of social and emotional involvement.

— *Grimacing.* Not uncommon; if noticed several times a day may reflect problem. Ask child in private why he makes faces.

Pulling at the ears. Probably not significant; may reflect some tension or emotional/social discomfort; suspect earache or itching.

Gritting of the teeth. Consider anger, intense concentration, frustration, tension; privately ask child if he knows why.

Being the oldest in the class. Generally not significant unless two years or more older; watch for teasing or rejection from other children.

— *Not knowing how to play with others.* Consult with physical education teacher; sometimes helps to put child with a child having better play and social skills.

Chewing the inside of the cheek. May just be nervous habit; ask child to stop.

Sucking teeth or tongue. May just be nervous habit; ask child to stop.

Chewing lips. May just be nervous habit; ask child to stop.

Twisting hair. Usually not significant.

Chewing hair. Usually not significant.

Not sharing. Talk privately with child about problem; channel other children into handling problem unless accompanied by other symptoms.

Does not participate in organized games. Consider emotional withdrawal, social isolation, lack of play skills.

Fear of getting hurt when playing. May be due to overprotection; gently encourage child to participate.

Not knowing how to lose. Talk with child about problem; let other children deal with the problem.

Preferring to be alone. May reflect isolation or withdrawal; if extreme, needs professional psychological attention.

Having few friends. Help child think about why others do not want to be friends with him or her.

Having no friends. Involve the child with you, then involve other children with you and child.

Refusal to talk to teacher. Start very, very gently.

Unwillingness to talk in front of class. Start with encouraging child to answer oral questions, even if he or she gives only one word answers.

Talking too much. Privately talk to child about problem; give positive consequences when child is quiet or brief.

Talking only in a whisper. May reflect fearfulness, emotional and social withdrawal.

Making strange noises. Not uncommon; handle as behavior problem.

Insisting on being first. Not uncommon; handle as behavior problem.

Bullying other children. Talk privately with child about problem; usually a bid for attention and social approval; handle very gently as behavior problem.

Starting fights. Not unusual if infrequent; if frequent then handle as behavior problem.

Cruelty to other children. Talk privately with child; arrange psychological evaluation; work gently but firmly with child.

Cruelty to animals. Talk privately with child; arrange psychological evaluation; work gently but firmly with child.

Temper tantrums. Child usually reponds to being ignored; firmly tell him to stop. Will help to consistently remove child from situation until calm.

Playing with matches. Initially respond with strong negative response; increase closeness and positive payoff in relationship.

Crying frequently. Start with closeness and increase positive payoff in relationship. At same time insist firmly that child stop crying. Ask child privately about problem.

Crying when spoken to. Increase gentleness and closeness in relationship; suspect child abuse or overly harsh parenting.

Refusing to look at others. Increase positive payoff in relationship; try to assign child special and desirable tasks.

Fear of men. Not necessarily significant; move slowly and gently with relationship.

Fear of women. Not necessarily significant; move slowly and gently with relationship.

Swearing. May be used at home; talk privately to child about appropriate school behavior.

Unusual fears. Ask privately about past "scary" events; initially encourage and gradually insist that child respond in spite of fear.

Pouting. Ignore if possible.

Lying. Increase closeness in relationship; treat as behavior problem.

Cheating. Increase closeness in relationship; consider overemphasis on success; gently handle as behavior problem.

Stealing. Increase closeness in relationship; handle as behavior problem.

Mood swings. Not uncommon; if extreme arrange psychological or psychiatric evaluation.

Being made fun of by others. Tell other children to stop.

Being upset by change in routine. Gently encourage and gradually insist that child accept change as part of life.

Wanting all the teacher's attention. Start with a lot of closeness in relationship; encourage relationships with children and other adults at school; gradually decrease emotional closeness in relationship.

Being very jealous. Talk privately with child about problem; generally ignore problem.

Possessiveness. Talk privately with child about problem; gently encourage child to be more sharing.

Feeling incapable of doing work. First consider why child thinks he cannot do work.

Feeling defeated before starting work. Place emphasis on getting started, with minimal attention to getting finished.

Feeling no good. Gradually build up self-esteem with success experiences.

— *Listless approach to work.* Look for distractions such as daydreaming, or emotional problems at home, tiredness, or physical problems.

— *Difficulty in concentrating.* First wonder why child might not want to concentrate.

— *Short attention span.* First consider why child might not want to pay attention; gently treat as behavior problem.

Fear of getting dirty. Start by asking child privately about problem.

Fear of teacher. Start with more emotional distance and work gradually to less emotional distance in relationship.

Fear of school. Ask child privately about problem; may reflect fear of separating from home.

Fear of failure. Suspect excessive emphasis on success, excessive experiences with failure.

— *Unfriendliness.* Start by being friendly toward and interested in child despite his or her unfriendliness.

— *Domineering attitude.* Be sure not to respond with anger or a dominating attitude of your own.

Much exaggeration. Talk privately to child about problem; let him know that you know that he is exaggerating.

Always wanting to touch another child or the teacher. Start with closeness in the relationship, touching back but gradually and gently discouraging the behavior.

— *Giving up easily.* Suspect a history of failure, excessive emphasis on achievement, unreasonable expectations on your part.

— *Disrupting the class.* Talk privately with child about problem and treat as behavior problem.

— *Giggling or laughing for no apparent reason.* May reflect serious emotional problems if frequent or continuing.

— *Put down of others.* Start by letting other children deal with the problem.

Being very critical of self. Encourage child and call attention to achievements and good points; be careful not to disagree with child when he or she accurately evaluates performance or achievement.

— *Being very critical of others.* Let other children deal with the problem.

— *Inability to accept criticism.* Treat reaction to criticism as behavior problem; suspect overemphasis on achievement or success; try making criticism milder and more gentle.

Not following school rules. First ask child privately about problem.

Underactivity. Suspect fear, emotional and social withdrawal; ask child privately about problem.

Inflicting pain on self. Potentially quite serious if recurs after initial experience of pain.

Hallucinations. Requires immediate medical attention.

Having only one friend. Perhaps talk privately with child and friend about why no other friends.

Not liking to be touched. Unusual in small children; be alert to other academic, social, or emotional problems.

Always thinking he/she is ill. Treat with firmness as a behavior problem.

Drumming fingers. Usually not significant; tell child to stop.

Not getting angry or laughing. Suspect emotional withdrawal and a lack of social and emotional involvement.

Fearing tests. Not uncommon; teach child a positive attitude toward tests.

Impulsiveness. Initially treat as behavior problem.

Removing part of clothes. Talk privately with child about problem.

Masturbating at school. Treat as normal behavior problem.

Not seeing consequences. Talk with child about problem; make positive or negative consequences more immediate and specific.

Teacher/child incompatibility. First talk with child about problem; gently and sincerely see if he or she has any ideas.

Not learning from previous experiences. Child may need clarification of what happened.

Making up stories to enhance own position.

Throwing things. Start by telling child to stop it.

Screaming. Start by telling child to stop it; say child's name and talk softly. Child may quiet down to hear you.

Kicking. Start by telling child to stop it.

Blackmailing other children. Most important to first consider nature of threat—injury? telling on child?

Biting. Start by telling child to stop it; your biting child is not appropriate even if it does deter behavior.

Sitting in one position for long periods. Not necessarily significant unless for half hour or more; may suggest emotional withdrawal.

Breaking other's things. Talk to child about problem; give child a way to replace object if possible; encourage apology.

Hiding other's things. Initially treat as behavior problem.

Hearing voices. Observe child closely; potentially extremely serious.

Compulsive lying. Not uncommon in small children; treat as behavior problem.

Tattling. Very difficult problem for teacher; try class discussion about what should be reported to teacher and what is just an attempt to get other kids into trouble. Usually encourage tattling child to handle problem by himself; consider both tattling child and reported situation before responding.

Wandering away. Insist that child listen to you, stay with group, and not go off alone; discuss dangers and reasons.

Thinking people do not like him or her. Not uncommon if only occasional; potentially serious if continuous.

Thinking people are trying to hurt him. Consider the possibility that they are; possibly a fearful and socially withdrawn child.

Thinking he or she is better than anyone else. Generally let other children deal with the problem.

Thinking he or she is not as good as others.

Hiding in corner or closet. Bring child back with group; look for other symptoms.

Putting things in the nose. Talk with child of possible consequences. Tell child to stop.

Putting things in the ears. Talk with child of possible consequences. Tell child to stop.

Defying authority. Talk privately with child; defiance may be justified.

Disagreeableness. Generally not significant.

Overreacting. Treat the excess as behavior problem. Consider possible emotional or social problems.

Inability to make a choice. Start by forcing minor choices—choose white cookie or brown cookie or go without; avoid "this one would be nice"; handle very gently.

Playing only with older children. Intellectually advanced children may relate better to children a year or two older.

Playing only with younger children. Intellectually slower children may prefer children a year or two younger; may reflect problem in social skills and involvement.

Having many superstitions. Ignore unless really interferes with activities and performance; discuss with parents.

Pack ratting and saving everything. Probably not significant.

Forced or artificial laughing. Probably not significant; may be a problem of social awareness and experience.

Boys having feminine mannerisms. Probably not significant; may need more relationships with men and boys.

Girls having masculine mannerisms. Probably not significant; may need more relationships with women and girls.

Carrying dangerous objects such as knife. Ask child privately why; perhaps need for protection is justified. If no reasonable need, then treat as behavior problem; if fears are justified, help child with the problem.

Cracking knuckles. Not significant; tell child to stop.

Kissing everyone, even relative strangers. Very gently and gradually discourage behavior; talk privately with child about dangers with *some* strangers.

Lying in fetal position when upset. Very gently treat as behavior problem.

Bringing security blanket to school. Ignore for two or three days; privately mention problem to child once a day for two or three days, then take blanket away from child when brought to school.

Sniffing glue. Talk with child and strongly discourage behavior first time; if it occurs again, professional counseling needed.

Using dope or unprescribed drugs. Immediate arrangements for counseling necessary.

Using alcohol. If amounts more than minor and very occasional, professional counseling is needed.

Smoking cigarettes. Discuss problem with child; treat as behavior problem. Professional counseling may be indicated.

Trying to buy friends. Start by talking to child about problem.

Compulsive neatness. Gently discourage excess in behavior.

Feeling unloved. Not significant if only occasional; if continuing, then work through your relationship with the child.

Feeling unlovable. Potentially quite serious if it does not gradually improve.

Sarcasm. Initially ignore, then gradually treat as behavior problem.

Secretiveness. Suspect emotional and social withdrawal.

Attempting suicide. Needs immediate mental health treatment.

Threatening suicide. Give emotional support and reassurance; mental health treatment probably needed.

Seriously injuring someone else. It may really have been an accident; if intentional or repeated, then professional counseling needed.

Thinking he or she is someone else. Not uncommon if child is pretending; if child seriously believes, then immediate mental health treatment required.

Preoccupation with death. May be a temporary reaction to death of pet, friend, or family member, but is potentially serious if it continues more than three or four weeks.

Wetting or soiling self. Child may be reluctant to use or ask to use toilet; not significant if occurs very occasionally; usually child just not responding soon enough to physical message of needing to use toilet. May reflect serious emotional problems.

Being youngest in class. Generally not significant; watch for other symptoms.

Withdrawal. Gently encourage more interaction.

Preferring to talk only to teacher. Talk with child about problem.

Making strange faces. Probably not significant; may reflect physical or emotional discomfort; may need to use toilet.

Crying spells. Start by asking child about problem; he may really have physical pain or discomfort. Talk quietly; child may quiet down to hear you.

III. Academic/Classroom

The signs and symptoms in this section generally represent intellectual, developmental, and other specific learning difficulties. In addition, they can indicate minor to serious physical problems and can be indirect manifestations of social and emotional difficulties. It is important to evaluate thoroughly possible physical, social, and emotional origins and implications as you consider the academic/classroom implications of these signs and symptoms. If possible, children reflecting these signs and symptoms should have both a thorough physical and psychological evaluation. If the latter is not possible, it will help for you to evaluate the child through developing achievement levels and isolating performance problems. You can evaluate his reading by starting with kindergarten material and gradually trying more difficult material until the child begins to have problems. The same approach can be used to determine the arithmetic level. In addition, watch for variability in a child's performance and ability. For example, does he do better on some kinds of things than others? Does he do better some days than others? Any time a child experiences academic/classroom difficulty, reduce the difficulty and complexity of the task until the child can perform without difficulty. Starting at that point, gradually increase the difficulty and complexity of work, moving with the child at his or her performance level.

If a child is unable to perform at even a minimally difficult level, a thorough psychological evaluation is critically important. Before coming to this conclusion, though, consider alternative ways of teaching the child. You can perhaps try the multi-sensory approach discussed in chapter two, carefully attending to what the child can do or is interested in doing and then encouraging and working with those areas, or anything else you can think of which might induce or encourage school learning. Do not overlook the possibility of talking with other teachers or school personnel (including psychologist, counselor, and nurse) who may have experience with this child or another with the same difficulty. All children can learn (at some level) about everything taught in elementary school.

In addition, it is important for you to be patient, persistent, imaginative, innovative, and confident that the child will learn if you and he keep trying in a positive and optimistic atmosphere. The signs and symptoms in this section tend to be more significant the older the child is. For example, they tend to be more significant in third graders than in second graders, in second graders than in first graders, and in first graders than in kindergarten-age children. Nonetheless, you should be critically concerned about a child who is unsuccessful in any of these grades. The argument that the child is too immature or not ready for school is seldom an adequate explanation. This is, in effect, an attempt to blame the child for the problem. He probably will not just grow out of it but very likely has a problem needing careful and caring evaluation and attention.

In addition to these general comments, some specific comments are included after many of the signs and symptoms. These comments should be combined with the general comments as you consider the specific signs and symptoms in this section. Finally, note that to say that a child is hyperactive does not really say anything particularly helpful about him. I hope your understanding of a specific child will be substantially more specific and explanatory. The term "hyperactive" has been used and misused so much that it has, for the most part, become a meaningless term frequently used to the actual detriment of children.

Sound substitutions. Probably not significant unless the child has fairly consistent difficulty with specific sounds, especially initial word sounds. Suspect hearing and/or speech difficulty; speak distinctly.

Talking in a monotone. Probably not significant; suspect hearing difficulty or emotional withdrawal.

Lisping. Quite serious if speech cannot be fairly easily understood; speech and hearing evaluation necessary if more than minimally present when child is seven years old.

Stuttering or stammering. Should only occasionally be seen in child of seven years or more; sometimes related to child being quite excited or talking too fast. Be patient and do not call a lot of attention to the problem.

Trouble identifying body parts. Treat initially as a simple learning problem.

Doing the same thing over and over. Probably not significant and related to enjoying activity or attempting to master it; may reflect emotional withdrawal or difficulty with social relationships.

Variation in quality and quantity of work. Some variation normal; occasional extreme variation fairly common. If extreme and continuing, consider physical or emotional problems.

Difficulty in remembering. Perhaps child does not really understand or know how to do the work. Real memory problems are uncommon; perhaps child prefers not to remember or sees no payoff in remembering.

Difficulty in reproducing simple shapes. Handle initially as a simple learning problem; try multi-sensory approach.

Difficulty completing assigned work. Assignment may be too long; no value in assigning child more work or more difficult work than he can or will do.

Overactivity. Bright and socially involved children frequently seem overactive; bored or underachieving children sometimes seem overactive. All children tend to seem either overactive or underactive at times. Start by telling child to stand still, sit still, or be still.

Squirming a lot. May need to use toilet, may be just excited; what makes the difference is if child is learning.

Distractibility. You, school work, and the assigned task may not be very interesting.

Daydreaming. We all daydream a lot. Why aren't you and school work more interesting?

Babytalk. Start by ignoring as child is exposed to other children and adults at school; gradually insist that child speak more appropriately.

Teacher ridiculing child. Always inappropriate.

Child achieving below ability level. A very complex problem; start with an evaluation of achievement levels and encourage continuing achievement. More than a little emphasis on "you can do better" may be quite frustrating and destructive to child. Place emphasis on achieving a little more and a little better instead of on some vague estimate of ultimate potential or ability.

Not enjoying learning. Why haven't you and other adults made learning seem more fun and interesting?

Sudden deterioration in quality of work. A complex problem; suspect physical, emotional, social, or family difficulties. Ask child about problem, be patient for two or three days, and then gradually insist that child's performance return to previous level.

Size of class. Frequently a real issue for teachers and for education in general; never a legitimate reason for a child not learning and developing.

Lagging behind in development. Child needs psychological and physical evaluation; may need special teaching approaches and expectations.

Earlier than usual development. If socially and academically advanced, the child may need somewhat more advanced opportunities and experiences. Double promotions or skipping grades rarely a good idea and should follow very thorough and careful evaluation and thought.

Excelling only in certain areas. Most children achieve at approximately the same level in all areas. A child who does quite well at some things and extremely well at a few things probably has no problem. A child who does relatively poorly in some specific areas needs help with those areas.

Slow learning. Never equate with *can't* learn.

Reversing numbers. Common in five and six year old children; initially treat as simple learning problem.

Reversing letters. Common in five and six year old children; initially treat as simple learning problem.

Reversing words. Common in five and six year old children; initially treat as simple learning problem.

Inability to repeat three numbers in sequence. Initially treat as simple learning problem in kindergarten age children; symptom should gradually disappear or only be very occasional by first grade.

Not hearing differences in sounds. A problem only if usual and continuing; suspect hearing difficulty; speak very distinctly when talking with child.

Limited vocabulary. Treat initially as a simple learning problem.

Not working independently. Try seating child away from others.

Not using time well. Try breaking tasks or assignments into smaller and less complex units.

Not organizing materials. A skill not usually taught; perhaps a classroom discussion would give children ideas on how to organize.

Inability to communicate ideas. Start by trying seriously to understand what child is saying. Verbalize his ideas in clear terms, and encourage him to express ideas more clearly. It may be a vocabulary problem, or may reflect some emotional withdrawal.

Being brighter than average. Can sometimes be a social liability; can be a real problem if teacher is not also brighter than average.

Learning more rapidly than other children. May result in child being somewhat bored and disruptive. He may be reluctant to complete assignments that are too easy and may benefit from a "quick finishers corner" with interesting games and other materials. He needs to learn to occupy himself and not disrupt others.

Boredom—no challenge. Being bored is a problem the child needs to learn to deal with in a way that does not disrupt or interfere with others. Puzzle books or special projects will be appreciated by child.

Memory lapses. We all forget or don't remember some things sometimes. The child may not have understood or known how, or perhaps was just not interested, or was interested in other things. Can be a very serious problem.

Excusing own poor performance. The excuse may be legitimate or justified. There may be too much emphasis on doing well. If excuses are not legitimate, then gradually insist that the child do better despite protests and excuses.

Not understanding numbers. Initially treat as simple learning problem.

Inability to memorize. May relate to difficulty concentrating, or to not understanding material to be memorized, or disinterest.

Not seeing similarities or differences. May reflect delayed conceptual development; initially treat as simple learning problem.

Poor penmanship. First consider the possibility that your standard is unreasonable or somewhat compulsive.

Speaking in sing-song rhythm. Consider the possibility of hearing or speech production problems.

Inability to speak. When a child does not talk or make noise, consider possibility that he or she either can't talk, has some emotional or social reason for not talking, or has some significant hearing or speech production difficulties.

Mouthing words without sound. Very common in children having some difficulty processing auditory or visual material. Having difficulty understanding what is being said or making a real effort to understand or remember what is being said is not necessarily unusual or significant. Gently call behavior to child's attention; look carefully for other symptoms.

Mumbling. Suspect fearfulness or apprehension. It may just be a bad verbal habit or may reflect lack of confidence in own ideas. Gently encourage child to speak louder and more clearly.

Skipping words in reading. Encourage child to read a little more slowly and carefully. Handle in a very gentle way and suspect the possibility of vision problems.

Skipping lines in reading. Encourage child to read more slowly and carefully. Handle very gently and suspect possible vision problems.

Repeating words or lines in reading. Encourage child to read more slowly and carefully; suspect possible vision problem. Repeating or skipping words or lines is not particularly uncommon as children learn to read.

Reading too fast to comprehend. Encourage child to slow down and read more carefully, and occasionally ask child to explain what he has read. Do not give undue emphasis to fast reading or undue attention to children who read fast. Set an amount of time for reading activities and avoid situations that encourage rapid reading in order to get to more desirable activities sooner.

Substituting words. Children who do this when talking usually reflect a somewhat limited vocabulary. Children doing this when reading usually are reading too fast, guessing or reflecting sight reading inaccuracies. Encourage child to slow down and read more carefully; suspect vision difficulties.

Adding extra words when reading. Usually reflects anticipation of what is written; encourage child to read more slowly and accurately.

Not recalling a story in sequence. Encourage child to read more slowly and to think about the topic or story as he reads. This also applies to picture stories. Difficulties with reading may interfere with understanding and remembering.

Lack of rhythm. With patience and interest initially treat as simple learning problem.

Inability to sound out words. Initially suspect simple learning problem with alphabet, letter sounds, or initial word sounds. Suspect hearing or vision difficulties.

Inability to handle money. May reflect undeveloped sense of value of money; may reflect difficulty with numbers and number concepts; probably reflects lack of experience with having and using money.

Lack of common sense. Remember that common sense is a complicated set of ideas, behavior, insights, etc., which have to be learned through teaching and experience.

Unawareness of current events and the world. Child's exposure and experience probably limited. Needs to spend more time with people who talk about current events and the world and more experiences where current events and the extended world have relevance to him.

Lack of a concept of time. Initially treat as simple learning problem.

Not finishing sentences. Perhaps child not used to talking with people who listen long enough or with enough interest to allow time for use of complete sentences; may reflect some social or emotional discomfort in expressing ideas.

Coloring only in black. Child may be color-blind; child may just like black; may reflect emotional difficulties.

Drawing or coloring only destructive pictures. Your interpretation may be somewhat biased. Child may be somewhat preoccupied with violence and aggression, or perhaps he has not thought of anything else to draw. Pictures may reflect a negative or destructive self-image or life orientation.

Answering inappropriately. May reflect lack of understanding, a problem in social awareness and skills, or a hearing problem.

IV. Environmental/Family

As we begin to think about the symptoms in this section, it is important to emphasize initially the fact that most parents love and care about their children, are vitally concerned about their welfare and well-being, and understand them as individuals far better than we do. Any time we are inclined to blame a child's parents or wonder why they do not relate and respond to the child differently, we should first think about our own motivations and justifications for such thoughts. The real likelihood is that the parents are doing as well with him as can reasonably be expected. Of course, some parents do neglect, abuse, misunderstand, and mistreat children. They are very much in the minority, though. Generally, the problems children are having will receive the combined thought and effort of the teacher, the parents, and the child. Our general focus should be less on why things are as they are and more on how to improve the situation for the child. As we talk with parents, this positive orientation is extremely important.

Some of the items in this section do not represent real problems in the sense that something needs to be changed. Rather, they represent situations which may cause the child to have unusual difficulties at school. In these cases, it is important for you to be aware of and understand the situation and its possible implications for the child. Given this awareness you can then best help the child through your relationship with him and through the influence you hold over his environment at school. Some of the signs and symptoms in this section require the involvement of outside agencies, professionals, and community authorities. Here it is critically important that you first solicit the involvement and cooperation of the parents. This will enable you to be more familiar with the overall situation and more sure about your understanding of the problem. With a few signs and symptoms and with a few parents, it will be necessary for you to initiate outside intervention with or without their cooperation. In those situations, it is very important to focus on the child and his needs and ultimate welfare. If this perspective is lost, it may be considerably easier to simply do nothing. If outside intervention is necessary and if you do nothing, the child may be the ultimate victim of your negligence.

Some of the signs and symptoms in this section are followed by comments which should be added to these general comments. In addition, the general comments at the beginning of Sections I, II, and III of this Appendix also apply to this section.

Fear of parents. Being careful not to make a "big deal" out of the discussion, you can gently and confidentially ask child about problem.

Fear of brothers or sisters. Ask child about problem; very gently and indirectly bring problem up with child's parents.

Poor school attendance. Parents may have difficulties which make it hard to get child to school. Helping them may in turn help child.

Frequent tardiness. Parents may send child on time but child may just not be getting there on time.

Coming to school hungry. Talk with child and parents about problem.

Unavailability of food at home. Talk with parents; may need to involve child welfare authorities. Check on free school lunches.

Picky or fussy eating. Probably not significant.

Clothing too small or too tight. Rapidly growing children frequently outgrow clothing before it is worn out; not a problem unless extreme.

Clothing too big. May have been given to family by someone or handed down from older brothers or sisters; not a problem unless extreme.

Clothing inappropriate for weather. Talk with child and parents; may reflect limited financial resources.

Limited cultural background. May need special experiences and help at school.

Coming from home where another language is spoken. May cause some difficulty reading and talking. Do not confuse with legitimate learning problem.

Coming from a broken home. Not necessarily a problem.

Separation from siblings. Sometimes seen with foster children, children living in institutions, children separated from siblings due to death or disability of parents, etc. Watch for specific symptoms at school such as emotional difficulties, social problems, learning problems, etc.

Lack of discipline at home. Child will tend to have difficulty accepting rules, limits, restrictions, etc. at school.

Lack of love at home. Child needs close, healthy relationship with you; overprotection and excessive sympathy on your part will not help.

Abuse by parents. If you even suspect abuse, you are obligated to report your concern to school officials and local child welfare officials.

Abuse by others at home. If you even suspect abuse, you are obligated to report your concern to school officials and local child welfare authorities.

Often being left alone. If you think this constitutes neglect of the child, discuss with parents. Report to school and child welfare authorities if your concern continues.

Being allowed to stay up very late. If more than occasional, discuss with child and parents.

Having to work very hard at home. May result in not having time for homework, play, rest, etc.

Overprotection by parents. Approach parents gently about problem.

Not being allowed to make decisions. Encourage decision-making at school. Approach parents gently about problem.

Not being allowed to play with other children. Be sure to talk with child's parents about problem and listen to their explanations.

Having no toys. May reflect limited financial resources; approach parents gently about problem.

Having no toys appropriate for age. Discuss with parents.

Never being read to. Not necessarily a problem.

Different ethnic background. You may need to help other children with their reactions or patterns of relating to the child.

Different family traditions. Provide recognition and acceptance of traditions.

Frequent school changes. Potentially quite confusing to child. Important to assess child's achievement level in various subjects and teach basics which may have been missed.

Frequent moves. Along with school and classroom problems, may also cause some social and emotional difficulties.

Parents drinking heavily. May contribute to abuse and neglect. If so, then you are obligated to report to school and child welfare authorities.

Parents abuse of drugs. May contribute to abuse and neglect. If so, then you are obligated to report to school and child welfare authorities.

Parental rejection of child. Child may feel unworthy or may seek acceptance elsewhere, including from unacceptable persons or situations.

Dirty home. Clean is relative to your standards. Unless home is a health hazard, probably not significant.

Home lacking in conveniences. Probably not significant.

Parents overdemanding. Child may react by refusing to cooperate.

Different religion than most children. Not significant. Be sure that you and everyone else at school shows respect for child's beliefs and values.

Coming from a very large family. Not significant.

Being an only child. May have more than usual difficulty with social relationships.

Blind parents. Not significant.

Deaf parents. Probably not significant; may contribute to somewhat delayed speech development.

Parents with severe speech impediment. Probably not significant; may contribute to problematic speech development.

Chronic illness in the family. Generally not significant; may contribute to attendance or adjustment problems.

Death in family. May have a temporary negative effect on child's social and emotional adjustment, school performance, etc.

Older than average parents. May actually be advantage for child in terms of economic situation, family stability.

Younger than average parents. May contribute to problems in terms of economic situation and stability of family; not necessarily significant.

Illegitimacy. Probably not significant. May affect attitude toward child of other family members; may cause some negative comments from other children, such as, "you don't have any father/mother." Be alert to problems if they occur, but do not assume that there will be problems.

Clothes inappropriate for school. Find out why; suggest what is appropriate.

Extreme wealth. May lead to some negative social attention from other children; adults at school may be inclined to give child more favored status.

Extreme poverty. Can contribute to a multitude of difficulties directly related to not having enough money. The only really bad thing about being poor is not having enough money.

Racial isolation. Especially in rural schools, it is not uncommon to find only one or two racially different children in a class or school. They may then be subjected to isolation and prejudice. You should be alert to any developing problems between them and the other children—and adults—at school.

Parent in jail. May affect child's self-concept and value placed on self; may result in negative social attention from other children and adults at school.

Socially unacceptable parent, e.g., loose morals. May cause prejudice or other negative social attention from other children or adults.

Poor table manners. School is appropriate place to teach this as well as other social behavior.

Moving from city to country or vice versa. No significance other than problems normally associated with being a new child in a school, e.g., having to make new friends, having to learn a new routine, perhaps having to use learning series different from one used before.

Being adopted. Generally not significant. If child was placed for adoption as a result of abuse or neglect, then those negative situations may have a carry-over effect to his present adjustment—emotionally, socially, academically, and physically.

Retarded sibling. Probably not significant.

Parents keeping child out of school. First find out why. If no reasonable or acceptable explanation, then insist that child be sent to school. If no improvement in attendance, then involve school officials and child welfare authorities if necessary.

Having been sexually molested. If being appropriately handled, then treat child as "normal." Such experiences may affect social and emotional adjustment as well as negatively affect classroom performance. If not being appropriately handled, then immediately involve school officials and child welfare authorities.

Parents not accepting child's limitations. First discuss problem with parents, initiating conversation in terms of child's strengths and abilities, and discussing child's limitations with tact and sensitivity. Be sure that you accept child's limitations only after developing certainty that he really does have the suspected limitations. It is probably better to expect a little too much of the child than to expect too little.

Crying when leaving mother. Gently but firmly insist that child separate from mother and that mother leave the school; assure child that arrangements have already been made for him to go home at the end of the school day; quickly try to involve child with other children or activities.

Parents being negative with child. Talk with parents about problem. Start by talking about child's strengths and assets, and very gently discourage their negative orientation to child.

Child blaming self for parent's problems. Talk with parents to see if they blame child. If so, then professional counseling probably indicated. If not, perhaps they can help child understand what causes problems. Be sure you let child know that you definitely do not think problems at home are his fault.

Sudden change in financial situation. May cause difficulty if change is from relatively better to relatively worse. Child may undergo some confusion and adjustment difficulties related to life-style changes, availability of opportunities, and other changes related to not having as much money.

Always being compared to siblings. If this occurs with adults at school, then try to minimize comparisons. Some positive comparisons may have good effect on child. May be necessary to talk with child's parents about the problem.

Coming to school much too early. Talk with parents to see if there is some reason why they need to send child so early.

Loitering around after closing. First talk with child about problem. There may be some reason why he does not want to go home immediately.

Apathetic or unresponsive parents. The first step is to be sure that you have tried to get their involvement in a positive and en-couraging way. Parental disinterest is uncommon; keep work-ing with them in an encouraging and enthusiastic way.

Parents becoming aggressive when approached about child's prob-lem. Be sure not to react with aggression or anger. Emphasize child's good points, just quietly listen until they have finished their angry comments, and then say something like "you surely have a nice son or daughter whom I want to understand better and I hope you will be able to help me with that."

Parents telling child he is stupid. Be sure that your approach to them does not have the effect of accusing them of being stupid for treating their child that way. Talk with parents about child's strengths and good points, get them to verbalize child's good points, and encourage them to tell child about both positives and negatives.

Being physically dirty. Children get quite dirty even between home and school in the morning. Talk with child and child's parents about problem.

APPENDIX II

Early Identification
Index

Starting in Chapter One, we have been developing the concept of a "symptom profile" for individual children. Figure 11 consolidates the symptom profiles developed in Chapters Two through Nine into an Early Identification Index that follows the format developed for the individual symptom profiles. In the top portion of the Early Identification Index, space is provided to enter specific data on individual children, along with data about the teacher of the child. The column headings for the Early Identification Index are the same as those for the symptom profiles in earlier chapters. Down the left-hand column, the hundred most significant signs and symptoms of early childhood difficulty observable by teachers at school are listed. In the remaining five columns, Xs have been placed, noting those categories which have the highest probability of representing a "causal" relationship to the particular sign or symptom. Of course, other categories may be causally related; but the categories in which an X appears are the "most significant" in a probability sense.

The Early Identification Index can be utilized by classroom teachers and within school systems in at least two ways. First, individual classroom teachers can use the index as a "symptom profile sheet" for specific children. If you have a child in your class about whom you are specifically concerned, you can complete the Early Identification Index and use it as a symptom profile for that child as you develop your treatment plan for him or her. In addition, it is recommended that you complete an Early Identification Index form for each child in your class about three or four weeks after the beginning of the school year. This will enable you systematically to consider each child in your class in terms of special problems and needs. About four months after the beginning of school, then, you can review the "symptom profile" for each child to see what progress is being made in reference to his or her difficulties, whether or not new problems have developed, and whether or not existing problems have become more complex. It is suggested that you use one color ink or pencil when the symptom profiles are completed at the beginning of the year and a different color the second or third time the profiles are reviewed. The different colors would, then, make it clear how the child is progressing, how the symptom pattern is changing, etc. Further, completing a symptom profile for each child two or three times a year will allow you to "identify" children with special needs and problems. This will be of real value to specific children. In addition, it will be a convenient way of fulfilling your professional and legal responsibility to identify "special needs" children.

In addition to the Early Identification Index being used with individual children and within individual classrooms, it has a strong potential as a very useful tool when used on a school-wide or school system-wide basis. For example, an Early Identification Index sheet could be completed by individual classroom teachers for all of the children, kindergarten through third grade, within a school or school system. The information developed by each classroom teacher about these children would be directly applicable to his or her work with them. In addition, the data can be collected and analyzed for the whole school or school system. At a less inclusive level, individual classroom teachers could forward Early Identification Index sheets on specific children who are having learning, social, emotional, environmental, or physical/organic problems. The data could be collected in part based on specific needs of the school. For example, the school could collect data on all of the children with learning problems.

If the data is collected on this partial basis, the school or school system can develop programming around the needs of these specific children. Also, the data will help in determining the extent of particular types of difficulties. If the data is collected on a universal basis within each school or school system, the aggregate data can be analyzed to develop a "symptom profile" for the entire school.

The form of the Early Identification Index is quite suitable for computer analysis. Each child's sheet should be coded so as to make it possible to identify the specific child. The data at the top of the sheet can be coded and entered. Similarly, each item on the index can be coded, with category references subcoded. For example, the first item could be coded "1." The five separate categories would then be coded 1.1, 1.2, 1.3, 1.4, and 1.5. This would allow for straight arithmetical counting of the prevalence of specific symptoms and specific causal components. Computer analysis could also be utilized to examine causal patterns, symptom patterns, the interrelatedness of symptoms with other symptoms, symptoms with causal patterns, and causes with other causes. In addition, these data can be analyzed in terms of their relatedness to and interrelatedness with the data developed at the top of the sheet.

At a minimum, a symptom profile could be developed for a school or school system by entering on a single sheet the number of children with a specific symptom. Across the columns, then, that number could be distributed in terms of causal categories. When this process is completed for all of the children using all one hundred signs and symptoms, careful visual or electronic analysis will clearly suggest those problems most needing intervention or remediation. Similarly, the summary sheet would suggest causal areas within which such intervention or remediation should occur. This process would allow administrators to develop a comprehensive program for responding to the needs and problems of the children within the school or school system. The data collection process could then be repeated at regular intervals as a way of measuring the effectiveness of remedial and/or corrective programs. Thus, the Early Identification Index provides a much-needed "needs" assessment instrument and procedure, important information about how and where to intervene, and a way of measuring the success of programs.

As emphasized at several points throughout this book, the Early Identification Index may not include a few signs and symptoms particularly prevalent within and important to a particular school or school system. This is due to the fact that the hundred signs and symptoms are the most significant in relation to all children five to eight years old. Within a particular geographic area, within a particular community, or within a particular school situation, there may be a few additional signs and symptoms that are of special importance. When using the Early Identification Index, though, it is strongly suggested that these "place relevant" signs and symptoms simply be added to the existing list of one hundred. The one hundred signs and symptoms on the Early Identification Index are of such importance and significance that none of them should be dropped. Also, there is nothing "magic" about holding the list at one hundred when using it within a specific classroom or within a specific school. You would, though, be strongly discouraged from expanding the list to include more than ten or so additional items. Extend it much beyond that and it would begin to become unmanageable.

Name: _____ **Date:** _____

Address: _____ **School:** _____

Age: _____ **Sex:** M F **Race:** White Nonwhite **Grade:** _____

Rated by: _____ **Years of teaching experience:** _____

Type of Class: _____ **General academic level of child**

(Circle 1) mostly A-B, C-D, or D-F

Please read each statement carefully and respond by circling the Xs to the right of the statement if you have observed that item in the child during the last two-month period. If you have not observed the item described in the statement during this period, do not circle the X (in other words, make no marks whatsoever if the statement describes a problem which is _NOT_ present).

CHAPTER 2

ITEM NUMBER	SYMPTOM	PHYSICAL/ ORGANIC	EMOTIONAL	SOCIAL	ENVIRONMENTAL	ACADEMIC
		PROBLEM AREAS				
1	Sudden deterioration in the quality of work	x	x			x
2	Seems to feel incapable of doing his/her work		x			x
3	Seems to feel defeated before even beginning to do his/her work		x			x
4	Seems not to be working up to ability		x			x
5	Cannot keep up with his/her peer group academically	x	x	x		x
6	Reverses and rotates numbers and letters	x				x
7	Consistently has difficulty identifying body parts	x				x

8	Easily distracted by surroundings and minor noises	x	x			x
9	Consistently looks at books or pictures upside down	x				x
10	Has difficulty applying him/herself	x	x			x
11	Has difficulty repeating three to five numbers in sequence	x				x
12	Appears to have occasional memory lapses	x	x			x
13	Frequently rocks in his/her desk or chair		x			x
14	Works inconsistently; seems to know something one day but not the next	x	x			x
15	Shows apparent inability to follow simple directions		x			x
16	Grasps his/her pencil or crayon too tightly, occasionally tearing holes in the paper	x	x			x
17	Scribbles when asked to draw a picture of a person		x			x
18	Shows an inability to draw a circle, square, or cross	x				x
19	Answers oral questions by completely changing the subject		x			x
	SUB SCORE					
20	Pulls out hair		x			
21	Repeatedly inflicts pain on self		x			
22	Shows constant nail biting, nose picking, or scratching	x	x			

CHAPTER 3

23	Frequently annoys others to draw attention to self		x	x		
24	Is repeatedly cruel to other children			x		
25	Intentionally seriously injures another child		x	x		
26	Shows repeated cruelty to animals		x			
27	Has consistent difficulty on school bus or on the way to and from school		x	x	x	
28	Has frequent temper tantrums		x		x	
29	Runs away from home or school repeatedly		x		x	
30	Seems not to learn from previous experiences	x	x			
31	Consistently fails to follow school rules			x		x
32	Frequently defies authority		x	x		
33	Steals repeatedly		x			
34	Is excessively or indiscriminately affectionate toward adults		x	x		
35	Seems unlovable		x	x	x	
	SUB SCORE					
36	Vomiting	x	x			
37	Difficulty swallowing	x				
38	Frequent or severe stomachaches	x	x			
39	Rash on face or other parts of the body	x	x			

CHAPTER 4

40	Frequent wheezing	x				
41	Frequent wet, productive cough	x				
42	Diarrhea	x	x			
	SUB SCORE					
43	Shows evidence of child's having been sexually molested		x		x	
44	Shows evidence that parents drink heavily or abuse drugs				x	
45	Is apparently abused by parents or others at home				x	
46	Parents seem not to accept child's limitations				x	
47	Parents become hostile or aggressive when approached about child's problems				x	
48	Parents belittle child or tell him/her that he/she is stupid				x	
49	Parents frequently keep child out of school	x	x		x	
50	Child reports parents do not allow him/her to play with other children		x	x	x	
	SUB SCORE					
51	Using one eye more than the other	x				
52	Frequent earaches	x				
53	Difficulty hearing	x				
54	Bleeding from the ear	x				

CHAPTER 5

CHAPTER 6

CHAPTER 7

55	Complaints of double vision	x				
56	Complaints of ringing sounds or sensations	x				
57	Frequent squinting	x	x			
58	Red or swollen eyes	x	x		x	
	SUB SCORE					
59	Has shaking, trembling hands	x	x			
60	Has frequent headaches	x	x			
61	Frequently wets or soils self	x	x			
62	Frequently expresses the feeling that he/she is no good		x		x	
63	Hears voices or sees things that are not there		x			
64	Often thinks people are trying to hurt him/her		x	x		
65	Has many unusual fears		x		x	
66	Seems to feel unlovable		x		x	
67	Tends to blame self for problems at home		x		x	
68	Has a preoccupation with death		x			
69	Shows frequent stuttering or stammering		x		x	
70	Shows frequent shivering or shaking when it is not cold	x	x			
71	Often expresses the belief that people do not like him/her		x	x		

CHAPTER 8

72	Usually seems to feel as if she/he is not as good as others		x	x	x	
73	Refuses to talk	x	x			
74	Has perspiring, cold, clammy hands		x			
75	Dislikes recess for fear of being hurt		x	x		
76	Frequently does not respond when others speak to him/her		x	x		
77	Is preoccupied with own thoughts and fantasies	x	x	x	x	x
78	Shows unusual reluctance to separate from parents		x		x	
79	Refuses to play with other children		x	x		
	SUB SCORE					
80	Bleeding gums	x				
81	Bluish tinge to lips, earlobes, or fingernails	x				
82	Shortness of breath after slight exertion	x				
83	Pain or burning when urinating	x				
84	Multiple or severe burns	x			x	
85	Unusual number of severe bruises	x			x	
86	Cuts or scratches that do not heal	x				
87	Reports using alcohol or drugs, or sniffing glue		x	x	x	
88	Eats odd things like soap or paint	x	x			
89	Swollen or painful joints	x				

90	Swelling of legs or feet	x				
91	Excessive drooling	x	x			
92	Unusually overweight	x	x		x	
93	Any signs of worms	x				
	SUB SCORE					
94	Frequent, rapid, jerky movements	x	x			
95	Brief or extended periods of blanking out	x				
96	Fainting	x	x			
97	Numbness of any body part	x				
98	Weakness of one side of the body	x				
99	Unusual staggering or lack of balance	x				
100	Convulsions, seizures, or unusual "spells"	x	x			
	SUB SCORE					
	TOTAL SCORE					

APPENDIX III

First Aid For Teachers

This first aid guide is intended to supplement the major discussions of symptoms and teacher responses presented in earlier chapters. You are specifically referred to chapters four, six, eight, and nine. This first-aid guide assumes that you are thoroughly familiar with the earlier discussions. Further, Appendix I covers and presents suggestions for dealing with an extensive set of physical/organic signs and symptoms seen in young children. Nonetheless, this first-aid guide can be used as a quick reference when preparing yourself to deal with first-aid situations in your classroom and for quick and easily accessible first-aid information when needed. Beyond this, you are very strongly encouraged to take advantage of the first-aid courses offered by your local Red Cross or through your local health department. As a minimum, you should take enough training to prepare you to deal with injuries where broken bones are a possibility, accidents where serious bleeding is involved, circumstances under which children become seriously burned, and situations where children either require mouth to mouth resuscitation or have their breathing blocked by some object lodged in the throat. It is likely that a representative from the Red Cross or from your local health department would be quite willing to come to your school to provide a training course for school personnel. As little as one hour of training could make the critical difference when a child is involved in a real emergency. Above all, remember that first-aid is the minimum essential emergency treatment to be used until proper medical attention can be obtained. Never do more than necessary to make the child safely comfortable and to prevent further injury or worsening of the problem.

Once you have become thoroughly familiar with the contents of this book—and of this first-aid guide in particular—and have had some first-aid training, you will want to prepare a first-aid kit for your classroom. First, keep in mind those things which you should *not* do in first-aid situations. Above all, you should not give a child any kind of medication nor put any kind of medication or preparation on the child's skin. Included on the "no list" are things such as aspirin, iodine, Mercurochrome, salve, burn ointments, etc. Next, never move or allow to be moved a child who *may* have sustained a broken bone as a result of an accident. Also, any child who has sustained a hard blow to the head should lie down immediately and should be *carried* to a comfortable place where he can rest.

With these cautions and suggestions in mind, you are ready to prepare your first-aid kit. It should include a list of the names, addresses, and phone numbers of the parents or guardians of all of the children in your class as well as notations of someone else to contact should you be unable to reach the parent or guardian. You should have a specific notation on that list that permission for emergency medical treatment is on file in the school office for each child in your class. Any exceptions *must* be indicated. Taped to the top of your first-aid kit should be the telephone number of your nearest emergency squad, your nearest hospital emergency room, and your area Poison Control number. If neither is available within your geographic area, be sure that your school has made effective emergency arrangements for children who have accidents or who become seriously ill at school. Above all, keep in mind the fact that this first-aid kit will be of no value if you cannot find it quickly when you need it.

The kit should contain the following: a roll of one inch and a roll of two inch sterile gauze, a supply of sterile gauze pads, a roll of adhesive tape, small adhesive bandages, prepared compresses or clean cloths that can be folded into compresses, a towel and washcloth, a bar of mild soap, small plastic bags into which ice can be placed, a pair of scissors, an oral thermometer which you are careful to sterilize after each use, a tongue depressor covered with adhesive tape, and a small flashlight.

The first-aid treatments which follow are divided into sections for easy reference. You should take time to thoroughly familiarize yourself with each section and with the appropriate first-aid response. Remember that, in a real emergency, you probably will not have time to look it up in the book.

Section I - Above the Shoulders

Even apparently minor injuries may, in fact, be extremely serious when they occur in this area of the body. Unless you are absolutely certain that the apparent injury is not serious and involves no hidden complications or problems, you should strongly encourage the parents to have the child checked by their physician "just to be sure." If you think that there is any possibility that an injury here may be more serious or may involve unseen complications, you should treat it as a medical emergency and follow through accordingly. If you have overreacted, people have been inconvenienced. If you are right, your quick and immediate response may save the child considerable difficulty.

Bump or blow to the head. Have child lie down immediately, carry him to a comfortable place, and keep him awake. If the swelling is more than minor, apply ice and arrange for immediate emergency treatment. Encourage parents to take child to the doctor if there is any dizziness, nausea, or continuing headache. The child should be awakened every hour for at least twenty-four hours unless the doctor feels it is not necessary.

Nose bleed. Have child lie down with head tilted slightly back, hold cold compress over child's nose and gently pinch closed the nostrils. If bleeding is profuse or does not completely stop within five minutes, then arrange for emergency medical treatment and contact parents.

Object stuck in nose. Do not try to remove object. Contact parents; be sure that they take child to physician.

Swelling of or around nose. Apply cold compress, suspect other injuries, and contact parents.

Black eye. Apply cold compress; contact parents.

Object in eye. Do not try to remove object. If natural tearing process does not wash object out in about two minutes, then arrange for emergency medical treatment.

Bloody or pussy discharge from eye. Arrange for emergency medical treatment.

Excessive tearing or itching of eyes. Apply cold compress; contact parents.

Obvious injury to eye—even minor. Arrange for emergency medical treatment.

Any discharge from ear. Contact parents; be sure that they have child seen by physician.

Swelling of or around ear. Apply cold compress, contact parents, and be sure that they have child seen by physician.

Object stuck in ear. Do not try to remove object. Arrange for emergency medical treatment.

Hard blow to ear. Apply ice if there is swelling, contact parents, and encourage them to have child seen by physician.

Earache. If pain is severe, contact child's parents.

Swelling of lip. Apply ice; contact parents.

Bleeding from mouth. Have child press corner of clean cloth against injured area if possible. Arrange for emergency treatment.

Toothache. Have child swish warm water around in mouth since food particles and some beverages occasionally cause the teeth to hurt, as does excessive cold in the mouth at times. Contact parents; encourage them to take him or her to the dentist if pain continues or recurs.

Swelling or redness of tongue or gums. Contact parents; encourage them to take him or her to physician.

Sore throat. Contact parents. Encourage them to take child to physician, since child may have strep throat or other serious infection.

Chipped, cracked, broken tooth. Contact parents. Encourage them to take him or her to dentist even if it is a baby tooth that is involved.

Loose tooth other than baby tooth. Contact parents and encourage them to take him or her to dentist.

Any cut on face, eye, ear, or inside mouth. Contact parents; be sure that the cut is evaluated by a physician.

Headaches. Have child lie down, place cold compress on forehead, contact parents, and encourage them to have the child seen by a physician. Headache may be a temporary reaction to eating or drinking something extremely cold. Small children should not get headaches from simply exercising too vigorously, running too fast, etc.

Section II - Breathing Difficulties

Child choking or strangling and unable to breathe. Stand behind child or kneel above him with his back toward you if he is sitting or lying down. Place one fist just under the child's rib cage, place other hand on top of fist, and jerk sharply toward child's back. The idea is to force the air in the child's diaphragm up through the breathing passage, dislodging any object possibly stuck in child's throat. Repeat maneuver two or three times. If breathing does not resume, have emergency squad called while you repeat maneuver to dislodge object in throat; or start trip to emergency room immediately while attempting to dislodge object. (Note: An emergency squad can usually reach you faster than you can get to the emergency room.)

Child's breathing stops as a result of smoke inhalation, inhaling water while swimming, or for no apparent reason. If there is a possibility of an object stuck in the throat, attempt to dislodge object as if child were choking or strangling. Perform mouth to mouth resuscitation until breathing resumes. Have emergency squad called while trying to reestablish breathing, or transport the child to the emergency room while trying to reestablish breathing.

Wheezing. Contact parents; encourage them to have child seen by physician.

Difficulty in breathing. Contact parents; treat as medical emergency.

Section III - Injuries to or Difficulties with Skin

It is important to remember that the first response to bleeding should be the firm application of a pressure bandage or compress to the wounded area. If there is no bleeding resulting from a cut, or if the bleeding is minor, running cold clean water on the cut will sometimes quicken clotting and will have the advantage of washing out the wound. Ice should always be applied to swelling areas or to burns.

Scratches. Wash area with soap and water; cover with clean bandage.

Cuts. Apply pressure compress if bleeding; wash in cold water if bleeding stops. Contact parents and treat as medical emergency if cut is more than minor or if bleeding does not stop in two minutes. Encourage parents to have cut evaluated by physician, especially if it occurs above the shoulders.

Bruises. Wash area with soap and water and apply ice. Contact parents.

Bumps resulting in swelling. Apply ice; contact parents.

Burns. Apply ice; contact parents. Treat as medical emergency if burn is more than minor.

Scrapes or floor burns. Wash area with soap and water and apply ice or cold compress. Contact parents.

Splinters or pencil lead in skin. Do not try to remove object. Contact parents and encourage them to have child seen by physician if injury is more than minor or if it involves pencil lead or other possibly poisonous substance.

Rash on any part of body. Contact parents; encourage them to have child seen by physician.

Dry or itching skin. Contact parents.

Any puncture wound. Wash with soap and water, apply ice if area begins to swell, contact parents, and be sure they have child seen by physician. Child may need tetanus shot or anitbiotics. Be sure physician knows what punctured the skin in case slivers or particles may still remain. Apply pressure compress if there is more than slight bleeding.

Section IV - Other

Sprained joints—ankle, knee, shoulder, elbow, finger, etc. Be sure that child does not use or put pressure on injured joint. Apply ice, have child lie down, and contact parents.

Any possibility of a broken bone. Be sure that you do not move or allow the child to be moved. Treat as medical emergency.

Extreme pain that continues after any accident. Treat as medical emergency.

Stomach ache. If severe, contact parents and treat as medical emergency. If mild, contact parents and encourage them to take him or her to physician. If it is a frequent problem with a specific child, be sure that the problem is evaluated by a physician and then follow his instructions and suggestions when problem recurs.

Getting too hot. Have child lie down, slightly elevate legs and feet, and apply cold compress to forehead. Contact parents.

Getting too cold. Be sure that child gets to a warm place immediately. Remove any wet clothing, have child lie down, and gently massage hands or other exposed areas of the body. Contact the parents and be sure that child is seen by physician if there is any continuing itching; numbness, discoloration of the skin, or soreness.

Vomiting. Contact parents, and encourage them to have child seen by physician if vomiting continues beyond eight hours.

Diarrhea. Contact parents. Encourage them to have child seen by physician if it continues beyond eight hours.

Convulsions. Have the child lie down on the floor and remove any chairs or other objects which the child might thrash into. Loosen the child's clothing around his neck and waist, place tongue blade covered with adhesive tape in child's mouth when it opens, and stay calm, since there is nothing you can do to prevent or stop the convulsion. Once the convulsion is over the child should be encouraged to lie down and rest for awhile. Contact the child's parents—they are probably already aware of the problem and will have advised you about how to deal with it when it occurs.

Fainting or passing out. Carry the child to a comfortable place where he can lie down, slightly elevate feet and legs, and place a cold compress on the forehead. Contact the parents.

Fever over 99°. Anytime a child seems a little flushed or ill, it is a good idea to take his temperature. If it is 99° or more, you should contact the parents. If the temperature is over 102° or under 98.6°, it should be handled as a medical emergency.

Possible or known ingestion of poison. Handle as a medical emergency. Call the area Poison Control number for specific advice as arrangements are being made to take the child to the hospital emergency room. Be sure to remember exactly what the child ingested, and take a sample of it with the child to the emergency room if possible. Have someone at school contact the parents and locate the emergency medical permission form. *Don't delay transporting the child for any reason—time is of the essence!*

Dizziness. Have the child lie down, slightly elevate his feet and legs, and apply a cold compress to the forehead. Contact the parents.

Hard blow to back or stomach. If breathing is interrupted and does not return within twenty seconds, administer mouth to mouth resuscitation. If any pain or discomfort persists after five minutes, then contact the parents and encourage them to have the child seen by a physician. If pain or discomfort is intense a few seconds after the blow, then treat as a medical emergency.

Bibliography

The material included in this bibliography comes from several different sources. First, the education literature used in developing the 450 signs and symptoms of early childhood difficulty, the basis for the research, is included. As indicated in the introduction, this education literature was not approached for the purpose of reviewing the presentation and development of signs and symptoms, but only for the purpose of extracting specific signs and symptoms of early childhood difficulty. Next, the literature used by the students who researched the one hundred most significant signs and symptoms is included. Additional material is included from the general fields of psychology, education, and medicine, which can be used to further study specific signs and symptoms as well as general areas of early childhood difficulty in school and school adjustment. In addition, a few specific references are included relative to handling health and first aid problems at school. Finally, some material is included on the recommendation of colleagues of the author. Overall, it is felt that this bibliography represents the "state of the art" in terms of recognizing, understanding, and dealing with early childhood difficulties within the school context. We hope that it will be of interest and help to you as you work with children.

Abrahams, Roger D., and Rudolph C. Troike, eds. *Language and Cultural Diversity in American Education*. Englewood Cliffs, N.J.: Prentice-Hall, 1972.

Adams, Don, and Gerald M. Reagan. *Schooling and Social Change in Modern America*. New York: David McKay, 1972.

Adams, Sam, and John L. Garrett, Jr. *To Be a Teacher: An Introduction to Education*. Englewood Cliffs, N.J.: Prentice-Hall, 1969.

Adler, Sol. *The Non-Verbal Child*. Springfield, Ill.: Charles C. Thomas, 1964.

Ahmann, J. Stanley, and Marvin D. Glock. *Evaluating Pupil Growth*. 2nd ed. Boston: Allyn & Bacon, 1963.

Almy, Millie. *The Early Child Educator at Work*. New York: McGraw-Hill, 1975.

Almy, Millie, et al. *Young Children's Thinking*. New York: Teachers College Press, 1966.

Ames, Louis Bates. *Child Care and Development*. Philadelphia: J. B. Lippincott, 1970.

Anderson, Carl L. *School Health Practice*. 3rd ed. St. Louis, Mo.: C. V. Mosby, 1964.

Anderson, Paul S. *Language Skills in Elementary Education*. New York: Macmillan, 1964.

Anderson, Richard C., and Gerald W. Faust. *Educational Psychology: The Science of Instruction and Learning*. New York: Dodd, Mead, 1973.

Anderson, Robert H., & Harold Shane, eds. *As the Twig Is Bent: Readings in Early Childhood Education*. Boston: Houghton Mifflin, 1971.

Arnheim, Daniel D., and Robert A. Pestoles. *Developing Motor Behavior in Children: A Balanced Approach to Elementary Physical Education*. St. Louis, Mo.: C. V. Mosby, 1973.

Baker, Harry J. *Introduction to Exceptional Children*. 3rd ed. New York: Macmillan, 1959.

Baker, Katherine R., and Xenia F. Faue. *Understanding and Guiding Young Children*. 2nd ed. Englewood Cliffs, N.J.: Prentice-Hall, 1971.

Baldwin, Alfred L. *Behavior and Development in Childhood*. New York: Holt, Rinehart & Winston, 1965.

Ballard, Allen B. *The Education of Black Folk: The Afro-American Struggles for Knowledge in White America*. New York: Harper & Row, 1973.

Bany, Mary A., and Louis V. Johnson. *Classroom Group Behavior: Group Dynamics in Education*. New York: Macmillan, 1964.

Baratz, Joan C., and Roger W. Shuy. *Teaching Black Children to Read.* Arlington, Va.: Center for Applied Linguistics, 1969.

Beard, Ruth M. *An Outline of Piaget's Developmental Psychology for Students and Teachers.* New York: New American Library, Mentor Book, 1969.

Beery, Keith E. *Models for Mainstreaming.* San Rael, Calif.: Dimensions, 1972.

Behrens, Herman D., and Glenn Maynard, eds. *The Changing Child: Readings in Child Development.* Glenview, Ill.: Scott, Foresman, 1972.

Bereiter, Carl, and Stegfried Engelmann. *Teaching Disadvantaged Children in the Preschool.* Englewood Cliffs, N.J.: Prentice-Hall, 1966.

Bernard, Harold W. *Mental Health in the Classroom.* Rev. of *Mental Hygiene For Classroom Teachers.* New York: McGraw-Hill, 1970.

Bernard, Harold W. *Psychology of Learning and Teaching.* 3rd ed. New York: McGraw-Hill, 1972.

Berry, Mildred Fresburg. *Language Disorders of Children: The Bases and Diagnoses.* New York: Appleton-Century-Crofts, 1969.

Bigge, Morris L. *Learning Theories for Teachers.* 2nd ed. New York: Harper & Row, 1971.

Binter, Alfred R., and Sherman H. Frey, eds. *The Psychology of the Elementary School Child.* Skokie, Ill.: Rand McNally, 1972.

Bishop, Virginia E. *Teaching the Visually Limited Child.* Foreword by Dr. Natalie Barrage. Springfield, Ill.: Charles C. Thomas, 1971.

Blackham, Garth J. *The Deviant Child in the Classroom.* Belmont, Calif.: Wadsworth Publishing, 1967.

Blackham, Garth J., and Adolph Silberman. *Modification of Child Behavior.* Belmont, Calif.: Wadsworth Publishing, 1971.

Blitz, Barbara. *The Open Classroom: Making It Work.* Boston: Allyn & Bacon, 1973.

Blumberg, Arthur. *Supervisors and Teachers: A Private Cold War.* Berkeley, Calif.: McCutchan, 1974.

Bolton, Barbara J. *Ways to Help Them Learn: Children, Grades 1 to 6.* Glendale, Calif.: International Center for Learning, 1972.

Bond, Guy L., and Miles A. Tinker. *Reading Difficulties, Their Diagnosis and Correction.* 3rd ed. Englewood Cliffs, N.J.: Prentice-Hall, 1973.

Boyd, Gertrude A. *Teaching Communication Skills in the Elementary School*. New York: Van Nostrand, 1970.

Braun, Samuel J., and Esther P. Edwards, eds. *History and Theory of Early Childhood Education*. Belmont, Calif.: Charles A. Jones, 1972.

Brearley, Molly, ed. *The Teaching of Young Children: Some Applications of Piaget's Learning Theory*. New York: Schocken Books, 1969.

Briggs, Dorothy Corkille. *Your Child's Self-Esteem: The Key To His Life*. New York: Doubleday, 1970.

Brown, Duane. *Changing Student Behavior: A New Approach to Discipline*. Dubuque, Iowa: Wm. C. Brown, 1971.

Bryan, Tanis H., and James H. Bryan. *Understanding Learning Disabilities*. Port Washington, N.Y.: Alfred Publishing, 1975.

Bucher, Charles A., and Evelyn M. Reade. *Physical Education and Health in the Elementary School*. New York: Macmillan, 1964.

Buckley, Nancy K., and Hill M. Walker. *Modifying Classroom Behavior: A Manual of Procedure for Classroom Teachers*. Champaign, Ill.: Research Press, 1970.

Byrd, Oliver E., and Thomas R. Byrd. *Medical Readings on First Aid*. San Francisco, Calif.: Boyd & Fraser, 1971.

Chapman, A. H. *The Games Children Play*. New York: Berkley, Medallion Book, 1971.

Clarizio, Harvey F., and George F. McCoy. *Behavior Disorders in School-Aged Children*. New York: Chandler, 1970.

Clarke, Louis. *Can't Read, Can't Write, Can't Talk Too Good Either: How to Recognize and Overcome Dyslexia in Your Child*. Intro. by Archie A. Silver. New York: Penquin Books, 1973.

Collier, Calhoun C., et al. *Teaching in the Modern Elementary School*. New York: Macmillian, 1967.

Craig, Eleanor. *P.S. Your Not Listening*. New York: New American Library, 1973.

Crow, Gary A. *Crisis Intervention*. New York: Association Press, 1977.

Cruickshank, William M., ed. *Psychology of Exceptional Children and Youth*. 3rd ed. Englewood Cliffs, N.J.: Prentice-Hall, 1971.

Daigon, Arthur, and Richard A. Dempsey. *School: Pass At Your Own Risk*. Englewood Cliffs, N.J.: Prentice-Hall, 1974.

Dreikurs, Rudolf, and Pearl Cassel. *Discipline Without Tears*. 2nd ed. New York: Hawthorn Books, 1972.

Dunn, Lloyd M., ed. *Exceptional Children in the Schools: Special Education in Transition.* 2nd ed. New York: Holt, Rinehart & Winston, 1973.

Engelmann, Siegfried. *Preventing Failure in the Primary Grades.* New York: Simon & Schuster, 1969.

Faas, Larry A., ed., *The Emotionally Disturbed Child: A Book of Readings.* Springfield, Ill.: Charles C. Thomas, 1970.

Family Guide Emergency Health Care. U.S. Government Printing Office, 1963.

Fine, Benjamin. *Underachievers: How They Can Be Helped.* New York: E. P. Dutton & Co., 1967.

Foss, Brian M., ed. *New Perspectives in Child Development.* New York: Penguin, 1974.

Foster, Walter S., and Norman C. Jacobs, eds. *The Beginning Elementary School Teacher: Problems and Issues.* Minneapolis, Minn.: Burgess, 1970.

Frostig, Marianne, and Phyllis Maslow. *Learning Problems in the Classroom: Prevention and Remediation.* New York: Grune & Stratton, 1973.

Funk, Hal D., and Robert T. Olberg, eds. *Learning to Teach in the Elementary School: Introductory Readings.* New York: Dodd, Mead, 1971.

Gardner, Richard A. *Therapeutic Communication With Children: The Mutual Storytelling Technique.* New York: Science House, 1971.

Gardner, William I. *Children with Learning and Behavior Problems: A Behavior Management Approach.* Boston: Allyn & Bacon, 1974.

Gearheart, B. R. *Learning Disabilities: Education Strategies.* St. Louis, Mo.: C. V. Mosby, 1973.

Gearhart, B. R., ed. *Education of the Exceptional Child: History, Present Practices, and Trends.* New York: Intext, 1972.

Getzels, Jacob W., and Philip W. Jackson. *Creativity and Intelligence: Explorations with Gifted Students.* New York: John Wiley and Sons, 1962.

Ginsburg, Herbert. *The Myth of the Deprived Child: Poor Children's Intellect and Education.* Englewood Cliffs, N.J.: Prentice-Hall, 1972.

Gnagey, William J., *The Psychology of Discipline in the Classroom.* New York: Macmillan, 1968.

Goldhammer, Robert. *Clinical Supervision: Special Methods for the*

Supervision of Teachers. New York: Holt, Rinehart & Winston, 1969.

Grahl, Ursula. *The Exceptional Child: A Way of Life for Mentally Handicapped Children*. London: Rudolf Steiner, 1970.

Gray, Jenny. *The Teacher's Survival Guide*. Belmont, Calif.: Fearon, 1967.

Greene, Mary Frances, & Orletta Ryan. *The School Children: Growing up in the Slums*. New York: Pantheon Books, 1965.

Grzynokowicz, Wineva Montooth. *Teaching Inefficient Learners*. Springfield, Ill.: Charles C. Thomas, 1971.

Hammill, Donald D., and Nettie R. Bartel, eds. *Educational Perspectives in Learning Disabilities*. New York: John Wiley & Sons, 1971.

Hammill, Donald D., and Nettie R. Bartel, eds. *Teaching Children with Learning and Behavior Problems*. Boston: Allyn & Bacon, 1975.

Hanninen, Kenneth A. *Teaching the Visually Handicapped*. Columbus, Ohio: Charles E. Merrill, 1975.

Haring, Norris G., ed. *Behavior of Exceptional Children: An Introduction to Special Education*. Columbus, Ohio: Charles E. Merrill, 1974.

Haring, Norris G., and E. Lakin Phillips. *Analysis and Modification of Classroom Behavior*. Englewood Cliffs, N.J.: Prentice-Hall, 1972.

Haubrich, Vernon F., and Michael W. Apple, eds. *Schooling and the Rights of Children*. Berkeley, Calif.: McCutchan, 1975.

Hawley, Robert C. *Value Exploration Through Role Playing: Practical Strategies for Use in the Classroom*. New York: Hart, 1975.

Heath, G. Louis. *The New Teacher*. New York: Harper & Row, 1973.

Helfer, Ray E., and C. Henry Kempe, eds. *The Battered Child*. Chicago: University of Chicago Press, 1968.

Hess, Robert D., and Doreen J. Croft. *Teachers of Young Children*. Boston: Houghton Mifflin, 1972.

Hetherington, E. Mavis, and Ross D. Parke. *Child Psychology: A Contemporary Viewpoint*. New York: McGraw-Hill, 1975.

Hewett, Frank M., and Steven R. Forness. *Education of Exceptional Learners*. Boston: Allyn & Bacon, 1974.

Hildebrand, Verna. *Guiding Young Children*. New York: Macmillan, 1975.

Huckleberry, Alan W., and Edward S. Strother. *Speech Education for the Elementary Teacher*. 2nd ed. Boston: Allyn & Bacon, 1972.

Isaacs, Susan. *Intellectual Growth in Young Children*. New York: Schocken Books, 1968.

Jessup, Michael H., and Margaret A. Kiley. *Discipline: Positive Attitudes for Learning*. Englewood Cliffs, N.J.: Prentice-Hall, 1971.

Johnson, Kenneth R. *Teaching the Culturally Disadvantaged: A Rational Approach*. Chicago: Science Research Associates, 1970.

Jones, Reginald L., ed. *Problems and Issues in the Education of Exceptional Children*. Boston: Houghton Mifflin, 1971.

Kagan, Jerome. *Understanding Children: Behavior, Motives, and Thought*. New York: Harcourt Brace Jovanovich, 1971.

Kaplan, Louis. *Education and Mental Health*. New York: Harper & Row, 1971.

Kirschenbaum, Howard, et al. *Wad-ja-Get? The Grading Game in American Education*. New York: Hart, 1971.

Krumboltz, John D., and Helen Brandhorst Krumboltz. *Changing Children's Behavior*. Englewood Cliffs, N.J.: Prentice-Hall, 1972.

Learner, Janet W. *Children with Learning Disabilities: Theories, Diagnosis, and Teaching Strategies*. Boston: Houghton Mifflin, 1971.

Lessinger, Leon M. *Every Kid a Winner: Accountability in Education*. New York: Simon & Schuster, 1970.

Ligon, Mary G., and Sarah W. McDaniel. *Teachers Role in Counseling*. Englewood Cliffs, N.J.: Prentice-Hall, 1970.

Long, Nicholas J., et al., eds. *Conflict in the Classroom: The Education of Children with Problems*. 2nd ed. Belmont, Calif.: Wadsworth, 1971.

Long, Nicholas J., et al., eds. *Conflict in the Classroom: The Education of Emotionally Disturbed Children*. Belmont, Calif.: Wadsworth, 1965.

Lovaas, O. Ivar, and Bradley D. Bucher, eds. *Perspectives in Behavior Modification with Deviant Children*. Englewood Cliffs, N.J.: Prentice-Hall, 1974.

Love, Harold D. *Parental Attitudes Toward Exceptional Children*. Springfield, Ill.: Charles C. Thomas, 1970.

Mager, Robert F., and Peter Pipe. *Analyzing Performance Problems; or, You Really Oughta Wanna*. Belmont, Calif: Fearon, 1970.

Merck Manual of Diagnosis & Therapy. 13th ed. Merck and Co., 1977.

Missildine, Hugh W. *Your Inner Child of the Past*. New York: Simon & Schuster, 1963.

Mitchell, John J. *Human Life: The First Ten Years*. New York: Holt, Rinehart & Winston, 1973.

Mordock, John B. *The Other Children: An Introduction to Exceptionality*. New York: Harper & Row, 1975.

Munsinger, Harry, ed. *Readings in Child Development*. New York: Holt, Rinehart & Winston, 1971.

Nerbovig, Marcella H., and Herbert J. Klausmeier. *Teaching in the Elementary School*. 4th ed. New York: Harper & Row, 1974.

Noar, Gertrude. *Individualized Instruction: Every Child a Winner*. New York: John Wiley & Sons, 1972.

Ornstein, Allan C., and Philip D. Vairo, eds. *How to Teach Disadvantaged Youth*. New York: David McKay, 1969.

Palmer, James O. *The Psychological Assessment Of Children*. New York: John Wiley & Sons, 1970.

Payne, James S., et al. *Exceptional Children in Focus*. Columbus, Ohio: Charles E. Merrill, 1974.

Purkey, William Watson. *Self-Concept and School Achievement*. Englewood Cliffs, N.J.: Prentice-Hall, 1970.

Ragan, William B., et al. *Teaching in the New Elementary School*. New York: Holt, Rinehart & Winston, 1972.

Rapp, E. Philip, and Philip Himelstein, eds. *Readings on the Exceptional Child: Research and Theory*. 2nd ed. New York: Appleton-Century-Crofts, 1972.

Ringness, Thomas A. *Mental Health in the Schools*. New York: Random House, 1968.

Rosenblith, Judy F., et al., eds. *The Causes of Behavior: Readings in Child Development and Educational Psychology*. 3rd ed. Boston: Allyn & Bacon, 1972.

Sanderlin, Owenita. *Teaching Gifted Children*. Cranbury, N.J.: A. S. Barnes & Thomas Yoseloff, 1973.

Sapir, Selma G., and Ann C. Nitzburg, eds. *Children with Learning Problems: Readings in a Developmental-Interaction Approach*. New York: Brunner/Mazel, 1973.

Schmuck, Richard A., and Patricia A. Schmuck. *Group Processes in the Classroom*, 2nd ed. Dubuque, Iowa: Wm C. Brown, 1975.

Sheffard, William C., et al. *Teaching Social Behavior to Young Children*. Champaign, Ill.: Research Press, 1973.

Smith, James A. *Setting Conditions for Creative Teaching in the Elementary School*. Boston: Allyn & Bacon, 1966.

Staats, Arthur W. *Child Learning, Intelligence, and Personality: Principles of a Behavioral Interaction Approach*. New York: Harper & Row, 1971.

Stewart, Jack C. *Counseling Parents of Exceptional Children: Principles, Problems and Procedure.* New York: Mss. Information, 1974.

Tanner, Laurel N., and Henry Clay Lindgren. *Classroom Teaching and Learning: A Mental Health Approach.* New York: Holt, Rinehart & Winston, 1971.

Torrance, E. Paul. *Gifted Children in the Classroom.* New York: Macmillan, 1965.

Van Osdol, William R., and Don G. Shane. *An Introduction to Exceptional Children.* Dubuque, Iowa: Wm C. Brown, 1974.

Volkmor, Cara B., et al. *Structuring the Classroom for Success.* Columbus, Ohio: Charles E. Merrill, 1974.

Wallace, Gerald, and James M. Kauffman. *Teaching Children with Learning Problems.* Columbus, Ohio: Charles E. Merrill, 1973.

Wallace, Gerald, and James A. McLoughlin, *Learning Disabilities: Concepts and Characteristics.* Columbus, Ohio: Charles E. Merrill, 1975.

Walzer, Stanley, and Peter H. Wolff, eds. *Minimal Cerebral Dysfunction in Children.* New York: Grune & Stratton, 1973.

Index

277